Twenty-Two
Foreigners
in Funny Shorts

Twenty-Two Foreigners in Funny Shorts

The Intelligent Fan's Guide to Soccer and World Cup '94

Pete Davies

RANDOM HOUSE NEW YORK

Portions of this work were originally published in different
form in the April 1993 issue of British *GQ* and in the June
26 1993 issue of *The Guardian Weekend.*

Grateful acknowledgment is made to Williamson Music
Company for permission to reprint four lines from "You'll
Never Walk Alone," by Oscar Hammerstein and Richard
Rodgers. Copyright © 1945 by Williamson Music. Copyright
renewed. International copyright secured. All rights
reserved. Reprinted by permission.

Library of Congress Cataloging-in-Publication Data
Davies, Pete, 1959–
Twenty-two foreigners in funny shorts : the intelligent
fan's guide to soccer and World Cup '94 / Pete Davies.
—1st ed.
p.   cm.
ISBN 0-679-77493-9
1. World Cup (Soccer)   2. Soccer.   I. Title.   II. Title: 22
foreigners in funny shorts.
GV943.D38   1994
796.334'688—dc20   93-41274

Manufactured in the United States of America
on acid-free paper.

2 4 6 8 9 7 5 3

First Edition

For Alan the Marxist Plumber

Acknowledgments

I would like to thank Brian Flynn, his assistants Kevin Reeves and Joey Jones, and all the players of Wrexham Football Club in the 1992–93 season. They were generous with their time, and great to watch.

My thanks are also due to Rogan Taylor, Janet Tiernan, and John Williams of the Sir Norman Chester Centre for Football Research at the University of Leicester—and to Chris in the library in Llangollen, who found me obscure books faster than I'd ever have thought possible.

Finally, some of the "Why America?" section in Chapter 18 first appeared in an article for the London edition of *GQ*, April 1993, while Chapter 23 was published in different form in *The Guardian Weekend*, June 26, 1993. My thanks for permission to reproduce this material here.

Note: Where dollar figures are cited, they have been converted at the rate of $1.50:£1.

Contents

Introduction

In June 1994, the biggest sports event on earth arrives in the U.S.A.—but because the sport in question is soccer, many Americans know next to nothing about it. So this book is written in the hope that, if you're coming new to the game this summer, I can help you to enjoy it. After all, the rest of the world will be watching—and we'd hate for you to be bored at your own party.

Along the way, I'll be explaining the rules. One reason soccer dominates the world as it does is the fact that the rules are transparently simple. The pitch is rectangular, the ball is round, you can't use your hands (unless you're the goal-keeper), and a game involves twenty-two foreigners in funny shorts kicking the ball (and each other) for ninety minutes. After this period, in the normal course of events, the Germans win, the losers riot, and the English slouch off muttering about who won the war anyhow.

But there's so much more to this than just the simplicity of the game. When Jeff Rusnak of the Fort Lauderdale *Sun-Sentinel* wrote "There is no greater drama in sports than a soccer team trying to validate its national character in the World Cup," he hit the nail on the head. Soccer is followed with a turbulent mix of anguish and passion in every corner of the planet—and when its finest exponents gather every four years to contest the World Cup, what ensues is nothing less than an epic of national affirmation. In soccer, more than in any other sport, the way you play is the way you are.

So the Brazilians are festive, the Italians are stylish but prone to dark neuroses, the English are decades behind everyone else and stubbornly unaware of it—and the Germans are as fast and well organized as the blitzkrieg.

On July 8, 1990, in the sweeping, seething bowl of the Olympic Stadium in Rome, the final of the 14th World Cup took place before a crowd of 75,000, and a television audience amounting to nearly half of all the people on earth. The Germans beat Argentina 1-0, and became World Champions for the third time.

On June 17, 1994, at Soldier Field, Chicago, they commence defending that title in the 15th World Cup: USA '94. This opener will be the first of fifty-two games played over the next four weeks in nine different cities: Boston, New York, Washington, Orlando, Chicago, Detroit, Dallas, San Francisco, and Los Angeles.

The accumulated television audience worldwide for these games—from Tokyo to Tashkent, Sydney to São Paulo, Stockholm to Soweto—is expected to exceed 32 billion. In America, 528 players, ten thousand journalists, and millions of fans will pelt round those nine cities in feverish packs, filling the great stadiums with noise, and putting on in God's country a spectacle the like of which it has never before encountered.

And, as I say, I really want you to enjoy it. But to help you do that, I need to give you more than just the rules, or the history; I need to give you the *culture* of this thing.

I need to tell you what I do on my Saturday afternoons.

Twenty-Two Foreigners in Funny Shorts

I

In the Fabric of Our Lives

January 23, 1993
Wrexham v. Walsall

Heavy gales blow in off the Irish Sea; wind rips over the Welsh mountains, dumping snow on the peaks and stinging drizzle in the valleys. A roof got blown off a school the other day—but wind's a feature of the winter round here.

In this unforgiving wind I leave home at two in the afternoon, and drive six miles east to where the Ceiriog Valley opens onto the Cheshire Plain. The trees along the winding little road buck and dance; the surface is littered with scraps and splinters of broken branch.

The valley ends at Chirk. I turn left on the main road and head ten miles north along the edge of the hills, the wind jolting and tugging at the car. On the road now I'm passed by other cars—cars with two, three, four people in each of them, people all going to the same place as me.

We're going to the Racecourse Ground in Wrexham for our regular fix. We're going to the Racecourse to sing and groan, to curse and cry out; to drop our heads in our hands one minute, and throw our hands in the air the next. We're going to the Racecourse for an act of communion more charged, more vital to British society than anything you'll find in any church in the country. We're going to watch Wrexham play soccer on a Saturday afternoon.

We spill from our cars, walking quickly, coalescing in urgent

bunches that block the traffic as we cross the roads. Red favors
are dotted through the gathering crowd, because red is our
color; in the parlance of the fan, We Are Wrexham. In a low
gray sky, cloud scuds off the green-gold hills along the western
horizon; the wind bats flags out stiff into the thin sharp rain.
We pack into the turnstiles. I pay $7.50 to go through the
Turf Entrance to the Kop; $7.50 to stand for two hours on a
concrete terrace lined with crush barriers under a corrugated
tin roof. It's 2:45. The game begins in fifteen minutes; in the
heart of the Kop where the lads are massed, the song, an
essential part of the soccer spectator's experience everywhere,
is in full and raucous swing:

> *Eeeeh-aaaay-eeh-ay-eeh-ay-oh*
> *Up the football league we go*
> *When we win promotion*
> *This is what we'll sing*
> *We are Wrexham*
> *Super Wrexham*
> *Gonna win the league**

And maybe we will, too.

Founded in 1873, Wrexham is the oldest professional soccer
club in Wales, and one of three Welsh clubs to play in the
English Football League. But Wrexham is a small town of
40,000 souls; it's a long way from here to the top.

The top flight of English football are the twenty-two clubs
of the Premier League. Tottenham Hotspur and Arsenal in
North London, Liverpool and Everton on Merseyside and,
above all, Manchester United—these are the glamour clubs,
where a player can be worth $5,000,000 or more, and make a
six-figure basic wage.

Beneath the top flight, where the money gets more modest,
there are seventy clubs in the three divisions of the Football
League. Wrexham are in the Third Division—and today, just
past midway in the nine-month season, we stand third among
the twenty-two in that Division.

It's a good place to be. In May, when the annual marathon
is over—when every club has played every other club at home

---

*Sung to the tune of the English standard "Knees Up, Mother Brown."

and away—the top three gain promotion automatically. The four clubs behind them must then contest lucrative but nerve-crunching play-offs, to earn the fourth precious spot in the next flight up. So here's what the top of the Third Division looks like, as we make ready to kick off against Walsall:

	P	W	D	L	F	A	Pts
Barnet	23	14	5	4	44	26	47
York City	24	12	9	3	42	25	45
Wrexham	23	11	6	6	41	35	39
Shrewsbury Town	22	11	4	7	32	26	37
Walsall	22	11	3	8	42	37	36
Cardiff City	22	10	5	7	39	31	35

P means games Played. W, D, L, F, and A mean games Won, Drawn, and Lost, with goals scored For and Against. For and Against matters because if you finish on the same points, the team that scored more goals places higher—and if you have the same number of goals as well as points, the team with the better goal difference places higher. Wrexham's goal difference is +6—which could use a little boosting.

But the number that really matters is the points. You get three for a win, one for a draw, and diddly-squat for losing—and as the points accumulate, they tell how thousands of people are in for mounting rushes of white-knuckle excitement as season's end approaches, and promotion begins to seem a thing you can dare to imagine.

And they tell how thousands of others must suffer agonies of apprehension as relegation looms, the Big Drop—which, if you're in the Third Division, means the stomach-churning prospect of a fall from Football League grace into the netherworld of the GM Vauxhall Conference, the feeder league for the four major divisions.

But for the majority—for many thousands more than the blessed at the top and the damned at the bottom—they tell how they've spent another slogging, soul-sapping season of wind and rain watching their team go nowhere; nine months watching them scuffle in midtable limbo with the gnawing, steady-growing certainty that next season they'll have to start all over, and do the same damn thing. The wind'll blow and the rain'll fall and the defenders are donkeys, and my mother's got a better first touch than that galumph in midfield, and that striker plays like he's wearing high heels, and that manager's a gormless toe rag . . .

But you keep on going. You keep on going because this isn't like an American sport where, if you finish nowhere, you start again next season against the same opponents anyhow. You keep on going because there's always the possibility of the unimaginable sanction—the appalling threat of being cast out to find yourself, next season, playing the likes of Stalybridge and Dagenham, decidedly unromantic teams in the Vauxhall Conference. You keep on going because, by your presence alone, you're willing your team not to inflict that cataclysm upon you. You keep on going because you are—and you will shout this out loud from the damp and steaming terrace so they never forget it—a Loyal Supporter.

And, of course, you keep on going because there's always the possibility of rapture. If things go right (please God, let things go right) then next season you'll be on a higher plane altogether, elevated in joy to a whole new universe—the Second Division. You'll be up there—whisper it soft—with Stoke City and Leyton Orient . . .

You think I'm daft? Maybe I am. But so are millions like me all around Britain, and millions more in Italy, Spain, France, Holland, Germany, Belgium, Poland, Paraguay, Brazil, Argentina, Algeria, Zimbabwe, Cameroon . . . this game, see—it's in the fabric of our lives.

The body that runs the game is FIFA, the Federation of International Football Associations; it lays claim to 170 million registered players. 528 of the best of these will play in the U.S.A. come summer '94, and I can't tell you how much I look forward to that—but right now, in the unglamourous lower reaches of the world's first Football League, it's nearing three on a Saturday afternoon at the Racecourse, Wrexham, North Wales. There's 5,324 of us here, willing eleven men in red to put goals past this other lot in black-and-white stripes from some dingy suburb of Birmingham. And we may not know much—but there's a few things we do know.

We know York City played Colchester United last night, and only managed a draw—so we know that, if we win, we'll be only three points behind York. And we know when we're through with Walsall this Saturday afternoon, come Tuesday evening we'll be back again—to play York.

* * *

When the PA system plays "Always Look on the Bright Side of Life" (from Monty Python's *Life Of Brian*), we know the moment is upon us—and when the teams come out the roar surges, the chants booming and thumping in the tin space of this barn where we stand. As the players warm up, spraying lazy passes round the turf one man to the next, the fans announce themselves:

> *Red Army! Red Army! Red Army!*

and pay tribute to favored individuals like No. 7 Gary Bennett, third-highest goalscorer in the division:

> *Psycho! Psycho! Psycho!*

The few hundred Walsall fans who've traveled over the border for the game, and who are now in the stand at the far end, must also be greeted in their turn:

> *We hate England*
> *Oh we hate England*
> *We are the England haters*

Then there's our anthem. Wrexham are sponsored by the local brewery, under the banner of a particularly unspeakable brand of beer named Wrexham Lager. So the lads sing out, to the tune of the hymn "Bread of Heaven," in the finest traditions of the Welsh male-voice choir:

> *Wrexham Lager*
> *Wrexham Lager*
> *Feed me till I walk no more*
> *Feed me till I walk no more*

Then, with an immaculate suddenness, all the great and rowdy noise falls absolutely still. The players from both teams stand, heads bowed, round the center circle. The two minutes of silence that follow seem to stretch for an eternity—and the roughest soul in the place wouldn't think for one second of breaching it.

The first British soldier to die in Bosnia was Lance Corporal Wayne Edwards. He was twenty-six years old, and he came from the village of Cefn Mawr just by Wrexham. He will be buried with full military honors a few days later. His town remembered him here.

Walsall make one sally toward our goal in the opening minute—then all the play is Wrexham's. The red shirts twist and turn, leap and run; immediately the crowd is caught up, tracing with experienced eyes and eager hearts the simple, aggressive patterns of soccer played the British way—one hundred miles an hour, no quarter given. In the fifth minute, the ball sails toward the Walsall goal; No. 10 Steve Watkin dives full-length, and pelts it off his head against the post. It comes out to No. 9 Karl Connolly; he tears down the left with the ball at his feet as Watkin scythes back through the center between two panicking defenders. Connolly sways away from the ball as he runs, not braking at all—and suddenly the ball's flying fast and low across the pitch now, clear into Watkin's sprinting path. He's timed the run to perfection; there's only the goalkeeper to beat, and he beats him decisively. Six minutes gone, 1-0 up—and all about me there's ecstasy, hands punching the air, inarticulate roars and screams of Yes! Yes! Yes!

> *The Reds are going up*
> *The Reds are going up*
> *So now you gotta believe us*
> *So now you gotta believe us*
> *The Reds are going up*

And, to the tune of "You Are My Sunshine":

> *You are my Wrexham*
> *My only Wrexham*
> *You make me happy . . .*

Who are these idiots in the black and white anyhow? Wrexham come close again, and again; the Walsall keeper has to dive, desperate, hands clawing air to keep the ball from the back of his net a second time—until out of the blue in the thirteenth minute, Walsall equalize.

1-1. And you have to understand that every goal the other guys get—every single goal against you, every single time—is replete with terrible potential. What if they get another? What if they take hold of this game now? Is this it? Is this the moment our season falls to pieces round our ears?

In this case, however, it isn't the season that falls to pieces, but just the game. After a red-blooded start, all that wind tearing in off the mountains under the murky sky takes over. The conditions, basically, become too awkward to be overcome any longer; the match degenerates for the next half hour into an aimless hoofing contest.

So another thing you should know about soccer is that it's not unusual for long stretches of many games to be boring. And I have two things to say about this.

First, you go out in a tearing wind and kick a round ball about, and try getting it to go where you want. Hell, you go out in a flat calm and try it. And now try it with big men striving all around you, with uncompromising physicality, to stop you doing any such thing. . . . Soccer, you see, is as fiendishly difficult as it's beautifully simple.

And second, that's another reason we go. Forget the partisan stuff about how we grew up with this game, and how the fortunes of our teams are a trough into which we pour our fervid emotions every Saturday, every season. We also go because, simply, we know how hard it is—so that we're thrilled, every Saturday, at those rare and precious moments when people infinitely more skilled than we'll ever be get this demanding game right. And when they do, a soccer stadium gets a charge of high-voltage mass excitement, an upheaval of keening, roaring, oceanic commotion that's like no other sensation I've experienced, in any other environment, in all the rest of my life.

So we go because we know, some days, it's going to click. We go because enough players on the team, some days, will hit that magic thing called "form," and then everything they try will come off. Every pass will arrive where it's meant to; every header, every flick, every backheel and lay-off will set up the next man, and then the next, and then the ball will go screaming in the net—and for all those afternoons of long-suffering loyalty, you will have your reward.

At halftime it's still 1-1. Nothing much has happened—a few niggling fouls, various bungles and errors to be wearily groaned at, and the customary crop of abominable refereeing decisions. (The referee, by the way, is always blind, corrupt, or both. Whoever you're playing he's on their side, and don't believe any lies in the program that say otherwise.)

In these circumstances, while the game turns into wind-swept human pinball, a crowd can amuse itself for a while—but in the end can only fall tetchily, disconsolately silent, muttering about the harshness of a fate that's doomed you to a lifetime of Saturdays at the Racecourse.

With fouls, perhaps, you can raise a bit of noise. If their man's down, the boys all yell,

Let him die,

and if our man's down, at Wrexham they'll inform the opponent who put him there that he's a

Dirty English bastard,

but even this meager sport palls. And then, slowly, the bile mounts, until frustration mutates into pitiless wrath, and you turn on your own team for having the gall to make you stand there and watch them be so bad.

Are you red or are you yellow?

In the second half, Wrexham come out more fired up—but still the crucial last touch isn't there. We're camped in their half, we have most of the ball, but we're not doing anything with it. The crowd sway between four-lettered condemnation, and yearning encouragement.

Then we score in the seventy-second minute, and again in the seventy-eighth—and what had threatened to peter out into resentful accusation turns in a twinkling to delirious, all-forgiving celebration. Wrexham 3, Walsall 1. As the clock runs out we cry, from our position of ineffable superiority:

Bye-bye Walsall
Walsall bye-bye

In the white glare of the floodlights under an indigo sky we leave the Racecourse well satisfied, buoyed up for York City in three days' time.

Round-Up

On a Sunday morning I buy two papers. I buy *Wales on Sunday* for a report on the game: "Sharpshooters Wrexham stay on the promotion trail after another battling performance." Then I buy a London paper, *The Independent on Sunday*— and here's what it tells me, on January 24, 1993, across four broadsheet pages.

The first thing I look for is a single column titled simply "Round-Up," summarizing news from the lower divisions. Tucked away among seven paragraphs, the sentence I want reads as follows: "In the Third Division, third-placed Wrexham beat Walsall 3-1 to narrow the gap on leaders Barnet to six points." And that's the extent of the notice paid nationwide to yesterday's doings at the Racecourse.

The lead article's about Manchester United. A second piece surveys feelings in the game about a new rule, forbidding goalkeepers to handle a ball passed back to them by one of their own defenders. (More on that later.)

Then there's a piece about the dilemmas confronting the England manager over team selection for a World Cup qualifier against the postage-stamp republic of San Marino, along with nine reports from the previous day's headline fixtures—nine matches at which the total attendance was 160,406 people.

And I do realize that, by American standards, an average crowd of 17,823 at the nine fixtures deemed most noteworthy around the nation may not, in fact, seem particularly impressive. Set aside the fact, however, that too many English soccer stadia are cramped inner-city urinals built way back at the birth of the game; set aside the fact that only belatedly have they tried to conform to civilized safety standards, with the limits on capacity that involves—and consider, instead, all the other fixtures a person wishing to watch live soccer yesterday afternoon in Great Britain might have gone to instead. This on a day, mind you, when there wasn't a full league program.

There were forty-five matches involving Premier League, Football League, Scottish League, and Vauxhall Conference sides. But results are also listed in my paper for games in five other cup competitions, and twenty-one other leagues, most of which themselves have at least two divisions—leagues with names redolent of mud and beer and hoofing on winter Saturday afternoons: the London Spartan, the Bass North West Counties, the Boddingtons West Midlands, the Press & Journal Highland, the Parasol Combined Counties . . . all in all, there are some 43,000 clubs playing soccer in 2,500 leagues in England alone.

The paper then carries results from the French, Belgian, and Dutch leagues, the Portuguese Cup, the European Under-21 Championship, a tournament in Hong Kong featuring Switzerland, Japan, Hong Kong, and Denmark—but I'll leave it there, because it's Sunday afternoon, and that means Italian soccer live on Channel 4. AC Milan are playing, the best team in the world, as of today fifty-one games unbeaten. . . .

All over England, all across Europe, all around the world, there are people playing soccer; it's in the fabric of our lives.

Bill Shankly, the manager who began Liverpool's twenty-year domination of the English game, once remarked how some people say soccer's a matter of life and death. But it isn't, he said. It's much more important than that.

2

Beginnings

The first officially recognized international soccer match was played between England and Scotland on November 30, 1872. The venue was the West of Scotland Cricket Club at Partick, near Glasgow; the score was 0-0.

The Football Association

Soccer began life centuries ago as a riot with a pig's bladder in the middle of it. In towns, it involved rude turbulence making its way down the alleys from one district to another; in rural areas, it pitched one village against another, and was fought out without boundaries across the miles in between.

Hundreds might participate, and death or serious injury were common. The ruling classes took a dim view of this, but despite a torrent of edicts and decrees, were unable to stamp it out. Industrialization did put paid to it for a while; people shoved into new factories in new towns had no place to play, and no time to play in. Paradoxically, therefore, while its previous "owners" were slaving in the mills, it was in the private schools of the aristocrats and the mercantile classes that the game carried on.

Education in these schools mostly involved beating the crap out of each other between Latin lessons. But in the early nineteenth century, with the need to produce sound chaps to go forth and boss the world around, educationalists began establishing a more disciplined framework for the learning process under the credo known as "muscular Christianity." Sport became an important part of education, and like the rest of education, it became more regulated—so upright fellows could now kick lumps out of each other in a more purposeful and comradely fashion.

But the different schools had different rules. Could you use your hands? What shape was the ball? Was kicking people OK? The chaps from Eton, Harrow, Shrewsbury, Winchester, Westminster, Charterhouse, and Rugby went up to Oxford and Cambridge, found they had different ideas on these matters, and set to scratching their heads over how to resolve them.

The first attempts to formalize a set of rules took place in Cambridge in the 1840s. The defining moment, however, came on October 26, 1863, when representatives of eleven London clubs met in the Freemason's Tavern in Lincoln's Inn Fields, and founded the Football Association.

The key arguments over the rules turned on handling the ball, as against "dribbling"—running with it at your feet—and on "hacking." Those who wanted the more deft, aesthetically appealing business of dribbling won the day, and soccer was born. Those who preferred a more in-your-face game, where you could run holding the ball, and be dispossessed by another guy booting you in the shins—that's hacking—went off grumbling that if you took out the manly violence, you'd find yourself getting beat by "a lot of Frenchmen" in no time.

This latter faction founded rugby instead—but both factions were gentlemen, alumni of the private schools, and many of the first clubs in the FA (all strictly amateur) were old boys' get-togethers. Writers, lawyers, army men, and civil servants, they could have had no idea as they drew up the rules that what they had begun, within a quarter of a century, would become the feverishly adored pursuit of British society in all its raw and rough industrial vigor.

The Field of Play

A hundred and thirty-one years after the organization of the world game began, the rules state that the field of play shall be a rectangle between 100 and 130 yards long, and from 50 to 100 yards wide. More specifically, FIFA decree that a World Cup pitch should be 115 yards long and 75 yards wide.

As it happens, you can't get a pitch that wide into Giants Stadium or the Pontiac Silverdome. In the first case, however, you could hardly have a World Cup in America and not go to New York—while in the second, the suggestion that netting GM as a sponsor might have anything to do with four games being held in Detroit is, of course, vigorously denied.

However wide the pitch, the object of the game you play on it is to put the ball in the other team's goal. You can use your feet or your head, or your butt if that's what gets in the way; what you can't use is a hand or an arm, here, or anywhere else on the pitch.

For a goal to be scored, the whole of the ball must cross the line. The goal is eight yards wide and eight feet high; the goalkeeper who guards it is the only guy who can use his hands. The area eighteen yards wide from each goalpost, and eighteen yards deep into the pitch from the goal, is the penalty area; the keeper can only handle the ball in this area.

If a foul is committed on an attacking player in this area, a penalty is awarded. Elsewhere if you're fouled, you get a "free kick"—possession of the ball with which to restart play, while opposing players retreat a minimum of ten yards.

But inside the penalty area—where a foul may mean you've been robbed of a scoring opportunity—you set the ball down on the penalty spot, twelve yards out from the goalmouth. This is known as a "penalty kick," more commonly, a penalty. Then you whack the ball at the goal, and there's no one but the keeper to try and stop it going in.

The player fouled doesn't necessarily have to take this kick. Every team has specialists—so penalties are hard to stop, and it's high drama when a keeper manages to do it. Attacking players, therefore, are naturally inclined to try and "win" penalties—which means your less-sporting types will hit Greg Louganis mode in the area the minute a defender so much as breathes on them. Hence the term "diving."

If you put the ball out of play over the sidelines, the other team throws it back in from the place it went out.

If the attacking side put the ball out of play over the goal line instead (i.e., behind the goal), the defending side restarts with a goal kick. Inside the penalty area a smaller area six

The Field of Play and appurtenances shall be as shown in the plan below.

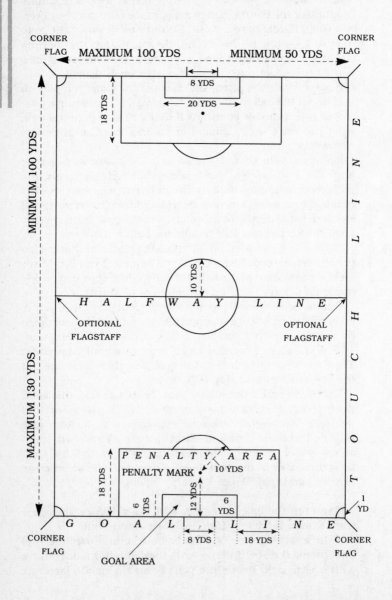

yards deep, and six yards wide from each goalpost, is the goal area; the goal kick is taken from here.

But if, under pressure, the defending side clears the ball over the goal line themselves, a "corner kick" is awarded. At each corner of the goal line, the corner area is a quarter circle where the attacking side puts the ball. They can then do what they like with it, but usually they'll flight it into the goal-mouth—and if they do it right, it's a chance to score.

Corner kicks are something managers can work on, drilling "plays" in the American sense of that word. From a corner, for example, the kicker might curl the ball over to a man at the near post, who'll head it on across the goal to a second man arriving at the far post, who rises in turn and thumps it in off his head . . . in theory.

As for free kicks within range—"range" wouldn't normally be more than twenty-five yards out. You can run plays for these, too—but what the fan likes to see is just some guy take a belt at it.

So, ten yards in front of him, the defenders deploy a blocking line, the "wall," between kicker and goal. The wall, however, will be no object to your quality free-kick merchant, who'll bend his shot over or around it with venomous insouciance, and deliver the ball inch-perfect to the top corner of the net. Ideally, it'll arrive at such blistering velocity that the first move the keeper makes is when he turns around to pick it up after-ward.

Historically, the finest exponents of the explosively swerving free kick are the Brazilians. A good Brazil-style free kick, the ball creasing through space, is a living demonstration of the theory of relativity. Don't blink, or you'll miss it.

Play kicks off at the start of each half from the center spot, around which the center circle has a radius of ten yards. That's because kickoff is, in effect, a free kick, so the other team stand ten yards off—i.e., outside the circle. Whichever team kicks off the first half, the other lot kick off the second; after a goal, the side scored against restarts from here too.

There's also a *D* marked out from the front edge of the penalty area, to a radius of ten yards from the penalty spot. That's so no defender can encroach within ten yards of the man taking a penalty.

And that's the field of play—so you send eleven of us and

eleven of them out on it, and then they run about like fiends for two periods ("halves") of forty-five minutes playing soccer.

The FA Cup and the Football League

On July 21, 1871, Charles William Alcock, the twenty-nine-year-old player, journalist, and secretary of the Football Association, proposed the following: "That it is desirable that a Challenge Cup should be established in connection with the Association, for which all clubs belonging to the Association should be invited to compete."

The FA Cup is the oldest tournament in world soccer. Fifteen clubs entered the first competition, all bar two of them from London; the final was held on March 16, 1872, between the Royal Engineers and the Wanderers, before a crowd of 2,000 at the Kennington Oval, a cricket ground. The Wanderers won 1-0, the goal scored by one Morton Peto Betts. In the next ten years the Cup was won by the Wanderers, the Royal Engineers, the Old Etonians, the Old Carthusians, Clapton Rovers, and Oxford University.

Then, in the final of 1882, something new turned up. Blackburn Rovers were not from the south, and they were not gentlemen. They lost—to the Old Etonians—but they were the first portent of a social revolution.

Three years later, a cup game between Aston Villa and Preston North End, both workingmen's teams, drew a crowd of 27,000; by the time the new century dawned, the crowd for the final was hitting six figures. Gentlemen still ran the FA—but the game they ran was now played by professionals, men from the backstreets and the factory floor.

The working class was demanding, and being granted, more leisure; they used it to play and follow soccer. The advent of the railways meant they could travel to play each other, while growing literacy and mass journalism meant they could read about it too. In the industrial north and in the Midlands, as well as among the proletariat of the capital, clubs sprang up like weeds—works teams, state school teams, teams born out of cricket clubs, or church teams organized by missionary members of the upper classes, bringing better health in the form of football to the rotten-toothed horde.

In 1874, Blackburn Rovers emerged as an old boys' club

from Blackburn Grammar School. In the same year, Aston Villa was born at the Villa Cross Wesleyan Chapel in Birmingham. Everton was founded in 1878 at the St. Domingo's Church Sunday School, and its great city rival Liverpool FC grew from that club too. Two years later, Manchester United began life as Newton Heath, a works team from the Lancashire and Northern Railway Company; Coventry City was a works team too, starting life at the Singer Cycle Factory in 1883, while Arsenal started out from the Woolwich Munitions Factory in 1886. Meanwhile, wanting something to do in the winter, members of Sheffield Wednesday Cricket Club founded a soccer club of the same name as early as 1867; fifteen years later, Tottenham Hotspur, Arsenal's bitter rivals in North London, also sprang from a cricket club.

In the season 1993–94, all these clubs were in the English Premier League.

Professionalism was legalized in 1885; the world's first football league began three years later, after the Scotsman William McGregor of Aston Villa wrote to six northern clubs suggesting it was time that the game became more organized. When the league got under way twelve clubs took part, all from the north and the Midlands—south of Birmingham, the game was still amateur. Of those twelve clubs, 105 years later, Everton, Blackburn Rovers, and Aston Villa we've met; eight others still play in the lower three divisions—and only one, Accrington Stanley, has fallen from the league altogether.

Goal nets and the penalty kick were introduced in 1891, and promotion and relegation in 1898; there were by then thirty-six clubs, in two divisions. Over the next thirty years the league went on growing; by 1923 it encompassed eighty-eight clubs, in four divisions. Among these were Wrexham, who joined what was then the Third Division North in 1921.

3

Endurance

January 26, 1993
Wrexham v. York City

The guy I normally go to Wrexham with is Alan the Marxist Plumber, and Chris the Music Industry Dropout will now characterize Alan the Marxist Plumber for you as follows:

"Alan's like one of those guys in a black-and-white Stalag movie, all the plucky Brits plotting away under the eyes of the Nazi commandant. Everyone's going round in rags 'cause the camp tailor's turning their clothes into fake German uniforms, and everyone's levitating all night, 'cause the planks they're supposed to sleep on have been spirited off to the underground workshop. And the toff major with the walrus tash comes to Alan and he says, 'Corporal. How's the Project coming on?'

"So Alan says, 'It's done, sir. Would you like to have a look?' And he throws open the secret doors at the end of the barrack hut and there in the hidden space, resplendent, finished to perfection, is the most inviting little bar you ever saw. It's got polished mahogany stools, glossy lines of gleaming optics, a shining chrome counter—just lovely.

"So the officer says, 'Ah. Very good. But the tunnel, Corporal. Where's the *tunnel*?'

"And Alan says, 'Blimey, sir. I didn't have anything left over for that.'"

* * *

In the Ceiriog Valley there are two kinds of rain. There's the rain that's actually rain, when water falls from the sky in discernible drops, spattering on the lanes and the fields; it gathers in thin, unceasing streams down the tracks off the hills, carrying drifts of leaves, twigs, pebbles, and earth into the channels round the houses. Outside of summer this can go on for days, gently remorseless, so the roofs and roads softly glisten all night in the streetlights, and porches fill with peoples' mud-slick boots, and their dogs become sodden, matted bundles, eyes peering through lank twists of wet fur.

Then there's the rain that isn't rain, the rain that's just wet air instead, rain that settles as a fine and permanent white mist. It rises in slow clouds along the course of the river, and wanders in slim veils through the trees on the slopes; when you walk out it materializes in a cool sheen on your face, mussing your hair, making your fingers slippery and your bones cold and damp. It wraps round buildings until there's nothing left but ghosts, then it slips through the walls, because now the stones are only shadows . . .

On this particular Tuesday evening, the rain can't decide which kind of rain it wants to be—but either way, it's wet. I set off with Alan and we know we're both thinking, as the wipers *tock-tock* across the windscreen, that we're totally daft. But when the visitors are second and your team's third, you've got to be there, right?

On August 29, Wrexham went to York for the second game of the season, and got stomped 4-0; by the end of November, tonight's situation was inconceivable. York were five points clear at the top; Wrexham were seventeen points adrift in thirteenth place. But in the weeks since then York have won only once, whereas Wrexham:

December 12	bt Scarborough	4-1	at home
December 18	bt Cardiff City	2-1	away
December 26	bt Crewe Alexandra	1-0	away
December 28	bt Chesterfield	5-4	at home
January 2	bt Shrewsbury Town	1-0	away
January 9	bt Torquay United	4-2	at home
January 16	lost at Barnet	1-3	oops
January 23	bt Walsall	3-1	at home

Alan says it's the best streak he's been on since he first went to football in Glasgow when he was nine—and he's been going for forty years. So in November, if they thought about us at all, in York they were probably laughing. But now they're looking over their shoulders and thinking, Crikey. Where did *they* come from?

It's 7:15. In the winter dark the floodlights are four brilliant blocks of white, and the rain looks beautiful. Against the black maw of the far stand and the navy blue of the dripping sky it flows in gauzy drifts of swirling whiteness, sheeting patterns of diamond translucence over the gleaming green of the pitch. We climb into the mass in the Kop; we are 6,894, the biggest crowd of the season.

But at a second glance the pitch doesn't look quite so good. A large area by the center circle is a boggy morass; there are patches of sodden mud everywhere. The teams splash about, warming up; Alan says he'll pop off for a piss, and pushes away down the stand. While he's gone the game begins, Wrexham surge forward, and win a corner kick; the ball's sweetly flighted in and as it hangs curling through the air, Connolly leaps like a salmon to head home at the near post. One minute gone, 1-0, pandemonium.

We're so brill it's unbelievable

Alan returns, grumbling; it's the fan's worst nightmare. It only takes a second to score a goal—so if you want your lot to get one you go for a piss, and they do, and you miss it.

Still, it's a marvelous start, and we go on attacking—but York, of course, no matter their recent travails, are still the second-placed side, and they can't be this battered for ninety minutes. Sure enough, slowly, they fight their way back in—until, with fifteen minutes gone, the play's even, and the ball breaking both ways.

Wrexham keeper Mark Morris leaps to pluck a high ball bare inches off the head of an incoming York striker, to avert a certain goal; another York strike fires in, shaving narrowly past the post. At the far end, the York fans rise—and the Kop, anxious, screams back at them,

Sit down, you lot

By now we've moved out from the middle of the stand, because the sight lines in there are terrible—but though our view is much better, we're also way out from under the big tin roof. Exposed to the Welsh winter sky, I have cold rain running down my face and my neck, while the game before us mires in the soaking mud. Alan says, "Bit dismal, isn't it?"

Another York shot flies narrowly wide. From the far end a faint cry can be heard:

We are York

A derisive jeer belts back at them:

> *It's nice to know you're here*
> *It's nice to know you're here*
> *Now fuck off home*

"D'you ever get the feeling," says Alan, "you're not watching a classic?"

Players slide yards on their butts through the greasy ooze, lifting showers of luminous spray. These are not ideal conditions for the exercise of fine judgment, or the application of exquisite ball skills. In the wind and rain, long passes intended to land in the path of the front men fly yards too far, and slither harmlessly away out of play.

And we have, at Wrexham, a notably gifted young winger named Jonathan Cross, a seventeen-year-old boy whose role in life is to beat men down the sideline—to "skin them," in the argot. Then, once he's slipped past like a wraith with the ball at his feet, and left them flailing and embarrassed in his wake, he races down the line in back of the defence, and crosses the ball to meet the strikers rushing in . . . it's what you go to see, that magic—but there's not much chance of it tonight. As the ball skids away from him once more, a bitter old man behind us now yells at him, "Stop mucking about!"

Alan shakes his head. "The kid's got two guys, one in his ear, one up his arse—what's he want him to do?" Then he says, "I tell you what. You want another goal?" He wanders off to take another piss—and Cross cuts inside from the line, and damn near scores one, too.

But he doesn't, and at halftime it's still 1-0. I go for a piss myself, in a foul brick shack under the humming tower of a floodlight stand; to get to it, you have to wade through diar-

rhea-brown puddles the size of Lake Superior. And why do we
do this? Why are we here? Back on the terrace I say, "Just
wait. Just think how it'll be in the spring. It'll be light in the
evening, and we'll stand here dry in the sun . . ."

"You never been in Wales in the spring?"

From the restart, we're all over them; the visitors fall back
in disarray. But still we don't score, and again, fifteen minutes
into the period, York have regrouped; now it's they who attack
all the time. And the game becomes frantic, desperate—because to stay second in the table, York must score; while to
go second ourselves, at all costs we mustn't let them.

Morris is forced into a series of increasingly breathtaking
saves. He tips a shot off his fingers inches over the crossbar,
falls to seize another on his knees in the mud as it rockets in,
until he's all that stands between us and two home points
thrown away—all that stands between us and the surrender
of a vital psychological opportunity.

We must have three points. We must go second. We must
deflate York City, and leave them wounded behind us . . .
so the night becomes a test of endurance, a succession of
onslaughts repulsed as we stand chilled, rain seeping into our
bones, miserable and anxious and praying for survival as the
Kop bellows for Wrexham to hang on, hang on . . .

Then, in the seventy-eighth minute, No.4 Gareth Owen digs
the ball out of the midfield mud and lofts it forward thirty
yards; as he does so, Steve Watkin rips round his marker into
empty space before York's goal. York's keeper sprints off his
line as the ball loops down between them—and it's certain
both men and the ball will arrive in the same place at the same
time. So the keeper lunges at Watkin's feet, and Watkin too is
diving, feet first at full speed—and Watkin's boot just makes
it there first. Off his toes he chips the ball high in the air over
the keeper's flying body, as the two men crash together in a
tangled heap.

But no one has a thought for them, as they lie winded and
bruised on the sodden earth—because the Racecourse now
falls silent, all eyes on that ball arcing slow and high through
the goalmouth air. 6,894 draw breath, waiting for a second
as long as eternity to see where that ball will come to earth
. . . and it comes to earth in the net.

It's a brave, finely taken goal. It's 2-0; the Kop erupts.
They've endured, and now their ambition knows no limit.

We're going up as fuckin' champions

There's only one team in Wales
Only one team in Waaaaaay-uh-uls . . .

With two minutes left, Cross lifts another pass over the defence, and Watkin tears through on it once more; he chips the keeper, a carbon copy. Wrexham win 3-0, and go second in the table.

So are we going to get promoted? Ha. It's January 26, there are seventeen games to go, and we won't know where we are until May 8. There's a great deal yet to be endured.

Round-Up

Tanzania withdraw from the African qualifiers for USA '94, the twelfth nation on that continent to do so. Defeated twice by Zambia, the Tanzanians have little chance of qualifying, and say they don't have enough money to continue.

A gunman in a red car pulls up at a soccer game in Soweto and fires on the players. No one is hurt. The remarkable thing is not that this should happen, but that the game is being played at all; the two teams come from rival Inkatha and ANC factions. A report on the incident compares the game to that played between British and German soldiers in no-man's-land, Christmas 1914—a match celebrated in the bittersweet pop song "All Together Now" by the Liverpool band The Farm. Not that the sport is always a bridge between nations; in 1969, a soccer match was the pretext for the outbreak of war between those two sorry countries, Honduras and El Salvador.

Stacey North, twenty-eight, retires from the game; a knee injury sustained in a reserve team match for Second Division Fulham puts paid to his career. Out of some two and a half thousand full-time professionals in the English game, only a handful leave it this way every year—but as the pace of the game increases, the injury count grows too. With frequent demands on the body to make abrupt brakes and turns, the most common injuries are to the Achilles tendon, the hamstring, the knee, and the groin. More rarely, legs are broken—and, very rarely, someone loses his temper and breaks someone else's jaw. But as contact sports go, soccer remains a relatively safe pursuit—unless, of course, someone pulls up in a red car and starts spraying the pitch with lead.

Wishing, perhaps, to avoid the gunfire, three South Africans come to England. David Nyathi of the Orlando Pirates goes on trial with Chelsea, Highland Park's John "Shoes" Moshoeu goes to Wolverhampton Wanderers, and Doctor Khumalo of Kaiser Chiefs tries out with Aston Villa. Chelsea already have a Russian goalkeeper, while Villa's winger Dwight Yorke is from Trinidad. You see why we call it the world game.

Blackburn Rovers, tucked in the bunch chasing Manchester United at the top of the Premier League, buy Norwegian defender Henning Berg from Lillestrom for $600,000. He's the eighth Norwegian international to come here; we also have three Swedes and four Danes. The Scandinavians represent an investment by big clubs approaching $9 million, money that might otherwise have gone to smaller English clubs to bring promising players up from there—and the smaller clubs need the money. Hartlepool are in court, appealing against a winding-up order; Doncaster Rovers have just avoided one, paying up most (but not all) of $105,000 they owe the taxman.

At Wrexham, we fear someone will buy Jonathan Cross, or Steve Watkin, or both. The manager says he's not selling—but they all say that.

No one buys foreign players like Italian clubs do, and no one has money like Italian clubs have to do it. They have the best Germans, the best Dutchmen, the best South Americans, you name it. The world-record price tag, however—$19,500,000—is on the head of home product Gianluigi Lentini, bought by AC Milan from Torino.

Two Englishmen play in Italy: David Platt at Juventus, and Paul Gascoigne at Lazio. Platt is an urbane and composed individual—but Gascoigne, aka Gazza, is not. He has the skills of an angel, the IQ of a stoat, and the story of the week concerns him belching on Italian TV. Watching a game between their clubs (both men were sidelined with injury), Platt and Gazza were approached by a TV crew for interviews. Platt replied politely, in Italian, that he had no comment to make at that time. Gazza belched. Italy was disgusted; the Italians don't go in for this kind of vulgarity. A member of parliament demanded that Gazza be sanctioned. Gazza's agent had the barefaced cheek to blame the TV crew, for "harassing" his player—but Lazio mean to fine him $3,500, or $13,500, depending on which paper you read. Either way, this would make it one of the more costly burps in history.

Gazza's in the news for domestic reasons too; his girlfriend has returned to England from Rome. It's reported that she can't be bothered with Gazza's beery buddies anymore, among them a fellow who goes under the cheerful sobriquet of James "Five Bellies" Gardner. And it's nice to know we have such an ambassador abroad, such a sterling role model for the nation's youth . . . but really, it's a shame. When Gascoigne lets his feet do the talking, he's the best thing England have got.

4

The World Game

"Once soccer gets a hold it's like a disease."
—Kayvon Bahramian, seventeen,
college student, met by chance on
the Amtrak from D.C. to Chicago
during US Cup '93

Wembley

The greatest stadium of them all was probably the Maracana in Rio de Janeiro, built for the fourth World Cup in 1950 with a capacity of 200,000. But it's a crumbling, rat-infested dump now, and Brazil doesn't play there any more. There are plans to turn it into a mall.

On their day Brazil play lovelier soccer than anyone else—but their domestic game is a corrupt and violent chaos, and the best players head for Europe the first chance they get. Of their twenty-one-man squad in the South American qualifiers for USA '94, fourteen make their living with clubs in Spain, France, Italy, Portugal, and Germany.

As with the best players, the finest shrines are in Europe. There's the Stadium of Light in Lisbon, the Bernabeu in Madrid, the Nou Camp in Barcelona—this last, seating 120,000, being home to the club that claims to be the biggest in the world.

Juventus in Turin (known as La Signora, the Old Lady)

might dispute Barcelona's claim. Owned by Gianni Agnelli, who owns Fiat and is unofficially the king of Italy, Juventus have 1,300 supporters' clubs, three of them as far afield as Shanghai, Baghdad, and Bangladesh—and they play their soccer in the Stadium of the Alps on Turin's northern edge, the mountains rising along the horizon beyond the Piedmont plain.

The Olimpico in Rome is a fine and gracious arena, while Milan's San Siro is just fabulous, an intense sci-fi brute of a place—but the Stadium of the Alps, built for Italia '90 (they're still arguing over who should pay for it) is something else altogether. As you approach it, all you can see is the roof, a glittering confusion of steel butterflies' wings suspended from what looks like the Golden Gate Bridge in a hall of mirrors— then you go in, and emerge inside on the top of three oval tiers, because the stadium's built down into an artificial hill. Put a big game in there, and the place is a cauldron.

But the original temple of the world game—the game's first grand home, the seed of all this epic progeny—is the Empire Stadium, six miles north from the center of London, the place we now call simply Wembley.

It was built in 300 days; it opened on April 28, 1923, for the FA Cup final between Bolton Wanderers and West Ham United. Officially, the capacity was 127,000 (today, it's an 80,000 all-seater) but 250,000 turned up for that game, and somehow or other four fifths of them got in. As the pressure mounted, the crowd spilled across the pitch until they covered it—but miraculously no one was seriously hurt, and the game eventually started forty-five minutes late. The occasion went down in history as "the White Horse Final," because a white police horse ridden by Constable George Scorey was prominent in the slow clearance of the field—and I suppose there are many who think that's just part of fond folk memory now.

But I expect there are many more who'll not be surprised for one minute to find that dangerously dunderheaded incompetence is nothing new in the management of English soccer. The FA's founders may have been bold and inventive Victorian pioneers, or they may just have been a bunch of toffs who fancied fixing up their leisure time better—but either way their successors long ago dwindled into a state of dullard smugness. It's a condition mirroring precisely the decline of the country whose national game they're supposed to represent—even as the rest of the world raced past, playing better soccer in smarter stadia.

England weren't beaten at Wembley until 1953, when an electric Hungarian side came and thrashed them 6-3. But thirty years earlier, as people milled in crushed chaos across the pitch on Wembley's opening day, the ecstatic contagion of the soccer bug had already spread far and wide around the world.

Getting to America

Twenty-four nations will contest USA '94—but the four-week, fifty-two-game festival they'll take part in is, in fact, only the final stage of a competition that goes on around the world for over two years.

USA '94 began on March 21, 1992, when Puerto Rico defeated the Dominican Republic 2-1 in the pre-preliminary round of the Caribbean Region, North. In all, 141 nations entered the qualifying stages; even allowing for dropouts, over 500 games were played before qualification was completed in November 1993. As hosts and champions, the U.S.A. and Germany have automatic places; among the twenty-two finalists joining them, the global allocation works out as follows:

Two sides come from Asia. At Italia '90 they were South Korea and the United Arab Emirates, both of whom went home after the first round—and whoever comes from Asia this time will probably go back home that quickly too.

There were also two African teams in Italy, Cameroon and Egypt. When Cameroon became the first side from that continent to reach the last eight, however, they earned Africa a third slot at USA '94 at the expense of one less place for Europe, and a good thing too. Cameroon were wonderful, playing a reckless, free-spirited game that enlivened Italy immeasurably—and it's to be hoped that at least one black African side will now come to America and do the same.

Between South America, Oceania, and the North and Central American and Caribbean region—a region known more easily by its ugly acronym, CONCACAF—things get more complicated. The CONCACAF countries have one definite place, while their second-placed finisher must play off against the winner of the Oceania group. South America, meanwhile, has three definite places, two of which virtually always go to Brazil and Argentina. They also have a possible fourth place, when their fourth-placed nation plays off against the winner of the CONCACAF-Oceania tie.

All of which adds up, one way or another, to ten countries joining the Germans and yourselves. The lion's share—the remaining dozen slots—then go to Europe. That's partly because Europe remains historically, economically, and actually the world's strongest soccer region—and then it's partly because, in Europe, there are just so many countries anyhow. Indeed, it seems sometimes there are more and more by the week.

The first European countries to qualify were Greece and Russia. Their progress was eased by the suspension from their qualifying group of what used to be Yugoslavia, the citizens of that wreckage being grimly otherwise engaged.

The Fever Spreads

Juventus was founded in 1897 by English residents and local students in Turin. FC Barcelona was established by the Swiss-born Juan Gamper two years later; four of the founding players were British, and their first game was against a team of British sailors in port with the Royal Navy.

The Chinese played a form of soccer as long as 2,000 years ago; all across Europe, "pre-industrial football"—a riot with a bladder—had been known since the Middle Ages. But once the English had formalized "The Simplest Game," it spread in that form, in particular through Europe and Latin America, within a couple of decades. Wherever Brits were trading, politicking, building railways, and starting businesses, they started cricket and football clubs too. Almost without exception, the locals rapidly decided cricket wasn't simple at all—but football, equally rapidly, proved to be the biggest English export success of them all.

Englishmen, or local nationals either educated or working in England, were involved in the formation of the first clubs in every country you look at. By the 1890s everybody in Europe was at it, from Austria to Iceland, from Paris to Palermo. AC Milan was founded, like Juventus, in 1898 by a coalition of locals and resident Englishmen. In the same year the Basque club Atletico Bilbao, Spain's oldest team, was established by people who'd learned the game in England.

In England, the heartland of the game was Lancashire, home to six of the twelve founding clubs in the Football League—and Lancashire's business was textiles. So it was textile men from that country who started the club in tsarist Russia that eventually became Dynamo Moscow. It was textile men in Romania, along with British workers in that country with Standard Oil, who got Romanian soccer started as well. Variants of the same story apply to Lisbon and Vienna, to Prague and Copenhagen, to Hamburg and Stockholm and Constantinople.

In Latvia, the president of the first football league was English. In Latin America, the Uruguayan club Penarol started life as the Central Uruguayan Railway Cricket Club, founded in 1891 by British workers with that company. Across the Plate River, meanwhile, tens of thousands of British expats were busy farming the fertile resources of Argentina; here, as in Brazil, they sowed the seeds for the most impassioned support the game has anywhere in the world.

The greatest player of all time is the Brazilian Pele, born Edson Arantes do Nascimento on October 23, 1940, in the little town of Tres Corações, a hundred miles inland across the Serra da Mantiqueira from the Atlantic. He is the only man to play on a World Cup winning side three times—at the age of seventeen in Sweden in 1958, again in Chile in 1962, and then in Mexico in 1970 with the Brazilian side universally acknowledged to be the greatest team of them all, a side that destroyed Italy 4-1 in the final with play of dazzling and unearthly verve and grace.

In 1,324 professional games, Pele scored 1,282 goals; he got ninety-three hat tricks (a three-goal game), had thirty-one four-goal games, five six-goal games, and once, unbelievably, scored eight goals in one match. He saw out his career with the New York Cosmos in the North American Soccer League, but before that his club in Brazil was Santos, on the Atlantic Coast by São Paulo—and Santos was founded in 1912, after a visit from the British Royal Navy.

5

4-4-2

The last time Wales made the World Cup finals was in 1958. In attack they had the formidable John Charles, "the Gentle Giant," a great success at Juventus; a man who once collided head-on with the goalposts and uprooted them. In the quarter-finals the Welsh met Brazil and for sixty-six minutes kept out everything the Brazilians could throw at them. Then Pele scored the game's only goal—he's said since it was the most important he ever scored—and Wales have never been back.

One man who'd be deeply happy if they got back for USA '94 is Wrexham's manager, Brian Flynn. At five four, he is a smiling elf of a man who played sixty-six times for his country. Now thirty-seven, he signed as an apprentice with Burnley when he was fourteen; he was in the top flight with Leeds for six years, then did the rounds of the lower divisions until he ended up at Wrexham in 1988. He played two years, then they offered him the manager's job. He remains on the playing staff—but, he said dryly, "I can't get in the team."

When Flynn took over, Wrexham were $750,000 in debt. In 1991, they finished last in the league; they escaped relegation only by the great good fortune that administrative rejigging that season meant no one went down to the Vauxhall Conference. But the debt was now clear, and he had young players worth $3 million out there; he said that, both for himself and for the players coming through, those lean times had been a learning process. So I asked if, having survived that process, they could win promotion—but he'd only say, "We're contenders. We've as good a chance as any. There's a long way to go."

Wrexham play 4-4-2, four defenders, four midfielders, and two forwards, and it looks like this:

No. 1
Mark Morris
goalkeeper

No. 2	No. 6	No. 5	No. 3
Barry Jones	Mel Pejic	Tony Humes	Phil Hardy
right back	center half	center half	left back

No. 11	No. 8	No. 4	No. 9
Jonathan Cross	Mike Lake	Gareth Owen	Karl Connolly
right wing	midfield	midfield	left wing

No. 7	No. 10
Gary Bennett	Steve Watkin
striker	striker

In theory, it's an attacking formation. In front of the keeper a "flat" back four defends, and when you get the ball, two wingers push up wide to feed the strikers (they "put in crosses"). So when the wingers push up, 4-4-2 becomes 4-2-4—and in a perfect world that puts you all over the other team like a rash.

England won the World Cup in 1966 playing soccer this way, and mostly the British have played it ever since. But you should bear in mind that while any system can describe your game plan, or be a tactical start point, it's only paper talk; it's 2-D. Once a match has begun, whatever system you go with can flow like wine or it can break like glass—and which way it goes is down only and entirely to the players.

Flynn said, "Systems are pie in the sky. You can play anybody in any position, and if they're no good on the day, you won't win. Systems just simplify things—they get players aware of their responsibilities on the pitch. That's all."

The team laid out above is the team he'd select on an ideal Saturday, injuries permitting, at this point in the season. As far as numbers go, the keeper's always No. 1; the left and right backs are usually 2 and 3, and to be honest, after that it's irrelevant. Some players like to wear a particular number, they get superstitious—otherwise, it's not an issue.

And Flynn plays 4-4-2 because his players are comfortable with it, they've grown up with it; it's the way he thinks he'll get the best from them. As for the assets he values at $3 million, they're Hardy, Owen, Watkin, Connolly, and Cross. But he said he wouldn't sell; given the position he was in now, he said, second in the table, "Would you?"

Mark Morris, keeper: "His job's to stop goals going in the net, pure and simple—and to control his eighteen-yard area to do that. He's the only one on the pitch who can use his hands, so he's got a massive advantage. Any balls coming in there in the air should—not always, but should—be his."

And what's Morris got?

"He's very good at stopping shots. He's pretty good at reading the game—assessing situations, and snuffing out the danger. He's not the best on dealing with crosses, because he's not the tallest—and because he has a weight problem he's not as agile, not as quick on his feet as he might be. But he's a good kicker, which is part of it—out of his hands, or on the floor."

I asked how he was coping with the rule change, now he couldn't handle back passes from his defenders any more, and Flynn said, "It's not been bad. But we didn't need to speed the game up here anyway, did we?" With the British, the game is played at a hundred miles an hour whichever way you're passing it.

Item: The Back Pass

It used to be that if a defender was under pressure, or if he just looked up and didn't fancy the options ahead of him, then he could turn the ball back idly to his keeper and get out of that jam. This was boring. So now you can still head the ball back to him, but you can't kick it. Or, to be more precise, you can kick it back—but if you do, the keeper can't handle the pass when it arrives. This means either the defender must play out of the tight spot himself, or, by turning it back, oblige his keeper to do it for him. This is good; it generates more action. Keepers might not like it—it gives them more work—

but I didn't pay money to watch them standing there holding the ball because their lunkhead defenders didn't know what to do with it.

Barry Jones, Phil Hardy, full backs: "The game's about playing together as a team, but it's also about playing your individual opponent, and getting the better of him. So the full back's job is to hold his winger, to stop crosses coming in from wide—that's the first job. Then they've got to combine with the center halves, cover one another—so they work as a unit, all four, with the keeper."

In essence, the back unit stops the ball coming our way, wins it, and sends it back up the other way. "By nature the full backs are defenders—then the bonus for them is what they can give to the team going forward. A lot of attacks start with your full backs. So not only have they got to be good defenders—they've got to be good passers of the ball too, short and long."

Of his back line overall Flynn said, "They're quick. They read the game. They're good tacklers. All four of them, without being the tallest, can compete in the air. And they all compete well generally—physically."

In the middle of the line Humes is the captain, "because he leads by example. He never shirks responsibility, and he's a good communicator. So he'll change things tactically, if he feels it's right—and that's what a captain does. I can't go out there and stop the match for five minutes; if things need altering, you can try to get messages out from the sideline, but it's difficult. And Humes is good at assessing what might need to be changed."

At Humes's side is Mel Pejic, at thirty-three the team's oldest man. "Mel's played at—no disrespect to him, but he's played at this level most of his career—and he knows our level, he's good at our level. Possibly, early on, he might have had a chance of playing higher, but it didn't come about, and he's enjoying himself now. In the twilight of his career."

Humes is twenty-six, Jones is twenty-one, Hardy's nineteen—so what's Hardy got, that puts him among the assets?

"The potential to play at the highest level." But when I asked him to define that, he smiled. He said, "What does the dictionary say *potential* means? You tell me."

Mike Lake, Gareth Owen, midfield: "Without being unkind, their job is to fetch and carry. They've got to have the physical ability to run long distances compared to the others, because they're expected to help not only the defenders but the attackers as well. So obviously the distance involved is the whole length of the pitch."

But Lake, just now, is not properly a Wrexham player. He is, instead, on loan from Premier League Sheffield United, and has been for nearly three months. Flynn wants to sign him permanently because "he's got good abilities, for someone so tall. Physically he's strong—and he's got very quick feet. We encourage players, obviously, when they're passing the ball, to use the biggest part of the foot, the instep—but he's got good ability to look up if he's passing it one way, to flip his foot and go the other way instead. He moves the ball quickly within his feet—his close control's good."

So why hasn't he signed yet? Flynn said, "He wants to sign, and we want to sign him—but if you've got something that's going for you, how d'you put a value on it? You can't. The fans like him, the players like him, he likes the way we play, he can see the potential here—but can you put that into cash? So it's down to the player. He's had a frustrating time at Sheffield; he's been there a few years, his second game he broke his leg, that knocked him back a bit—and he's not a regular there, which he hoped he would be. . . ."

Lake's twenty-six; Owen, twenty-one, is another asset. And Flynn says he won't sell players to another team, so I put the question a different way. In a few years' time, would there be a lot more people who'd know about some or all of these five players?

"Oh yeah. Obviously Cross is getting a lot of attention because he's seventeen, and he's scoring goals—and Watkin's scoring goals, and people always look at strikers. Hardy, he's as good as them all—but he's a left back, and left backs don't hit the headlines, so you won't get as much for him as you will for Cross. That's the way it is."

As for Owen, "He's got all the abilities to be a top midfield player. His one weakness is that he's very poor at short passing, at seeing a short pass. Sounds daft, doesn't it? Because that's the easiest one there is. But he needs to play with people; he needs to link up with people more."

Now we're into the glamour zone—the people who make the goals, and the people who take them. Connolly and Cross, wingers—one's twenty-three, and the other's just a kid.

"They've got flair, a lot of flair. I say to the pair of them, especially Cross, be unpredictable—because if a defender knows what you're going to do, he's won the battle. If he doesn't, you have. It's like a dance, quick-quick-slow, slow-quick-slow—if you go at defenders at the same pace all the time, they can read you. But Cross is a natural. Obviously we work with him, show him how to do things—but a lot of it's natural talent, he can do things without thinking about it. He's got a good football brain."

Cross played for the first time last year, aged sixteen, but Flynn said he considered playing him in a friendly game at fifteen; he knew he was that good. "But we knew he was going to be big; it would have been a bit too much pressure."

So how's he coping? How's his temperament? In a word central to the lexicon of British soccer, has he got *character*?

"He's seventeen going on twenty-seven. He's a man. I've got another kid in the reserve team who's played in the first team, he's nineteen, but he's nine in the head. But Cross, he's a man in everything that he does. Sky's the limit."

For every talent like Cross, there's ten more that fall by the way. Or a hundred, who knows? Ticking them off on his fingers, Flynn said, "The pitfalls are drink. And at his age, women—and then, believing what other people tell him, other people than us. If he believes what we tell him, he'll go a long way—but if he believes people outside the game saying he's the best thing on earth, he'll come unstuck. He's just learning his trade, learning it well—but you've got to get trust. We had a kid I released last year, got in the first team, similar ability—and he went to pot. Out at night, girls, clubs . . . he's playing Sunday league football in Runcorn now."

Connolly has traveled the other way. He never played in the pros before Wrexham; he was working in a chip shop in Liverpool, playing Sunday morning football. So what did Flynn see in him?

"Tricks—he's got the tricks of an older professional. Then both of them, surprisingly for wingers, are good in the air. And they've both got good vision, good awareness, they can see what's about them. Then they're both good passers, good crossers of the ball. Connolly's not as good a crosser as Cross is, and he's very weak on his right foot—Cross is comfortable on both feet, but strongly left-sided—"

Stop the tape. What does it mean, when a player's "strong

on his left foot"? When you're streaking down the sideline, and your job's to play the ball in across the face of the goal to your strikers, naturally you'll make the pass with your outside foot, so you're turning into the direction of the pass. Hence Connolly, weak on his right, plays down the left side, so it's off his stronger left foot that the ball comes in.

Restart. What about defence, when the other side have the ball, and the wingers track back to help out their full backs? Flynn laughed. "They're not very good. Not the best. Very willing, the pair of them. But sometimes they can be a nuisance." And one of the problems with 4-4-2 is that the wingers have to come back at all—but we'll get to that.

Cross and Watkin got on the team late November, back when Wrexham started climbing. Since then Cross has six goals from fourteen games, and Watkin has eight. But Gary Bennett's played nearly the whole season, and in twenty-nine league and cup games he's scored eighteen times. That's respectable.

"We got Bennett from Chester, for nothing. He's twenty-nine, and technically not as good as some of the others—but he has a great belief in his ability to score goals. He laughs and jokes . . . the way we train, it all involves the ball, using the ball, working with the ball. So Bennett comes and says, Oh look, let's run, I'm good at running. Never mind this football, let's just run . . . but he knows where the goals are.

"Watkin's younger, twenty-one—but he's a late developer. Hardy was in the team at seventeen, Cross, Owen—Watkin's been here as long as them, but he didn't get in the team till he was twenty. But when he was eighteen, my contacts with the PFA [the player's union] said, D'you want somebody to go to New Zealand for six months? So I sent him. And before I sent him he was five eight, five nine, skinny little kid. Then he came back and walked through the door and I thought, *Ooooph.* Not the same person, this. He'd grown in his shoulders, he'd put on two inches, and he'd come out of himself. He's a shy lad, he's still quiet—but the independence brought him out a bit more."

So as goalscorers, what have the two of them got?

"Any goalscorer will tell you they don't know. It's a knack, and you can't explain knacks. You don't think about it—when you start thinking about it, that's when you don't score. But they complement each other. And Watkin's ability, his technical ability—he's very good with his back to goal, he's involved in the buildup, he can turn people. Bennett's different, he wants the ball played in front of him, especially played in behind defenders—he's good at going at people."

In other words, Watkin has more skill on the ball. He can take it with his back to goal and some hairy arsed defender on his neck, and he can turn and slip round that guy—or he can shield it, hold it up to feed to other people—while Bennett's faster, and just likes tearing on through. Psycho . . . but either way the two of them, just now, are scoring goals. They're the front two men in the 4-4-2, doing the thing that, finally, we all go to see.

February 20, 1993
Wrexham v. Gillingham

We've played away from home twice, won one, drawn one. Cardiff have gone second, Wrexham have dropped to third. We've made the semifinals of the Welsh Cup—and our opponents over the two legs of that fixture will be Cardiff. So now February fades, and Gillingham come to town—twenty-first in the league, without an away win all season. But the Gills won't roll over and die for us, they don't want to be relegated; there are no easy games.

At least the weather's perking up. The sun's shining through creamy clouds in a bright blue sky, Wrexham win a corner straight from the kickoff, and it seems we're going to enjoy ourselves—which just shows you how wrong you can be.

The Gills win a corner, the ball floats in, Morris jumps to claim it—and drops it. In the ensuing scrap a defender saves him, scooping the ball over the crossbar. Troubled, the crowd try putting Gillingham in their place:

You're going down to the Vauxhall Conference

And after that they fall silent, because for a long while now nothing happens, nothing at all. There's no urgency, no penetration; Watkin and Bennett spend long periods invisible. The ball wanders to no purpose round the middle of the field, and thick gray clouds come to cover the sun. The crowd, vexed, begin rhythmically demanding the obvious:

Attack! Attack! Attack!

But we don't. Cross is quiet, and a few injuries cause delays that kill for good any faint notion that there might be something to watch here. The men with the magic sponges trot out to tend the bruises.

All we are saying
Is give us a goal

Nobody does, and the first half ends, and the second half begins, and Alan goes for a piss. So then Cross wriggles through two guys, and fires a shot in the side netting—a shot at goal! I'd half forgotten what that looked like. I try the goal-stimulating method myself, wandering off to the foul brick shack—where the puddles have dried up outside, only for a vast new one to form in the doorway instead, a great pool of undigested beer that you could maybe jump across, if you were Carl Lewis—and when I come back, sure enough, we've put the ball in the net. But it's disallowed; Watkin was offside. I'll explain offside later, but right now it's just one of those days—and the crowd is angry with it.

What the fuck
What the fuck
What the fuck is going on?

Watching me take notes Alan asks, "Have you used the word torpid there yet?"

Cross looks jaded. He's seventeen, and he's tired; Flynn substituted him last week, and now he does it again. He sends on John Paskin, a big man from Cape Town, and he does more in five minutes than Cross did all game. With fifteen minutes left we get a corner, then another; Connolly curls it over, Paskin leaps and heads home. The roar that rises is one of purest relief. 1-0.

We get another corner, and their keeper drops it. Two yards out from an empty net, Lake thwacks the loose ball high against the crossbar—but the crowd are so pleased something's happening, anything, that they readily forgive him.

Sign him on!
Sign him on!

Then, with ten minutes to go, Psycho snakes into the area, and a despairing defender trips him. He gets up and comes to the crowd grinning, fists clenched, thumbs up; he pelts the penalty home and we're 2-0 winners, and it's afternoons like this that get you promoted. You play like sleepwalkers for seventy minutes, it's a total dud, and you win the thing anyhow.

Item: Substitutions

Each entrant to the World Cup brings a squad of twenty-two. You name eleven to start each game, and five more to sit on the bench. Any two of these can go on as a substitute at any time in the game, either as a tactical replacement, or because someone's injured. As for the player taken off, that's it—once you're off, you're off.

Generally, one of the five on the bench will be a back-up keeper. But a manager will prefer not to use him, because once a game's begun his subs are about the only way (except for halftime which Flynn calls "the most important ten minutes of my week, every week") in which he can directly alter what's happening. So unless the keeper's injured the manager will use his substitutes to make changes in the outfield. A crude example: if you're holding a narrow lead with ten minutes left, you might pull out a forward, and play an extra defender—or, if you're behind and getting desperate, you'd do the opposite.

A real example: against the Gills, with a tired young winger, the 4-4-2 wasn't penetrating a packed and obdurate defence, so Flynn took Cross out, and stuck on a third striker instead. 4-4-2 became 4-3-3—because if we were going to win that game, the way to do it was to pack up playing fancy, and punch a hole through the middle instead.

Bad News

Barnet and Cardiff both won; Wrexham stayed third on 52 points. In the program, Flynn said the target was 60 points as quick as possible; I asked him why, and he said, "All I'm saying is, once you've got 60, you've got a good chance of at least making the play-offs—and once you've got something, it's easy to go for the next thing, isn't it?"

But, I said, it wasn't a good game, awful first half—and he laughed. "We've played worse than that. But give Gillingham credit—they got so many men behind the ball, they made it difficult to break them down. And they've drawn their last five away games, so they've set their stall out, haven't they? Let's not lose, that's their attitude—'cause they're down the bottom of the league. So we had to be patient."

Now Barnet and Cardiff both won . . .

"Doesn't matter. Doesn't concern me. It's what we do that matters. If we keep winning, nobody can catch us."

But he wasn't as happy as he might have been; Mike Lake had gone back to Sheffield. He'd gone because a player in the Third Division won't normally earn more than the national average wage—$300 a week, or less—and Lake wanted more. It was bad news, and Flynn was disappointed. "I think he'll realize he's made an error. Just when he'll realize it, I don't know. But I think he will."

And next Saturday, he has to take a team to Bury. He won't have Lake, and he won't have Humes either; the captain's totted up enough disciplinary points (which you tend to do as center half, knocking strikers about) that he must now begin a two-match suspension. So Flynn doesn't know what he'll do; he'll watch the reserves play on Wednesday, and decide after that who's on form. And, he said, "I might change the system, because it's Bury; they scored six last Saturday. So"—he laughed—"I'll play eight at the back."

But what he's thinking of doing, in fact, is playing a sweeper—playing 5-3-2, instead of 4-4-2. And since most of the teams at USA '94 will do that too, we'll look at it in more detail a little later.

Round-Up

Hard times in eastern Europe. The indispensable *World Soccer* magazine reports that Polish side Hutnik Warsaw have signed a Russian—and paid for him with a TV set and a VCR. Another club took two players from Kiev in Ukraine, and sent back in exchange a lorryload of potatoes.

* * *

It could be worse. Sarajevo say they'd like to play some invitation games—but they can't get out of the city to play them. Radovan Karadzic, the slippery villain who leads Bosnia's Serbs, was formerly the team psychologist—but, says the manager, "He wasn't very good. The players fell asleep whenever he gave pep talks." Now he keeps them awake shelling them instead.

Hard times in the Third Division, too. To pay wages, debts, and a $75,000 fine for "financial irregularities," leaders Barnet confirm that their entire playing staff is up for sale. But Barnet are weird. Manager Barry Fry has been sacked and reinstated so many times I've lost count, and has said publicly that the club's chairman, who keeps sacking him—a scalper named Stan Flashman—should do the club a favor and sack himself instead. As for the fire sale, Fry says, "I won't encourage any bids. I'd hate to throw promotion away." And at Wrexham, of course, we'd love them to do just that.

No such trouble in Italy. AC Milan's rival in that city, Internazionale, buy Dutchmen Wim Jonk and Dennis Bergkamp from Ajax of Amsterdam. The combined fee tops $15 million.

In the Premier League, Manchester United are second, two points behind Aston Villa. They might have been five points behind—with eight minutes left last Saturday, they were 1-0 down to Southampton—but then a prodigiously gifted nineteen-year-old Welshman named Ryan Giggs scored two goals in two minutes. The tabloids dub him "the Prince of Wales," but United manager Alex Ferguson won't let the press anywhere near him. He will only say, "His talent is maturing bit by bit. In four years' time we'll be able to say what the finished article is." Southampton keeper Tim Flowers, however, is not so reticent. "Speaking as a fan, I thought he was pure magic. Speaking as a member of the keepers' union, he's an absolute nightmare. He goes down the wing like a snake, sidewinding all the way, and you never know if he'll cut inside and shoot, or dip outside and cross. It's frightening what he could achieve."

In Liverpool, meanwhile, another stadium falls silent. After two ten-year-old boys are charged with the abduction and murder in that city of two-year-old Jamie Bulger, 36,680 people keep a minute's silence in his memory. Fans hold up a banner saying R.I.P. JAMES; it's on the front page of every paper the next day. The country is bewildered by the crime, fearful that it betokens some terrible slide further toward moral vacuum. A Liverpool policeman who sometimes has a drink in the valley shakes his head and says sadly of the children in his city, "Half of them are junkies. They don't know what they're doing any more."

Moral vacuum? When the opponent's keeper is in goal at our end, here's what the Kop chants each time he takes a goal kick:

> *You're shit—ha!*
> *Fuck off—ha!*
> *You've got AIDS—ha ha ha!*

There are people in boardrooms who don't behave much better. Our game is run, it often seems, by greedy, fractious nitwits. The dispute of the day concerns FIFA's World Youth Cup, kicking off in Australia on April 7. That weekend, Arsenal, Sheffield Wednesday, and Tottenham Hotspur have FA Cup quarter-finals, and all three have key players wanted by England for the Under-20's in Australia. If they don't release them, they can be fined. There is a permanent source of friction between clubs and national teams. United didn't release Ryan Giggs for a Welsh friendly with Ireland last week; they said he had a thigh strain. Three days later, he put two goals past Tim Flowers.

Qualifiers for USA '94 continue around Europe. Northern Ireland travel to Albania, where some of the party stay in a hotel with no power, no food, no running water, and cardboard in the windows where the glass ought to be. The Ulstermen win 2-1, and get out as quick as they can.

In Nicosia, Belgium beat Cyprus 3-0; with six wins out of six, they look certain to go through to the finals. The Welsh are in this group, along with Romania, Czechoslovakia, and the Faroe Islands—and there's only one other slot behind the Belgians. So can Ryan Giggs grace the American stage, and Wales make it to the World Cup for the first time since 1958? Looks a long shot right now.

Meanwhile, the English story of the day continues to be Gazza. After belching on Italian TV, he's now farted at the Italian press. Furthermore, after a poor performance for England against San Marino, it's concluded that he is simply "too fat." He is, says one paper, "a bona-fide wobble-bottom"—so all we can talk about now is whether he's drinking himself off the rails.

All we can talk about, that is, when we're not grieving for Jamie Bulger. The flowers pile up where he died, in mute and mystified memorial.

6

The First World Champions

"Other countries have their history. Uruguay has its football."
—Uruguayan manager Ondino
Viera, 1966

Uruguay 1930

The Fédération Internationale des Football Associations has 178 members, so since they started they've been putting on fat at a rate, give or take, of two nations a year. The organization was the brainchild of French journalist Robert Guérin; the founding members were France, Belgium, Denmark, Holland, Spain, Sweden, and Switzerland, and they first met in Paris in 1904. The English, despite exporting the game to all points of the compass, still thought an international meant playing Scotland—but they joined two years later, and the FA's treasurer, D. B. Woolfall, was elected president.

By the time of the first World Cup, the FA had pulled out. The specific reason was a conflict over the definition of amateurism; a more general cause was the belief that Johnny Foreigner didn't know which way was up, a belief more pompously formulated in England's 1928 letter of withdrawal: "The great majority of the Associations affiliated with FIFA are of comparatively recent formation, and as a consequence cannot have the knowledge which only experience can bring." As another consequence, the English missed the first three World Cups, and they didn't rejoin FIFA for another twenty years.

Meanwhile, the men who made the World Cup were also French: Jules Rimet, FIFA president from 1920 to 1954, and Henri Delaunay, FIFA secretary from 1919 to 1956. The idea of the tournament was current by 1924, when Uruguay came to the Paris Olympics and won soccer gold with eye-opening grace and ease. By 1928, when they took gold again in Amsterdam, it was plain that the Olympics weren't big enough for soccer; the professional game needed a party of its own.

Uruguay said they'd pay the costs of all who cared to come; they said they'd build a Centenary Stadium, so the tournament could mark the hundredth anniversary of their nationhood. Europe, peeved that they weren't hosting the first party themselves, said thanks but no thanks. It was a three-week voyage—and only France, Belgium, Yugoslavia, and Romania (their squad selected by King Carol) had the stomach or the decency to show up.

The other participants in the 1930 World Cup were Argentina, Bolivia, Brazil, Chile, Mexico, Paraguay, Peru, and the United States. U.S. soccer was coming to the close of its "golden age," when the eastern seaboard's American Soccer League—with teams like Bethlehem Steel, Brooklyn Wanderers, the Fall River Marksmen, and the Providence Clamdiggers—drew crowds averaging 6,000 through the twenties.

Many players in this league, and most of the national side, were emigrant Brits; in Montevideo they beat Belgium 3-0, Paraguay 3-0, and advanced to the semifinal. And unless you're a soccer freak and a stat hound, I'll bet you didn't know that the United States were in the last four of the first World Cup.

Argentina trounced them 6-1; Uruguay demolished Yugoslavia by the same score, and the first final was on. 90,000 filled the Centenary Stadium two hours before kickoff; after trailing 2-1 at halftime, Uruguay won 4-2. Across the Plate River an enraged mob in Buenos Aires attacked the Uruguayan consulate, and could not be dispersed until the police started shooting. Welcome to world football.

Referees

The man who took charge of the first World Cup final was a Belgian named John Langenus. Under FIFA's auspices today, a million referees run 20 million games every year—and why any of them do it, frankly, I can't imagine for one minute.

Among British crowds, the referee is known as "the wanker in the black"—though, sadly, it's no longer the case that he automatically wears black now that referees, like players, are dressed in ever more luridly colored uniforms. I say sadly, because "the wanker in the cerise/aquamarine/vermilion" doesn't have the same ring—but whatever the color, this is a man with a job from hell.

He has two linesmen to help him. They trot up and down the sidelines waving their flags when the ball goes out of play, and saying who gets to throw it back in. They also wave when they think a man's offside—but while they draw the ref's attention to that, or to any other misdemeanor he's not seen (as in, I'll just whack this bugger in the throat while the wanker in the tangerine's not looking) the ref's judgment is always final.

Now, you try jogging about among twenty-two fast, fit men busy crunching one another, and make sure they all do it by the book. You'll see it's not surprising that referees make mistakes. And some say it's high time they had recourse to replay cameras—but I'm opposed to this.

Soccer is not about justice. It's a drama—and criminally wrong decisions against you are part and parcel of that. "We was robbed" [*sic*] is integral to the fan's phrase book; there must be games where you leave aggrieved, or the games you leave enraptured could never be so sweet. And then, the sport goes on forever, like a rolling wheel—so you get robbed, OK, you'll be back—and the brew, next time, will be all the spicier for the memory of that theft to be avenged.

Besides, if the ref was always right, how could we shout at him?

If a foul is committed, the ref blows his whistle and the team sinned against gets a free kick. When the run of the ball, however, means play can continue with an advantage to the side sinned against, the ref should let it pass ("play advantage"); the essence of his job is to let the game flow with a minimum of interruption.

Under orders from FIFA to come down hard on the wicked, it's got tougher for refs to do that, and they're getting more picky. In Britain, we're not inclined to approve of this; it's a man's game, and namby-pamby foreigners writhing about on the turf in quest of Academy Awards is not the done thing. Namby-pamby foreigners, meanwhile, asked for an opinion of our game, will often say that they admire its physical nature.

This is a polite way of saying we're unskilled morons who play like cavemen—but it is generally acknowledged that we don't go about our business with malice. We don't spit in our opponents' faces, hack them when they're not looking, rake them when they're down, or jab elbows in their windpipes when the wanker in the bile green's gone walkabout.

Uruguay and Argentina, on the other hand, have unsavory reputations for this sort of cynical provocation. In the quarter-final of the 1966 World Cup at Wembley, Argentina's behavior against England was famously disgraceful. Amid a welter of fouls, the Argentine captain Antonio Rattin pursued the German referee around the park in a permanent lather of protesting intimidation, until the referee sent him off—and Rattin, for ten eternal minutes, refused to go. The English manager called them "animals."

Scotland's manager applied the same term to Uruguay after a brutish encounter at Mexico '86. In Italy four years later, Uruguay said they were reformed, and they were. Argentina, however, turned up sly and dirty as usual, and achieved the dubious distinction of being the first team to have a man sent off in a World Cup final. Not satisfied, they had a second man sent off soon afterward; so, not for the first time, a referee spent long minutes with his whistle in his mouth and his finger pointing to the sideline, surrounded by a jostle of baying maniacs.

FIFA's report on Argentina in 1966 said, "The referee would have been justified in bringing a charge against certain players for assault." It is, like I said, a job from hell.

Away from malice and dementia, what's a foul? According to the rule book, it's one of ten Bad Deeds:

A player should not intentionally kick an opponent,
trip him,

jump at him,
charge him "in a violent or dangerous manner,"
charge him from behind,
hit him,
spit on him,
hold him,
push him,
or handle the ball.

None of which, in the red mist of high-speed, high-tension international play, are the most clear-cut of matters to judge—but in essence you play the ball, not the man.

And obviously, now and then, someone does something so blatantly injurious and malevolent, whether he's near the ball or not, that unless you're having an eye test at the time, it's clear as day you send him off. Otherwise, all I can say is I'm glad I'm not the wanker in the black who's got to judge it.

A run-of-the-mill foul results in a free kick. If it's something more serious, however, the ref will show you the yellow card—you've been "booked." That's a caution; do something book-able twice, and you're off.

And if you do something Really Bad—if you set out with the clear intention, let's say, of chopping the other man into hamburger on the spot—then the ref shows the red card and that's it. No appeal, off, *now*.

"Foul and abusive language" comes under the heading of Really Bad—so don't tell the ref about his parentage. Leave that to the crowd.

Along with the cards, there's a suspension system. In World Cup play, if you get a red card—or if, over the course of two games, you get two yellow ones—then you're barred from the next game. This has one interesting consequence. If you've got a yellow card, the next lot you play will know about it—and they'll know you'll be inclined to tread more carefully as a result. Or if the next team you face are Argentina, they'll throw themselves to the ground every time you go anywhere near them.

And in case you think I'm being snotty about sneaky folk from other nations here, I'll point out that the winners of FIFA's Fair Play award at Italia '90, awarded to the team with the best disciplinary record, were England.

Italy 1934

Uruguay didn't show up for the second World Cup. They were piqued because Europe didn't go to theirs, and they were embroiled in a players' strike anyhow. But sixteen other countries were there—after another sixteen had been knocked out in qualifiers—and one of them was Egypt.

There would not be another African finalist until Morocco got to Mexico in 1970. Soccer in Africa today is an enormously potent force; the final of the 1993 Under-17 World Championship, for example, was contested by Nigeria and Ghana, and continental competition at club and national level is followed with vivid fervor. But in the early days, the game prospered in those countries where England traded a great deal more than it did where England ruled. In the summery dominions of India, Australia, New Zealand, South Africa, and the West Indies, colonial types preferred to play cricket, while in less-developed parts of the Empire, there was no urban culture in which soccer could breed. And, of course, there was no more desire that the indigenous people should engage in soccer's unruly gatherings than there had been that the peasants should do so in the Middle Ages.

Those who had more equal relations with the English, however, started teaching the country that invented the game some lessons. England suffered its first defeat abroad in 1929, losing 4-3 in Spain; how they would have fared at the World Cup is, of course, impossible to gauge—but the managers of the two favored teams, Italy and Austria, were both men who'd learnt from the English, and then taken their knowledge further.

Juventus's rival club in Turin is Torino, set up in 1906; the club's guiding light was Vittorio Pozzo, who'd studied English in Manchester and become close friends with one of the players at Manchester United. In 1934, he was running the Italian team.

As for the Austrians, managed by the equally Anglophiliac Hugo Meisl, they were known across Europe as the "Wonder Team." In England in 1932 they lost 4-3, but they were an unsettling surprise all the same. With their skill, their teamwork, their finely timed running both on and off the ball, they confounded the heavier English, one of whom said admiringly afterward, "If only they knew how to finish!" And these were, perhaps, prophetic words.

The 1934 World Cup, with sixteen countries, had a straight knockout format. In the first round, Egypt put up stubborn resistance against Hungary before losing 4-2. Among the other losers were Brazil, Argentina, and the U.S.A.—trounced 7-1 by the Italians—so those three came a long way to play one game.

It was apparent by now that this was not an attractive competition. Under Mussolini's greedy gaze, Pozzo's Italians could be as ugly as they were organized; describing the baleful atmosphere of the times, John Langenus would later say, "Italy wanted to win, it was natural, but they allowed it to be seen too clearly." In the quarter-finals, they kicked lumps out of Spain; when it went to a replay, only four of the Spanish side were fit to start the second game. Austria, meanwhile, beat Hungary 2-1 in what Meisl described as "a brawl, not an exhibition of football."

The two sides then met in the semifinal; on a muddy surface inimical to their crafted game, what few chances the Austrians made for themselves they didn't complete, and the Italians won 1-0. In the final in Rome, they beat Czechoslovakia 2-1 in extra time, and soccer had its second world champions. But it hadn't been pretty—Pozzo's side took the aggression and discipline of the English and, pushed by their political masters, went over the limit into thuggery. When the new champions subsequently met the English at Arsenal's ground in North London in November 1934, the match would go down in history as "the Battle of Highbury." There was a broken toe on one side, a broken nose on the other; England won 3-2, but in the circumstances it didn't mean much. As one of the English players remarked later, in a trenchant tone of wounded prejudice, it was "a bit hard to play like a gentleman when somebody closely resembling an enthusiastic member of the Mafia is wiping his studs down your legs."

Happily, however, the Italians these days play a more beautiful game altogether. And while the British for the most part persist with their 4-4-2, what the Italians play for the most part is the sweeper system.

7

The Sweeper System

The 4-3-3 deployed by Wrexham to break down Gillingham, and by England to destroy San Marino in a World Cup quali- fier three days later, is an assault formation. England used it because they expected "to fill their boots"; to have a goal feast.

You could fit the population of San Marino into Wembley three times over, and still leave empty seats. In England, there are 2,250,000 registered players; in San Marino, there are 1,033. They've had international credentials since 1990; before this game they'd played 12, lost 12, scored 2 goals, and conceded 53. They have two full-time pros, from the lower reaches of the Italian league; the rest are just regular guys. The keeper drives a bus; another of their players is Gazza's postman in Rome, and Gazza probably makes more in a week than the Sammarinese do in a year. So England played a 4-3-3.

And there are mean souls who say San Marino and their kind should play a pre-qualifying round before troubling the likes of England in their Empire Stadium. But I say let them play—why shouldn't they have a day out? When the Faroe Islands played Wales in spring 1992, they turned up in their fishing boats, and good luck to them. (They lost 6-0.)

The Sammarinese came by plane, saying on the way they'd be happy if they could hold the score to 5-0. And England's 4-3-3 looked like this:

Chris Woods
(Sheffield Wednesday)

Lee Dixon   Des Walker   Tony Adams   Tony Dorigo
(Arsenal)   (Sampdoria)   (Arsenal)   (Leeds United)

David Batty   Carlton Palmer   John Barnes
(Leeds United) (Sheffield Wednesday) (Liverpool)

Paul Gascoigne
(Lazio)

Les Ferdinand   David Platt
(Queen's Park Rangers)   (Juventus)

In this formation, when England have the ball, Palmer holds the middle, and Barnes or Batty go forward; they're wide men, but with license to roam and cut in. As for Gazza, his role in the front three is to play "in the hole" behind the forwards, an attacking midfielder linking middle to front.

England won 6-0, and it was widely considered a triumph for San Marino. One goal was dubious—it was debatable whether the whole of the ball had crossed the line—while three more only came in the final minutes, when the Sammarinese were exhausted. On top of which, the bus driver saved a penalty. So, sure, the whole game was played in San Marino's half—but for much of it England huffed and puffed against ten defenders, which, given the gulf between the sides, wasn't really good enough.

And it's hard being an international footballer, because in the big soccer nations you're expected unthinkingly not just to win every game, but to do so by towering margins, in scintillating style. Anything less, and the cruel jeers of enraged legions of Loyal Supporters will cascade mercilessly in your ears. For example: England performed dismally in the last European Championship, Sweden '92. After Sweden beat them in their last game, one of the tabloid headlines they came home to said: SWEDES 2, TURNIPS 1.

* * *

Most of the world, most of the time, play neither 4-4-2 nor 4-3-3. Most of the world, instead, play 5-3-2 when they haven't got the ball, and 3-5-2 when they have. It's called the sweeper system, and it looks like this:

keeper

sweeper

center half   center half

right back   left back

midfield   midfield   midfield

striker   striker

Brian Flynn: "A sweeper is an extra man behind your two central defenders—which means your two wide defenders need to be more advanced for your attacking play. It's a pyramid, or a triangle—and it's insurance down the middle of your defence. So if it works well, when the opposition's got the ball, the sweeper rarely touches it—but when it's not working, then he's forever covering people, making tackles, doing this and doing that. And then, when you've got the ball yourself, he's your spare man—so instead of your wide men supplying your ammunition, your initial forward ball, you expect the sweeper to do that. He's your starting point then."

So when might Flynn play a sweeper?

"If you look at the opposition, the style of play they have— if it's direct and it's long, I'd play a sweeper against that. I've played it once this season, at Lincoln, because they're direct and they're big, they're physically big—and we drew 0-0, so it worked. Very few chances either end—but it served its purpose. A point away from home."

I got the impression it hadn't been pretty. The "long game" generally isn't—"long" meaning you don't bother playing the ball to feet through midfield, but just hoof it as high and as far forward as you can, as often as you can. Ireland are the principal international exponents of this, and it's horrendously difficult to play against—the whole point being that you're not really playing football at all, you're just preventing more skilled opposition from playing instead. It's a frantic heave-ho, brain-numbingly ugly to watch—so Flynn, I presumed, combating Lincoln's lumpen long game, played a sweeper as a more defensive approach than his normal, swashbuckling brand of 4-4-2.

"With the players I've got, yes. Because Hardy and Jones, they're not bad going forward . . ."

But they're not naturally creative; they're not wing backs.

"Wing back" is a relatively recent coinage, and denotes (as the term suggests) an attacking defender. In the past, defenders were just that—big guys, tacklers, "stoppers." They weren't there to play football—they were there to stop the other lot playing it, and then hoof it up front.

In the modern game, however, everyone on the field should be able to play—they should be "comfortable on the ball." So for the sweeper system to work offensively, as opposed to just being a defensive measure to contain the likes of Lincoln, you need full backs who are quick and skilled, and who like to go forward. When you've got the ball, they become wingers—wing backs—and then 5-3-2 turns into 3-5-2.

Faced with this, 4-4-2 can start to creak. Your midfield's outmanned, your wingers backpedal, your strikers get cut off. . . .

Look at it this way. With 4-4-2, your back line's flat, and once it's broken that's that—you're through on the keeper. With 5-3-2, however, your center halves can "mark" individuals (i.e., play man-to-man defence), rather than covering zones—and if they're beaten, there's still the sweeper to tidy up behind them. So a back four's glass, but a sweeper system's rubber. Hit one, it breaks; hit the other, it bounces back at you. You lose the ball—and next thing you know, you've got the sweeper feeding the wing backs and they're tearing up in your face. Thus, the great merit of the system is its flexibility; although, like any system, it is by no means fail-safe.

The creator of the role is one of the all-time greats, Franz Beckenbauer, who won the World Cup for Germany as a player in 1974 and as a manager in 1990—and in one version or another, most countries have followed his example.

In recent times, the finest player in the part has been Franco Baresi of AC Milan and Italy, a player said by one Italian manager to be "on first-name terms with the ball." And he's one reason Milan's unbeaten run was extended (by early March 1993) to the astonishing tally of fifty-six games.

But we must return to the proviso that systems are starting points, not miracle cures. Many say, for the most part rightly, that the Italian league (awash with sweepers) is a finer, more cultured spectacle than the blood and thunder you get in Britain. But like his predecessor Vittorio Pozzo, Arrigo Sacchi, who took Milan to the top of that league and now runs the Italian national side, is a fan of the English game—and AC Milan often play 4-4-2. So ultimately, in soccer, it's not what you play, it's how you play it, and with whom.

To sum up: The sweeper system, which on paper is apparently more defensive (five at the back), can in fact be a liberating pattern, releasing all bar your three central defenders to go forward in unpredictable, potentially uncontainable ways. And 4-4-2, which on paper looks more devil-may-care, can end up being a defensive struggle—because if the other team start pegging you back, your wingers end up retreating all the time to help out their full backs, and then there's no one to supply the front men.

So there's nothing intrinsically wrong with one system or another; as ever, it's down to the players on the day. But while 4-4-2, as played with attacking panache by Brian Flynn's Wrexham, is fine in the hurly-burly of the Third Division, when it comes to the highest levels of the international game, you'll have a hard time cutting the mustard with it against teams who lock you out with a sweeper.

March 6, 1993
Wrexham v. Hereford United

February ends in chill blasts from the Arctic. On Saturday, March 27, Wrexham go north of Manchester to Bury; snow falls before the game, and the wind chill's well below zero. With Lake gone, Humes suspended, and Bury on a roll, Flynn plays Pejic as a sweeper in a five-man defence—and Bury win 3-1.

Flynn shrugs. "They caused us more problems than I thought they would. They played three up front, no winger—but they're on a run. They were just better than us."

At halftime we were 2-0 down; we went back to 4-4-2. It may sound odd (you're losing, so you thin out the back), but the idea was to cause more trouble in their half so their front men got less ball to cause trouble in ours—not that it worked.

Flynn said, "It didn't make much difference, because they got a third goal early on. Then they relaxed a bit, so we got a consolation—but the better team won on the day."

And why weren't we any good on the day?

"Because too many players didn't perform. But I regard it as a one-off. Certain players had a bad game, and I know they won't perform like that again. They've got enough character not to do that again."

In the fabric of our lives, Part 2: Bryn the Man with the Video Van does his rounds Wednesday and Saturday evenings, renting out movies for the village VCRs. So the Wednesday after the defeat at Bury I'm going back into the house with a tape and Bryn says, "Did you hear? He got his man."

It takes only a nanosecond to decipher this remark. Bryn's a Wrexham Gold Bond agent, taking 75 cents a week off me for the club's prize draw—and what he's telling me on my doorstep on a Welsh winter evening is this: that Brian Flynn's signed Mike Lake after all. I asked Flynn how he got him and he shrugged and he smiled. He said, "Compromise."

Three days later, Lake puts the ball in the net against Hereford United. It's disallowed for offside, but it hardly matters—we're one up already and the second's coming anyhow, a beauty of a goal, a rapid and gracious exposition of what the game should be about.

The ball comes to Connolly in the center circle. Feinting outside, he sends his marker that way, lays off a short pass across the circle to Lake instead, then sprints forward. Completing a deft one-two, Lake gives it back to him as he advances, the precision of the interchange leaving a second man beaten—so Connolly's free, heading deep into the left side of their half. Ahead of him, Bennett moves into that side of their penalty area; Hardy tears up the wing from left back, outside of these two. Connolly gives the ball forward to Bennett; he takes it with his back to their center half, edging goalward from the corner of the area, the marker hustling hard on his shoulder. So, looking up, he pushes the ball out to Hardy, then turns into the man on his back. Hardy, cutting in from the wing, gives it back to him—and Bennett's able this time to take the ball from the side, and ahead of him. He swerves goalside of his marker, bearing in from a tight angle, while Watkin streaks up at the far post. The keeper hesitates, holding his line; he doesn't come out to Bennett, as he expects the

ball to zip across in front of him to Watkin. So Bennett fires—
and as the ball flies past the keeper, it's the first time in the
entire move it's left the ground.

Which is how it ought to be. Four players were involved (not
counting the defender whose clearance to Connolly began the
move in the first place), and between them they played five
sweet passes to feet before Bennett finished. It wasn't the
absolute ideal, because not all five passes were made with the
first touch—"one-touch football" being the Brazilian paradigm—but in the Third Division, this was class. Hereford
managed nothing like it all game, and it was a good measure
of Wrexham's superiority thoughout. Cross scored the first on
four minutes, after half an hour we were 2-0 up. . . .

And yet we went home disappointed. It should have been a
rout, but it stayed 2-0. As Alan put it, a game that started full
of promise went "all pear-shaped on us."

The weather was back from bitterly freezing to merely cold.
Under a dull gray sky 5,280 came to the Racecourse, and for
thirty minutes we got what we came for. Hereford, nineteenth
in the table, were reduced to a series of desperate hoiks out of
a buckling defence as Wrexham spilt all around them. There
were passes connecting, crosses sailing, defenders flailing—
and as each shot fired in the ground fell silent, all eyes tracing
the flight of the ball while their keeper leapt like a salmon, the
last thin line between Hereford United and an ignominious
thrashing. Lake was winning the midfield tussles (to uproari-
ous applause), while Pejic at the back was fiercely solid. And
we went 2-0 up . . .

> *Everywhere we go*
> *People want to know*
> *Who's that team in the red and white?*
> *Wrexham Wrexham we're all right*

Then the referee went crazy. For the remainder of the game,
certainly, Wrexham eased up—but they weren't helped by a
string of calamitously inept decisions, the last in the closing
minutes being a failure to give a penalty that was, quite simply, incomprehensible. By the end, I figured we'd been robbed
three times; when I asked Flynn how many penalties he
thought we should have had he said, "At least two."

So with the referee's help the game lost its flow, the score stayed stuck, and the crowd stood fizzing with helpless rage. Mostly we still attacked and attacked—but if they're reduced to knocking you over in the area and you get nothing for it, after a while you start wondering why you bother.

Then Cross got brusquely sandwiched between two opponents, and went down clutching his ankle. You could hear panic in the stands, men begging for play to be stopped. After lengthy treatment he was helped off the field, hobbling—and when we use the term "campaign" to describe the long march of the season, the military reference is precise. It's war out there. We left that day feeling anxious for Cross, and generally disgruntled. We'd got three points, stayed third in the table—but we'd only scored two, when we should have had five.

I said to Flynn, we should have had way more than two.

"Yes. I don't like being disrespectful to the opposition, because we've been where they are now, but it was too easy for us—and when you're winning that comfortably, it's hard not to get complacent."

The referee didn't help.

"He had an off day. I've seen him before, he's experienced, and if he sat down now, I'm sure he'd realize he'd had a bad game. I'm sure he would."

There were some scandalous decisions . . .

"He's only human."

Managers report on every game to the authorities, and mark the referee out of ten. But, Flynn said, "You don't say he was hopeless, you've got to be constructive. And then, his decisions are his opinion—so he's not wrong, is he? The referee's never wrong."

What, even if he's blatantly wrong? When a guy trips over his own feet miles from any of our players, and gets a free kick for it anyhow?

"He gave that decision, and in his opinion he was right. 5,280 people thought he was wrong—but who's the one that matters?"

How many marks did you give him?

Flynn laughed. "Not many, I can tell you that."

Three days later, Wrexham would go to Darlington—and Flynn would have Tony Humes back from suspension. He was, he said, "Delighted. Our last ten games we've lost two, and both of them Tony wasn't playing."

What about Cross?

"He's all right."

So, with twelve games to go, I asked again: Are we going to get promoted?

"We're in a very strong position; we've got a very good chance. Every ten games I analyze how we're going, and you can turn statistics any way you want, but the first ten games we got fifteen points, the second ten we got eighteen, and the third ten we've had twenty-two. The first ten games we conceded eighteen goals, the second ten fourteen, and the third ten, it was ten. And conceding ten in ten—averaged out that's still a goal a game, that's not good enough—but if you look at it, out of ten games we've had four clean sheets, and that's a good ratio. We've been thumped twice by three goals away from home, that's all—so take that out, and we're hitting the standards we're looking for. Of course, it's all ifs and buts—but we've made progress all the way. And," he added, "we're top scorers in the division."

But defences will start packing in tight, now we get to the final stretch.

"We'll always score goals. We've got the players who can do that."

So how does he feel?

"I think we'll do it."

But how does he *feel*?

"I feel good. I feel the players are relaxed. It's pleasurable."

Because, as a young manager, he's not been here before.

"No. But I've been at the other end, and that's worse."

Round-Up

On February 27, every stadium in the country falls silent. Three days earlier, Bobby Moore died of cancer. Moore captained England ninety times, and led them to the World Cup in 1966; he's remembered for that, and for being the greatest defender of his day in all the world, and for being a gentleman. His smiling embrace with Pele, swapping shirts after their classic encounter in the 1970 World Cup in Mexico, is published in every paper; the tributes flow in. Franz Beckenbauer, speaking on television from Germany, tells how the news was broken there, and how they remembered him, and how Moore had become a good friend.

In the wake of Moore's death, the club v. country dispute over players for the World Youth Cup is resolved. The clubs back down; the players will go.

I was seven when England won the World Cup, a shade too young, and it wasn't that which got me into soccer; it was Chelsea winning the FA Cup in 1970. Chelsea then were glamour, they were the King's Road and pop stars—but now they've gone thirteen games without a win. On the wrong end of a thrashing at Blackburn the Chelsea fans sing, to the Vera Lynn tune,

> *We'll win again*
> *Don't know where*
> *Don't know when . . .*

I lived in London for eight years during my twenties, and went to Chelsea a good part of that time—but I went off them when, at the height of the hooligan psychosis in the mid-eighties, the club's chairman suggested installing electrified security fences to contain the fans. His customers, for Chrissake.

Alan's a Chelsea fan; when his family moved from Glasgow to London, that was where he went to watch his football. He remembers how, in the days before television, *Pathé Gazette* would film the crowd; before the game they'd come round the stands and whip them up, and get footage of people whooping and cheering, which they'd then use to cut in after a goal. So one time Alan watched Tottenham beat Chelsea, and a day or two later he went to the cinema—and there on the news he saw himself, a Chelsea fan, artificially cut into the film, leaping and cheering *for a Tottenham goal*. Decades later he still smarts over this, and wonders if it's possible to sue.

The Japanese FA, proposing plans for their bid for the 2002 World Cup, say they'd like to hold it in sixteen stadia, as opposed to Italy's twelve, or America's nine. They are, they say, a compact country, with decent transportation, they have the facilities—but can they play? Twenty-nine Asian countries contest qualifiers for USA '94 in May through October 1993;

the venues are Amman, Beijing, Tehran, Damascus, Qatar, Singapore, Seoul, Beirut, Kuala Lumpur, Riyadh, Dubai, and Tokyo. And then, I guess, we shall see.

> "Your mission is part of the confrontation between Iraq and the Forces of Evil embodied by the U.S. and its allies."
> —*Al-Qadissiya* newspaper, Baghdad, on Iraq's World Cup qualification campaign.

The International Board, the body that oversees the rules of the world game, meets in Hertfordshire. Because the English originally codified the game, the four "home unions"—England, Scotland, Wales, and Northern Ireland—each have a permanent seat on this board, while the other four seats rotate between other nations. But the board, in effect, is a rubber stamp for FIFA's executive. Fearful of losing those four seats (which, after all, are now wildly anachronistic), the British would probably say OK if FIFA secretary Sepp Blatter said, From now on we'll play underwater. As it is, he says we should have kick-ins from the sideline instead of throw-ins—and the board agrees for this to be experimented with in an Under-16 tournament in Turkey, and then an Under-17 tournament in Japan. And if that works, the Hungarian League will try it.

It's crazy. It devalues free kicks and corners, and it'll slow up the game—because now, every time the ball's out of play, everyone'll have to run upfield into set piece mode before it can come back. What's worse, however, is that in pursuit of more mayhemic goalmouth action, it'll mean less time spent playing football to get the ball in the goalmouth in the first place—which I thought, myself, was the idea of the game.

Official USA '94 merchandise is launched in Britain; baseball caps, tracksuits, hooded sweatshirts, and the rest. The president of Time Warner Sports Merchandising claims globewide sales of World Cup goodies will reach a billion dollars.

The inaugural championship of Tadzhikistan is indefinitely postponed due to civil unrest.

Thirty-four scouts watch Barnet's table-topping job lot beat Gillingham. When the deadline for transfers comes up in two weeks, will Barnet have anyone left to play for them?

* * *

Another troubled club, Birmingham City, in Chapter 11 since their previous owners went bust, are bought by a pornographer. Strange visions rise of what they might start selling in the club shop . . . but a precedent's been set here already. National Heritage Minister David Mellor ("the Minister for Fun") lost his job after the revelation that he'd been having an affair with an actress. We learnt, among other things, that he liked to do it in a Chelsea shirt. There's glamour for you.

In Liverpool, on March 6, they fall silent again. In 1989, ninety-five Liverpool fans were crushed to death against the security fences at Hillsborough. One who didn't die was Tony Bland, kept alive ever since in a Persistent Vegetative State. After long legal process, his parents win the right for their son to be allowed to die. Liverpool mourn their ninety-sixth loss.

After Hillsborough the fences are gone, and the grounds slowly improve. Tottenham Hotspur visit Manchester City's Maine Road in the FA Cup quarter-finals; City proudly unveil a $9 million new stand. With Spurs winning 4-2, two hundred City fans spill out of this stand and invade the pitch, presumably seeking to have the game called off. It takes fifteen minutes of police dogs and horses to get the situation in hand and play out the game, and these ugly images are seen on television all over Europe.

In the fabric of our lives, Part 3: The day after the ruckus at the Maine Road quarter-final, I visit a friend in the Oxfordshire village of Middle Assendon; he's late back from work, so I go for a beer in the Rainbow Inn. In the bar, I find two guys each putting a five-pound note in an envelope—a bet on the outcome of that evening's Derby County–Sheffield Wednesday match. And one of these two guys is a seriously fat geezer who happens to be a Tottenham fan, and who was at the disrupted game the day before—so after his side had won, he says, he went to evensong in the first church he could find. So I ask, was he upset over the trouble? Or was he just a religious guy? "Nah," he says. "I was just praying to me old Dad for a result in the semi."

8

From Darkness into Light

In May 1938, England played Germany in Berlin. The
Germans would stand for the British national anthem; the
English, in return, were obliged to give the Nazi salute.
Irked, they won 6-3.

France 1938

Three weeks later, the best thing about the 3rd World Cup
was the Swiss turning over Germany in the opening round.
This wasn't quite as neat as Jesse Owens's gold medals at the
Berlin Olympics, but if the Germans had had a good tournament, God knows what Goebbels would have done with it.

Hitler had gobbled up Austria, and along with everything
else he'd gobbled up their soccer players; when the game finished tied 1-1 and had to go to a replay, the Germans fielded
three of them. At halftime in the second game, they were 2-0
ahead—then in the second half the Swiss scored four, and
the Germans went home.

In Marseille, Norway pressed the Italians hard; the champions scraped through 2-1 after extra time. Elsewhere, the hosts
beat Belgium, the Czechs beat the Dutch, Hungary strolled to
a 6-0 win over the Dutch East Indies, and Sweden got a bye—
but the best contests of the first round featured Cuba, making
their only World Cup appearance to date against Romania in
Toulouse, and Brazil tackling Poland in Strasbourg.

Brazilian soccer hadn't yet arrived at its dazzling peak—black players had only come into the game in the previous decade—but by now they knew they were good, and their approach in France was one of cocksure nonchalance. By half-time they were 3-1 up, then the Polish got a grip, and after ninety minutes the score was 4-4. Extra time finished 6-5 to Brazil, and I'll bet the crowd had a fine time that afternoon.

As for the Cubans, no one gave them a prayer—so when they tied the Romanians 3-3 it was a big surprise. Even more surprising, the Cuban keeper was terrific, yet when it came to the replay they dropped him. And even more surprising than that, the keeper said they'd win the replay 2-1 anyhow, and he was right.

It often happens that when unfancied outsiders arrive fired up and cause an upset, they get overwhelmed by where they find themselves and blow up. Sure enough, in the second round, Sweden beat Cuba 8-0. As the massacre proceeded, one French reporter gave up and quit work on the grounds that, "Up to five goals is journalism. After that, it becomes statistics."

In the other quarter-finals, Hungary sent the Swiss home, Italy put out the hosts 3-1 before a Paris crowd of 58,000, and Brazil had a punch-up with Czechoslovakia in Bordeaux. Two Brazilians and one Czech were sent off; among a variety of injuries, two Czechs ended up with broken limbs. For what it's worth, the score was 1-1. By a peculiar contrast, the replay was a model of decorum; Brazil won 2-1, and felt so assured that they'd do so that the players and officals not involved set off for the semifinal before the game had even started.

Hubris: in Marseilles, the Italians beat them 2-1. And in Paris, Hungary demolished Sweden 5-1—so now only the Hungarians could stop Italy becoming the first nation to de-fend a World Cup title successfully.

As it turned out, Norway, France, and Brazil had all been stiffer challenges; the Italians finished the job with plenty of fuel left in the engine. Hungary were not yet the team they would become in the fifties; they did score twice, but it was Pozzo's Italy who had the skill, the stamina, the power. They won 4-2, and no doubt Mussolini grinned from ear to ear.

So were Italy the best team in the world? They were the best team who showed up, certainly—but the World Cup before World War II was never quite the complete affair. The English and the Scottish hadn't deigned to dignify it with their presence; England would have been potent contenders, while Scotland, like Uruguay, were a small nation abundantly blessed with talent. They beat England as often as not, and even today the record between them over 112 games shows 46 wins for England, and 41 for the Scots. Then as now, the English league tapped a rich vein of Scottish playing and managerial ability—so either side might have made a good showing.

The Uruguayans, still engaged in fractious disputes over the domestic management of their game, didn't turn up either; nor did the Argentinians, who bid to host this tournament and when they didn't get it stayed home in a huff—a fit of petulance that caused another riot among the deprived fans of Buenos Aires.

One other nation wasn't there to challenge Italy—Spain, which, between Franco and the Republicans, was too busy being the Bosnia of the late thirties.

It wasn't a happy world, what with soccer teams giving the fascist salute before they went about their business—and we can only pray that sixty years later, when the World Cup returns to France in 1998, we shall not find ourselves in a similar situation.

The Structure of the Tournament

In organizational terms, there are three principal differences between France '38 and USA '94. First, the modern World Cup has a guaranteed twenty-four participants, as opposed to the fifteen who made it to France. Second, it only goes to a knock-out format after eight teams have been eliminated in a first phase that is more complex. And third, the overbearing demands of the world's television schedules mean that when a game is tied it's no longer possible to take it to a replay.

In America, of course, the notion of a tie is anathema. What's the point of sitting there all that time—or, at Wrexham, standing—if you don't get a winner? (I shudder to think what you'd make of cricket, in which an international match can last for five days and still end in a tie.) As for the notion of a 0-0 tie, this is culturally inconceivable, yes?

In fact, a 0-0 tie can be a white-knuckle heart-stopper—there's no reason why a low-scoring soccer game should be any less exciting or intriguing than its baseball equivalent can be. But there's a more specific reason why we're happy to see ties as part of the furniture in soccer's regular domestic round.

When you're playing a season of forty-two league games, some of those games (in Wrexham's case, only seven so far out of thirty) are bound to be ones in which yourselves and your opponents are evenly matched on the day. In that case, to go away from the occasion with a point apiece is simply fair and square—you add the point to your tally and move on. In the first phase of USA '94, covering thirty-six of the fifty-two games, this philosophy also applies.

The twenty-four teams are drawn into six groups of four; six teams are seeded to head each group, so the big guns don't knock each other out early on. On FIFA's all-time rankings—headed by Brazil, the only nation to have competed in all fourteen World Cups—the big guns, the ultimate six seeds, read as follows:

rank	country	app.	games	W	T	L	Pts.
1	Brazil	14	66	44	11	11	99
2	Germany	12	68	39	15	14	93
3	Italy	12	54	31	12	11	74
4	Argentina	10	48	24	9	15	57
5	England	9	41	18	12	11	48
6	Uruguay	9	37	15	8	14	38

The Soviet Union, France, Yugoslavia, Hungary, and Spain come next; the United States rank twenty-eighth, level with Denmark and the now-evaporated East Germany. At any given World Cup, however, seedings are weighted toward more recent performance, so that list isn't necessarily the six seeds we'll get this summer—assuming those six all qualify in the first place.

Whoever's seeded, each team plays every other team in its group; the first phase of the World Cup thus consists of six six-game mini-leagues. For a win under this dispensation, you get two points; you get one point for a tie, and if you lose you get zero.

When it's over, if two teams have the same points, the team with the better goal difference (goals scored minus goals conceded) places higher. One result of this is that in their last group game a team can take the field needing to score a hatful if it's to have a hope of staying on.

And when it's over, the worst eight go home. Or, put another way, the top two finishers in each group go through, along with the four teams with the most points (or the best goal differences) in third place.

If it sounds complicated, that's because it *is* complicated—and when the last round of the group games is on, and news of each goal comes in, you can hear fingers working the calculators round the world as panicked fans work out the permutations. The reasoning behind it is, first, you don't want teams traveling halfway across the planet, as Argentina, Brazil, and the U.S.A. did in 1934, just to play for ninety minutes. And second, the more games you play, the more money everyone (mostly FIFA) gets to put in their pockets.

The remaining sixteen then play a knockout—but because replays don't suit TV, you need a result. So if you're tied after ninety minutes, you play thirty more minutes of extra time, fifteen minutes each way; and if it's *still* undecided after that, you have a penalty shoot-out.

The exhausted teams collapse in a heap in the center circle, and five from each side take turns to go and fire one penalty kick each at the opposing keeper. If you're still tied after ten kicks, you take two more, and two more, and you carry on until somebody misses.

It is extremely dramatic. After two hours of deadlock, the stadium holds its breath ten times over to see who holds the key. And in a situation where the keeper has nothing to lose—because a penalty kick, in theory, should get converted every time—each kicker is, literally, being put on the spot before the eyes of all the world.

However, it's also a profoundly unsatisfactory way to resolve a game of football. The drama is ersatz; it settles the issue with little or no reference to the match that's preceded it, and reduces the world's greatest game to bingo. Everyone involved, players and fans alike, deserves a replay; what they get is a lottery.

But, I guess, it's good TV.

Brazil 1950

During the war Jules Rimet kept the trophy under his bed; it now bore his name. The 4th World Cup at which it was contested was, like the host nation, an organizational mayhem, and a fabulous one. It had a preposterous format, which also happened to be wildly advantageous to Brazil, and it suffered a continuing spate of small-minded and ill-tempered withdrawals. But you could also make a case that it was the first proper World Cup, in that while only thirteen nations took part, there was at least a semblance of balance about them. Six nations came from the Old World, seven from the New—and those who didn't turn up missed a tournament featuring the greatest upset in the history of the game, and one of the greatest final games, too.

Absurdly, however, that great last game wasn't technically a final—technically, there wasn't a final at all. In the early days, the host association had a lot more say over how the thing was run than it does today—and compared to the crystalline clarity of FIFA's World Cup now, what Brazil went in for was murky and lopsided.

There was to be no knockout element; there would instead be four opening pools, as in the present day's opening phase, and the four winners then passed into a finalists' pool. On paper, this meant that when the last game came to be played, it could perfectly well have been an irrelevance; the title might already have been decided elsewhere. Happily, however, it didn't work out that way.

As to who had the worst reason for not showing: it's hard to pick between them, but for infantile pique Scotland probably shades it over Argentina. Argentina were in a huff again, but Scotland's huff was positively otherworldly. The British associations had rejoined FIFA in 1946, and had secured its financial survival the following year by organizing a match between Great Britain and the Rest of the World at Hampden Park in Glasgow. Dubbed the "Match of the Century," the British selection won 6-1 before a crowd of 134,000—while the gate put the then very sizable sum of $45,000 into FIFA's parlous postwar bank account.

Back in the fold, it was decided that the "Home Championship" contested every year between England, Scotland, Wales, and Northern Ireland would now serve as a World Cup qualifying group, from which the top two would advance to Brazil. When Scotland came second behind England, however, they announced that if they couldn't go as British champions, they'd not be going at all—and despite attempts to persuade them otherwise, they stuck their heads up their kilts and went sulking to the glens.

Germany had the plainest reason for not being there—this soon after the war, they hadn't yet been allowed back into FIFA—while France's excuse had the merit at least of being practical. The way the groups were organized, Brazil played all bar one of their games in Rio, while the visitors had to haul butts and baggage back and forth round the Amazon from one game to the next—in France's case, two thousand miles up the coast from Pôrto Alegre to Recife—which they felt, in Brazil in 1950, was a little bit rich.

To compound the farce, when the French pulled out, precisely two contestants were left in their opening pool. So Uruguay played Bolivia, chewed them up 8-0, and there they were in the final four.

Other entrants had more work to do, and none more so than Italy, whose presence in Brazil was a mute but noble rebuke to the meaner souls who stayed away. Twelve months earlier, the plane carrying Vittorio Pozzo's beloved Torino from a game in Lisbon crashed, killing every player, among them eight internationals. In the wake of this horror, the squad cobbled together to replace the gutted national side went to Brazil by boat; in their group they faced Paraguay, and a powerful Swedish side managed by a lively and progressive Englishman, George Raynor. Paraguay were no obstacle; the Swedish were, Italy lost 3-2, Sweden went through, and Italian clubs—already the most commercially and internationally minded in Europe—promptly picked up eight of the Swedish players.

More attention, however, was given to the other two groups, each with a full complement of four; attention that focused on the two most-favored teams. Brazil were in one group, playing at home before a crowd fanatically desirous of victory, and England were in the other—the game's original nation appearing at last in the World Cup finals.

In the enormous Maracana, still unfinished, a feverish crowd scrambled in over the builders' rubbish to greet the home side in a tumult of fireworks. They watched their heroes tear an intimidated Mexico to bits 4-0 without breaking sweat, and went home thinking, no doubt, that they could samba all the way to the Jules Rimet trophy. But the intense, prideful politics that plague Brazilian football then reared its head. Hopping down the coast to São Paulo, the side to face Switzerland was changed so that players from that city could take their turn, and the obdurate Swiss tied the unsettled hosts 2-2.

This meant that victory was essential in their last group game with Yugoslavia. They got it, but it was a squeeze—their first goal came after three minutes, when the Yugoslavs still only had ten men on the pitch. The eleventh was being treated in the dressing room; when he came out they made a game of it, before going down 2-0.

Brazil thus joined Uruguay and Sweden in the final four, albeit a tad less convincingly than expected—and the fourth to join them would, of course, be England.

In 1946, England had made the kind of leap into the present so typical of the FA, catching up with everybody else, just as everybody else moved on; they appointed the country's first team manager, Walter Winterbottom. Previously, the team was selected by a committee, the committee largely composed of club chairmen; old buffers inclined to pick players from their own clubs either out of pride, or because they were ignorant of anyone else's players. The committee didn't go away after Winterbottom's appointment, either, so although he himself was an astute coach, idiot rumblings against new-fangled concepts (like coaching) persisted, and the manager had still to argue the case to his masters for the eleven men he'd like to pick.

Nonetheless, the men he could pick included some very good players, among them Stanley Matthews, the "Wizard of Dribble"—now thirty-five years old and sixteen years into his international career, but still considered the finest winger in the world. And England, in 29 games between the end of the war and the Brazilian World Cup, had won 22, lost only 4—so these, surely, were big-time contenders.

England benched Matthews, beat Chile 2-0 in the Maracana anyhow, then traveled 250 miles inland to a small stadium in Belo Horizonte. Here, they played the U.S.A.—500-1 outsiders from a country where pro soccer had long since turned up its toes, a motley collection with a Scottish manager who coached at Penn State, and a Scottish captain who'd emigrated to the United States eighteen months earlier, after ending his pro career with, of all clubs, Wrexham.

The left back was from Belgium; the striker Joe Gaetjens was from Haiti. The Spanish had already beaten them 3-1 in Curitiba; a number among them stayed up late into the night before the game, drinking to the certain defeat that awaited them.

On thirty-seven minutes, Gaetjens rose to meet a long ball

into England's area. Whether he meant to do what he did is disputed to this day—did he head it, or did the ball just hit him? Either way, it went in the net. For the rest of the game, England camped in the American half, hit the woodwork repeatedly, were repeatedly denied by a brave American keeper named Borghi, and lost the game 1-0. One of the English players said afterward, "Bloody ridiculous. Can't we play them again tomorrow?"

It's the biggest earthquake of a result ever recorded. England went back to Rio, picked Matthews, lost 1-0 to Spain, Spain went through, and England left for home appalled and bewildered. The Americans lost 5-2 to Chile in Recife, and doubtless went home happy as hell anyhow.

They would not be seen at the World Cup again for forty years. Nor, after twenty years, would Joe Gaetjens be seen again; he disappeared in his native island, presumed a victim of the Tontons Macoutes.

What followed was the beginning of modern world soccer; Brazil hit their stride, and no one had seen anything like it. England, typically, didn't see it at all—when they'd been put out, every journalist and official went home with the team, as if the rest didn't matter. What they missed was the future of the game.

It wasn't that Brazil had some cunning new game plan, there was no blackboard innovation—soccer at its best, after all, is far more an art than a science—and Brazil now raised that art to new peaks. They were athletic, explosive, intricate, with lightning reflexes and uncanny balance; they had panache, daring, and a supreme confidence that if they only touched the ball once—with the head, the chest, the knee, the foot, no matter—it would go where it was meant to, where the next man in turn was moving onto it, primed and ready to weave the next spell. In front of huge crowds transported into rapture, they took Sweden to pieces, 7-1; they brushed Spain aside, 6-1, and Uruguay didn't look to be any more of an obstacle.

Uruguay had fast forwards and stout defenders, but against both Sweden and Spain they were 2-1 down at halftime. With luck and resolve, they beat the Swedes 3-2, tied Spain 2-2, and went on to the Maracana. So a draw would be enough to give Brazil the World Cup; for Uruguay, having dropped a point against Spain, only a win would do.

The home crowd had no doubt the trophy was theirs; they were whipped on in their triumphalism by Rio's state governor, who gave an insane speech hailing victory before the game, raving on about a team with "no equals in the terrestrial hemisphere." The game began, and Brazil danced and surged forward, and wave upon wave of elegant assault broke against the rocks of the Uruguayan defence. Their keeper was courageous and acrobatic, their center halves ferocious and resolute; shot after shot was blocked, saved, cleared, until halftime came and the score was still 0-0. In the closing minutes, the Uruguayans had begun to break out and make moves of their own—but two minutes into the second half, they were a goal behind.

They might have collapsed; instead they took the game to Brazil, and after it had swung back and forth, with twenty-five minutes remaining, they leveled the score. Still the World Cup was Brazil's—but the tide now was with tiny Uruguay, and with eleven minutes left they brought the treasure home to port. Aghast, the Brazilians streamed forward until every one of them was in Uruguay's area—but the game was up and it was 2-1 Uruguay, and an impassioned, roller-coaster match ended in a stunning victory. The trophy went back to Montevideo and soccer, out of the troubled thirties and the nightmare of the war, came roaring and jubilant back into the light.

As for Brazil, victims of hubris a second time, they would learn the lesson and return.

9

Different Climates, Different Cultures

"It's a game of athleticism, a game of power and competition and strength. Anybody who thinks football is just a game of deftness of touch without those other things *wouldn't win*."
—Bobby Robson, England Manager, 1982–90

Something came up that may have struck you as odd: Gary Bennett coming to Wrexham and, on discovering that in training Flynn works with the ball, asking instead if he couldn't just run. But if you play the game with a ball, I hear you say, how could you train for it without one?

Herein lies the principal debate in the British game. I'm actually fortunate to have at my club a man who wants his team "to play football." I'm fortunate, to put it another way, that Flynn's committed to "the passing game"—to the game played with the ball to feet, by players among whom skill and invention is encouraged. I'm fortunate because in this, if not exactly a rarity, he's bucking the trend—and with a different manager, our lives in the Kop could be very much worse. We could be watching Route One every week.

Route One is the long game, "sticking it in the mixer"; superfit leviathans thundering round the park, their ideas limited to lofting the ball into the other lot's penalty area as often as possible, then seeing what turns up when it lands. The most unflinching exponents of this bulldozer method are Wimbledon, the Crazy Gang; they barged into what's now the Premier League a few years ago, and somehow they've hung on ever since. But despite being three flights higher, they've lately been drawing crowds smaller than we get at the Racecourse—which gives you an idea of how much fun they are to watch.

So if you want to figure out the way different people play, what it comes down to, put crudely, is this: Where the sun shines you'll find artists, with their minds prone to wander, and where the rain falls, you'll find hairy-arsed cavemen disciplined into not having too much mind in the first place. Of course, I'm simplifying. The English have minds, and they can wander as far afield as anyone's; it would be a gross slur, moreover, to say they have no skill. Equally, for all their peerless skills, the Italians can be as hard as nails—while the perfect team, obviously, has a full and balanced mix of art and muscle both. But to understand different soccer styles, it remains the case that the Renaissance happened in Italy, and the Industrial Revolution in England—and when either country plays soccer, that's the way it tends to look.

In Britain it rains and the wind blows, and by the middle of the season half the pitches are swamps, so if you go out and play at a hundred miles an hour you'll just be warmer. But if you're playing in Naples or Marseille or Barcelona, for the best part of the season the skies are more clement, and if you go running your butt off all you'll get for your pains is dehydrated. At Mexico '86, England forward Gary Lineker lost ten pounds of his body weight in one game.

So the style of play preferred by the Latin nations tends to be slower and more thoughtful. It's "possession football," and requires more craft, more technique on the ball if you want to keep it—which is how come the Italians are artists. And I'm not saying that, compared to the amphetamine rumpus you get in England, at an Italian game you can sit and watch the grass grow—but they do take more time about things, and think them through a little more, and they'll let you have the ball in your own half; generally they'll not bother trying a tackle until you've crossed the center line. But then, once they've got it back from you, they'll break into attack out of the sweeper system with moves that may not be slower than an English attack, but will most likely be more measured, more incisive, more directed.

If the English are martial and the Italians are clinical, the Germans are both. The Germans are engineers; they play football the way they make cars, fast, solid, efficient, reliable, and stylish. And you have only to look at their market share—in cars, in World Cup finals—to figure they must be doing something right.

Then there are the Dutch—a mystery zone. Here we have, on the face of it, one of the world's more boring nations—and yet they keep on producing devastating teams. Even more odd, the surest way on earth to start an argument is to put two Dutch soccer players in the same room; the only thing they might conceivably agree on is that the manager should be sacked. Then they come out and thrash you.

The greatest Dutch player of all time is Johan Cruyff, now the manager of FC Barcelona. In the seventies his side played "total football," meaning that all of them went everywhere—every one of them could play, and they switched positions around among themselves until you didn't know who was coming from where. But when Cruyff was asked how he played the way he did, he first said he didn't know. Then he said maybe it was because he did the wrong thing all the time.

The Dutch won the European Championship in 1988, thanks in part to the awesomely skilled trio of Frank Rijkaard, Ruud Gullit, and Marco van Basten. It's no small part of Milan's success since then that, after that tournament, they bought all three of them.

The fact is, the Dutch are smart. They come on boring so nobody will notice or bother them, then they quietly run one of the world's more progressive and amiable societies, a society their soccer reflects admirably.

It's less admirable that the English style reflects, equally well, a society mired in antique notions and structures. The English don't just play biff-bang-wallop the way they do (what Alan calls "kick, bollock, and bite") because the weather's grotty and they want to keep warm; they also play that way because soccer is the working-class game, and the working class are the poor bloody infantry, and the last thing the toffs want from the poor bloody infantry is independent thought. So there is, in England, a long and depressing record of national managers not fielding the country's more talented players—on the grounds that they might, heaven forbid, have ideas of their own, and not do what they're told.

A different example of this is that it's considered a noteworthy thing when an English player takes his services abroad and learns the language of his employers—whereas Dutch players tend, like their countrymen in general, to be readily multilingual, and no one feels the least need to remark on it.

So we have in Britain an ossified, officers-and-men approach that helps to explain why the game is, in fact, one of the few industries we have left. We are grumpy, conservative, profoundly suspicious of genius—and when we do find genius and it goes off the rails, as Gazza threatens to do every other week, we nod sagely and say that we told you so.

The Italians, by contrast, are more inclined to admire individual panache. On a good day they play as they dress or eat—beautifully—and on a bad day they play as they govern themselves, hysterically bickering.

Knowing these differences, I have little doubt that the true soccer aficionado could watch a game between two sides wearing neutral colors and still have a good guess, before the game was much advanced, where the two sides had come from. Soccer, in short, is an expressive sport—and the way you play speaks volumes about the way you are.

But of course, in the end, this is generalization. At USA '94, how each side represents their nations' qualities will still come down, ultimately, to twenty-two players and one manager. They'll be themselves, and if what they do is brave or beautiful, then that bravery or beauty will reflect well on their country. If what they do is ugly, however, they'll have let their country down, but it hardly means their country's ugly too—which brings us to the strange case of Argentina.

Of the major South American sides, Brazil we've already met in their first great incarnation—and still today, whenever we see the men in the gold and green, we start dreaming again. They bring music to the stands, and romance to the field; whenever Brazil are in the big time, the possibility of magic is reborn as each World Cup unfolds, and we hope for joy from them every time, for unpredictable cheek and impossible daring. But Argentina . . .

At Italia '90 they clawed their way to the final with malevolent resolve, psyching opponents out of their way in penalty shoot-outs in both the quarter and the semifinals—then they played the final like they wanted a shoot-out there too. They didn't try to win—they clung on with bloody nails, hacking and diving, griping and scowling, barging the referee in vituperative packs until the red cards came out, and they got in the record books for all the wrong reasons again. The performance was so grisly that an American journalist, wondering how USA '94 could ever succeed if soccer was like this, wrote: "If this was a fish, you'd throw it back."

That team, however, could not be said to have represented Argentina—it could only be said that they shamed her. So if you play well, your merits in doing so may be merits peculiar to your country—Brazilian fantasy, Italian style, German invention masterfully organized, or plain English bloody-minded refusal to give up. But if you play foul, you don't show us the worst in your country. You show us the worst in us all.

March 13, 1993
Wrexham v. Lincoln City

Barnet still haven't paid the fine for their "financial irregularities." "We're living on a time bomb," says manager Barry Fry.

Cardiff win at Colchester and go top. The game is interrupted by a hundred Cardiff fans invading the pitch, which has people in Wrexham shaking their heads at the stupidity of the South Welsh. Why do it, they ask, when you're winning?

As for bloody-minded refusals to pack in, Wrexham go to Darlington and nick a 1-1 draw, Mel Pejic scoring in the eighty-ninth minute. It's a fighting result—throwing your center halves up in the other lot's area, still scrapping at the death for a point away from home.

But Mark Morris said bluntly, "First half we were crap, the worst we've played all season. So we went in halftime, and the gaffer gave us a bollocking. He told us what we'd been doing all season, what's given us success—short balls, getting it wide, passing it—we weren't doing it."

Briskly reminded what they were about, in the second half, "We battered them. But we had four or five chances and we weren't scoring, and to be honest I thought we wouldn't do it. Then Mel nips up last minute, the corner comes in, bobbles about a bit, and he slams it top corner. That's a point."

Next up, Lincoln—eight games in three days. I said, "Don't you ever find yourself thinking, I'm *knackered* . . ."

"You can't. It's mental now, isn't it?"

* * *

As a fan, Morris likes to watch 4-4-2; with the wingers, you've got crosses whipping in from everywhere. As a keeper, on the other hand, he'd rather play against big boots down the middle every time; with the ball coming straight at him, it's easier. And that's what Lincoln do; they take Route One.

Mid-March, and it's Ray-Ban time already. Under an unseasonably warm and cloudless sky we walk through the parking lot behind the Marston Stand, where the visitors sit; through the corrugated tin we can hear their plaintive grunts:

> *Inngg—ger—luh—uhnd*
> *Inngg—ger—luh—uhnd*

and in the Kop they're laughing.

> *Can you hear Lincoln sing?*
> *I can't hear a fuckin' thing*

But the first chance is Lincoln's. Hardy's gone up the wing, so when they hoof it out there's only Pejic back to cover. Their No. 10 skins him, flashes the ball into the side netting, *oooph* . . . and at their end they're breaking up our attacks, flying in on people's feet, then lofting it forward. Their strikers are both fifteen feet tall. Another satellite launch of a pass attempts to reach them—and lands on the roof of the stand.

Bennett ducks and weaves, and gets his feet sawn off at the ankles; Lake hits the crossbar. The ball comes out, gets slide-ruled back in, and Psycho chases it studs first onto their keeper. We have fireworks potential here—but tactically, the analysis is simple. If we keep the ball on the ground, we win— we slice them up. If they keep it in the air, they win—they hammer us down. And just now it's 50-50.

And the difference in style is striking. The ball sails in again and Hardy collects, trapping it deftly on his ankle, slicing it fast and neat along the floor to Watkin, two touches, it's out wide to Connolly—and he's brought clattering to the ground. So we wait awhile for the ball to achieve reentry, collect it again, and then it's pass and move, pass and move. It's about us trying to play and them trying to stop us, and after fifteen minutes culture's winning.

Then the scoreboard says York have gone 1-0 over Barnet. "So," says Alan, to the humming sound of 5,246 people instantly calculating goal differences, "we've got to win now."

Because we're on 56 points, and so are York—and it's only a narrowly better goal difference that's keeping us third.

There are goalmouth melees at both ends. We win a corner, then another.

> *We're gonna score in a minute*
> *Score in a miiiii—ih—nit*

But we don't. Their keeper tips one shot out, gathers another in his midriff; up our end Morris is flying high among the crashing heads, the ball coming in like artillery. From London the news is now Barnet 1, York 2—but the news here at halftime is 0-0.

Two minutes after the restart, Lake wrestles his way through a midfield morass of lunging carcass and limb, playing one-two, one-two with Connolly. Giving it and taking it as they duck through the tangle, Lake gets free and makes thirty diagonal yards toward their area. Connolly goes across and behind him toward the penalty spot; Lake swivels, scoops it onto Connolly's head, and the winger buries it in the net. 1-0.

> *You're not singing*
> *You're not singing*
> *You're not singing any more*

So now we hit a purple patch. Their keeper's thrown this way and that, and you can hear the breath rushing out at the thrill of Cross running at them, and each surge of free men through their lines draws great roars of hope and happiness:

> *And it's Wrexham, Wrexham*
> *Wrexham FC OK*
> *You're by far the greatest team*
> *The world has ever seen*

Lincoln are playing their desperate pinball again, but when you do that going backward, sooner or later someone's going to have you—and when the ball drops down from another moon shot to their scrambling right back, Bennett's on him like a wolf. He plucks it off his toes, streaks to the goal line, cuts in, crosses on the deck; their keeper crashes into Watkin in the goalmouth, the ball spins out, and Owen arrives like a freight train to pelt it in the bulging net so hard it looks like it's coming out the other side and heading off into town for a drink. 2-0.

Going up, going up, going up

We're playing one-two's in their area now, they're falling all over themselves; they don't know where they are, let alone where we are.

Gwwwaaaaahhhhhhhnnnnnn SKIN HIM!

Party time—and the scoreboard says BARNET 1, YORK 3. So when it's over they open the gates down by the turnstiles; we funnel our way out past the deathburger stall into the road, bunched and jostling, and all around us are men and boys with little radios glued to their ears. In front of me there's a scrawny youth and suddenly I see his eyes roll and go wobbly, and to no one in particular he cries out in pain:

"Fuckin' ell. We've dropped a place. Fuckin' York beat fuckin' Barnet 5-fuckin'-1. Fuck. Fuckin' gone over us on goal fuckin' difference. Fuck. Fuck fuck fuck."

Alan says, "Well, there's a sickener. You run your lungs out, win 2-0, and drop to fourth anyway."

And the prospect of getting mired in the play-offs is too terrible to bear. Between third place and fourth, the difference is between going to heaven straight off or being stuck outside knocking on the gate, and not knowing for three more weeks if we'll get in.

I asked Flynn how he felt when he heard the York–Barnet result—knowing he's won 2-0, and dropped a place anyhow.

He said, "I didn't feel any sense of disappointment. We've played three in a week, we're unbeaten, we've scored four at home—and 5-1, that's a freak result. There'll be a few more of those before the end. Besides, I know how it happened: Barnet, if they're losing, throw five men up front and try retrieving it. So they've conceded two goals, eighty-fourth minute, eighty-ninth minute, and it looks terrible—but Barry Fry's just said, go on, up you go. Might as well lose 5-1 as 3-1, that's his attitude. It won't worry Barry, and it won't worry his players."

So he doesn't think the wheels are coming off down there? At a club, after all, that's only just arrived out of the Vauxhall Conference—a club that play their soccer on a sandpit, with a scalper for a chairman who keeps sacking his manager, and the league breathing fire on their tails for a fine they can't pay, and all their players up for sale . . .

"They thrive in adversity, Barnet. They've no right to be where they are, but they're there all the same."

No adversity at Wrexham—so are we going up?

"I've got that feeling. That feeling's still there."

Round-Up

In the chase for the Premier League title, Manchester United do the difficult thing—they go to Liverpool and win—then they visit bottom club Oldham Athletic and lose. But come the run-in, the bottom clubs are as hard as the top ones; they are, in Alan's words, "fighting for their children's shoes." Meanwhile Tottenham go to Aston Villa and holds out for a 0-0 draw—so United and Villa have 60 points apiece, with United on top by the slender thread of one goal.

In Italy, Milan are out of sight. A 2-0 win over Fiorentina is their fifty-seventh League game unbeaten—and as a win in *Serie A* gets you only two points, their lead of eleven over Inter is now patently unassailable.

In Australia, sixteen nations contest the World Youth Cup. The first phase is four groups of four; the top two from each make the quarter-finals. England's in with Turkey, South Korea, and the U.S.A.; Turkey are European Youth Champions, while the English have all the players they wanted, so the other two haven't a prayer. The U.S.A. are 50-1 outsiders. Opening results:

England 1	South Korea 1
Turkey 0	United States 6

An in-your-face score if ever I heard one.

Phil Hardy is called up by the Republic of Ireland for their Under-21 squad to play Germany. Given the ease with which you can qualify as Irish—trace one grandparent and you're in—this means, Alan says, "he must have been born somewhere." The story's told of a player new to the Irish side standing before the match while the national anthems are played, and he turns to the player next to him and says, "This one goes on a bit." So the other guy whispers, "Shut up. It's ours."

* * *

More results from Australia:

South Korea 1	Turkey 1
England 1	United States 0

Ah well.

A minor earthquake in the World Cup qualifiers:

San Marino 0   Turkey 0

It's San Marino's first international point—but in soccer, anything can happen. Someone might even beat Milan one day.

The tiny Pyrennean principality of Andorra, previously administered under joint Franco-Spanish sovereignty, votes in a referendum to become fully independent. They say they're aggravated at EC bureaucrats meddling with their tax privileges; people hopping over the border for duty-free booze and cigarettes is, along with skiing, their principal source of income. But me, I figure they heard the San Marino result; I figure Andorra wants to play international soccer too.

Milan's unbeaten league run is 57; in all competitive fixtures, it's 42—they're 330 days without a loss. So in the first leg of the Italian Cup semifinal they go to Rome, where Roma beat them 2-0. Roma's president rushes to the Olimpico to congratulate his side—from his hospital bed, in his pajamas. And next thing you know, San Marino'll beat someone. Andorra, maybe.

In Japan, the curtain-raiser for the inaugural season of a new pro league pits Yomiuri Verdy against Nissan FC Yokohama Marinos in the Tokyo National Stadium. There are 60,000 seats—and 900,000 applications to sit in them. Playing striker for Nagoya Grampus 8 will be Gary Lineker—he's into his thirties, he's too smart to spend his time being knocked about in the English brawl any more, and the job pays a seven-figure salary.

The first phase wraps up in Australia:

England 1	Turkey 0
South Korea 2	United States 2

England top the group; the USA go through past the Koreans on goal difference. 50-1 outsiders? Your coach, by the way, is English.

Aston Villa travel to Manchester United for the season's biggest game so far—the summit meeting, the Thriller with the Villa. The game lives up to its billing, the sides electrically inseparable at 1-1. United stay top.

Gazza plays a blinder for Lazio against Milan; this one ends tied as well, 2-2. The press, who've had Gazza coming home in a beer barrel any minute, decide Lazio might keep him after all.

World Youth Cup quarter-finals:

England 0   Mexico 0
(England win 4-3 on penalties)

Australia 2   Uruguay 1
Ghana 3   Russia 0
Brazil 3   United States 0

Bummer of a draw, guys.

And the season has eight weeks to run. It's Tuesday, March 16, and for their fourth game in eleven days, Wrexham are in Cardiff to play the first leg of the Welsh Cup semifinal. From one side of the world to the other—from South Wales to New South Wales—like a rolling wheel the game goes on.

10

The Galloping Major & The Little Bird

"I had never suspected that the World Cup would be such a
test of nerves."
—Gustav Sebes, Hungarian Deputy
Minister of Sport

Switzerland 1954

The first televised World Cup had sixteen entrants, a four-
pool first phase from which eight went home, and a knockout
thereafter. It didn't matter; everybody knew the Hungarians
would win anyway.

Behind the Iron Curtain there was, of course, no such thing
as professionalism. Instead you put your best players in the
army, formed an army club for them to play at (in Hungary's
case, Honved), and then let them go to it with whatever support it took to promote the greater virtues of the socialist man.
Ideology aside, however, Hungarian coaching methods, in
terms both of technique and of fitness, were unquestionably
more intensive and more intelligent than any yet seen. This
would count for nothing, obviously, if your players were
duds—but the Hungarians weren't, and among many fine
talents they had Ferenc Puskas, the "Galloping Major."

In Helsinki in 1952 they won Olympic gold; the following
year they came to Wembley. Before the game one England
player said of Puskas, "Look at that fat little chap. We'll murder

this lot." The Hungarians scored in the first minute; the little fat chap got two. And it wasn't the fact of the 6-3 scoreline so much as the manner of it; England, said *The Times*, were "strangers in a strange world, a world of flitting red spirits." Six months later it was worse; at the Nepstadion in Budapest, the Hungarians won 7-1.

Like Pozzo's prewar Italians only more so, Hungary took the superior technique of the Continent, fused it with what was best in Britain (physical force, fearless finishing), and the alloy was perfection. They were not Brazil—no one else could be, no one else has that environment—but they were the best thing Europe had ever made. In their opening group in Switzerland they beat Korea 9-0, Germany 8-3, and advanced to a quarter-final against—who else?—Brazil.

Brazil, meanwhile, had done what they often do when dazzling shine alone hasn't brought them the prize. They brought Didi, whose unreadably bucking, bending free kicks were called "falling leaves" (by Mexico 1970, this Brazilian speciality would be known more prosaically as "banana kicks"), but they left behind the front line that had wrought the magic four years earlier. Feeling that in Rio pure artistry had been undone, they now came harder, prepared to fight when the game was against them, and not just to play when the flow of it was theirs. And fight, in Berne, is precisely what they did.

Puskas wasn't playing; the Germans had kicked him (deliberately, said Puskas), but after eight minutes Hungary were 2-0 up anyhow. After seventeen minutes Brazil got one back, and at both ends the hacks and punches started flying. In the second period Brazil equalized; Hungary made it 3-2, one player from each side was sent off after a fistfight, Hungary got a fourth goal, a second Brazilian got a red card, and when it was over Brazil assaulted the Hungarians in their dressing room. Amid the flying blows one Hungarian had his cheek slashed; Brazil's captain was similarly injured, allegedly by Puskas breaking a bottle in his face. No players were punished by either side, everybody blamed everybody else, and Brazil went home.

At thirty-nine, Stanley Matthews was still playing for England. The "Ageless Wonder" swerved on and on; the first man named European Footballer of the Year, he would play his last professional game—still in the top flight—five days after his fiftieth birthday in 1965. But after their drubbings at the hands of Hungary, English confidence was low, and the FA was daily berated. As one journalist wrote, "Do we really need a panel of nine to pick a team of eleven?"

Uruguay, meanwhile, were more than capable of defending their title. Their defence was the same that had locked out Brazil in the Maracana; in attack was Schiaffino, who had scored there. They warmed up with a 2-0 win over the Czechs, then met an ineffectual Scotland; Vittorio Pozzo said brusquely of the Scots that "they will die in the sun." Sure enough the Scots watched bewildered, and Uruguay scored seven.

In a fine quarter-final England were harder, and Matthews was brilliant; he made one goal, hit the post, and had another shot saved. But Schiaffino shone brighter; Uruguay won 4-2. England went home prouder this time, but still baffled.

Italy were equally baffled; the days of Pozzo's iron management were over, they turned up a bickering rabble, and were eliminated by Switzerland. The hosts then lost a bizarre quarter-final 7-5 to Austria; in Geneva, meanwhile, the unfancied Germans raised eyebrows with a 2-0 defeat of the more gifted Yugoslavia.

The Germans were strong and disciplined, but, newly back in the fold, they had few credentials. Even when eyebrows hit hairlines after they demolished Austria 6-1 in the semis, it hardly seemed important; in Lausanne in the other semi, Uruguay had met Hungary in one of the great games of all time, and the outcome would surely determine the destiny of the fifth World Cup.

Puskas was still unfit; Uruguay's experienced captain Obdulio Varela was also unavailable, after an injury picked up against England. But both squads were far too rich to be undone by one injury, and cleanly, beautifully, they flew at each other. At halftime, Hungary had a two-goal advantage; Uruguay, as in Rio, refused to lie down. With fifteen minutes left, Juan Hohberg pulled a goal back; when he hit a second, and Uruguay went level just three minutes from time, his colleagues leapt on him in such a frenzy of joy and relief that they knocked him unconscious.

In extra time, Hohberg hit the post; Hungary were more precise, and scored twice. Again, they had beaten South American opposition 4-2, but this time there'd been no ugliness about it and their manager said simply, "We beat the best team we have ever met."

A better team, certainly, than Germany; in the final, as against Brazil, Hungary went two up in eight minutes—but they'd made a mistake. Puskas was playing—and as the game proceeded, it was clear that he still wasn't fit. Hungary stuttered; the game swung, and was still young when the Germans were back in it 2-2. Hungary, stung, now played fast and furious; the German keeper was kept as acrobatically busy as Uruguay's keeper had been in Rio; what he couldn't save was kicked off the line, or fell away off the woodwork. The missed chances began to tell, the Hungarians tired, and with seven minutes left in a game to which they'd clung against the odds, the Germans scored their third and decisive goal.

They were the third nation to win the World Cup; they would be back, too, and far stronger than this. But like their economy, climbing miraculously out of the wreckage to which Hitler had led them, they served early notice to the postwar world of German resolve.

As for the Hungarians, they could point to the German who kicked Puskas in the opening round, when they had been so patently superior, and claim that kick was the most important of the tournament. But one man is not a team, and the truth is that the Hungarians, after cresting the final ridge and setting eyes on the summit, let their legs go beneath them at the prospect.

Munich

In Europe in the fifties there were three great teams: Hungary, Real Madrid, and Manchester United. In Europe today, the paramount club challenge is the European Cup, the Champions' Cup, contested by the league champions of each country—a competition born in the fifties in the heyday of those teams. And as with many good things in soccer, it was the idea of a Frenchman.

Friendly meetings—"friendlies"—with big clubs from other countries were already established as lucrative attractions; a four-game tour to Chelsea, Arsenal, Cardiff, and Glasgow by a thrilling Dynamo Moscow side immediately after the war drew 270,000 fans. But in December 1954, after the Swiss

World Cup, when Honved of Hungary visited the English league champions Wolverhampton Wanderers, this was recognized as a clash at the peak.

Honved had six of the men who'd been the toast of the World Cup they didn't win, among them a fit Ferenc Puskas. The Hungarians went two up early on, as seemed by now to be a habit. But this wasn't summer in Switzerland, it was winter in Wolverhampton, and now it started pouring with rain. Across sheets of water and bogs of mud, Wolves played a fiercely aggressive "kick and rush"—the long game, basically—and crashed back against a soaked and flailing Honved until, submerged and pulverized, Honved could hold out no longer, and were beaten 3-2.

The English were jubilant; English was best again, and the Wolves manager called his players "champions of the world." In Paris, however, Gabriel Hanot, editor of the sports paper *L'Équipe*, drew a different lesson. For years he had dreamed of a pan-European competition; now, he said, if Wolves wanted to say they were the best, then let there be a tournament in which that claim could more properly be tested.

In April 1955, Hanot invited eighteen clubs to a meeting in Paris (from England he invited Chelsea, soon to take over as champions from Wolves) and the European Cup was born. And it was a tremendous idea, everyone could see that—except the slack-witted xenophobes who ran the Football League, who promptly leaned on Chelsea not to take part. They felt that playing around with foreigners in some pie-in-the-sky Euro-fad might distract a chap from his rightful business in the English mud; the idea that a chap might learn from it was, of course, too silly for words. Indeed, the idea that a footballer might learn anything at all other than to do what he was told wasn't just silly, it was threatening; he might learn, for a start, that in Europe they paid a player a proper salary.

Chelsea humbly acquiesced; the first European Cup went ahead without them, and was won by Real Madrid. It was won by Real Madrid, in fact, in all the first five years of its existence, and after the tanks rolled into Budapest in 1956, one of the players who helped them achieve that great record was a refugee by the name of Ferenc Puskas.

But it might not have been so.

Matt Busby, from a mining village in the Scottish county of

Lanarkshire, played his football before the war in Manchester; when the war was over, he went back there to take up the reins at United. The stadium at Old Trafford was bomb-damaged; players had lost the best years of their careers, and seventy-five of them had lost their lives. In the aftermath, as English soccer struggled back to its feet, Busby built the first of three great teams—but the second, the team he fashioned in the mid-fifties, was something else again.

The Red Devils, the Busby Babes—they were gorgeous, elegant, electric, a team without parallel in the English game. They won the league championship in the spring of 1956 by a racing margin of eleven points, and, unlike Chelsea the year before, Busby would not be denied a tilt at the greatest prize a club could win by some bunch of fuddled clots at league HQ.

In the fall of that year, they entered the second European Cup. Each tie was played over two legs, home and away; at Old Trafford they played Anderlecht of Belgium, a side with six Belgian internationals, and beat them 10-0. The Belgian captain said, "The best teams of Hungary have never beaten us like this. They were fantastic; they should pick the whole team for England." The average age of the United side that day was twenty-one.

They beat Borussia Dortmund, and Atletico Bilbao; trailing 5-3 from the away leg of the latter tie, they won it with a 3-0 victory at Old Trafford before 70,000. "They play with such passion we were simply overwhelmed," Bilbao's captain said.

In the semifinal they met Real Madrid. Real didn't have Puskas yet, but amid a host of Spanish internationals they had the great Argentine Alfredo di Stefano, and the French winger Raymond Kopa; in the Bernabeu they had a crowd of 125,000, too. They won the first leg 3-1; United could only tie the return in Manchester 2-2 and thus, in their first attempt on the trophy, they fell short of the line. But Busby only said, "A great experienced team will always beat a great inexperienced team." He knew they would be back.

League champions again, the Babes returned to Europe the next season. They put out Ireland's Shamrock Rovers, winning 6-0 in Dublin; Busby's biographer Eamon Dunphy watched them do it as a boy on the terraces, and remembers that they were "unbelievably grand," that his "blood ran cold with a shiver of delight."

They beat Dukla Prague; in the quarter-final they faced Red Star Belgrade, and could only beat them 2-1 at Old Trafford.

The away leg was a battle, but they tied it 3-3, went through 5-4 on aggregate, and again they were in the semifinals. A year older, a year wiser, they were the finest side English soccer ever produced—and were still so young.

On the way back from Belgrade, on February 6, 1958, after a refueling stop at a snowbound Munich airport, their plane crashed on takeoff. Twenty-one died instantly, and two more in hospital later; among them were eight of the players.

Busby's assistant Jimmy Murphy would say many years later, "If I close my eyes and meditate, I can still see them playing."

Sweden 1958

Hungary were not Brazil, but they beat them. After the tanks came, Hungary weren't Hungary either—what use is smart coaching, when your best players have fled the country? But Brazil, after their foul display in Berne, were very much Brazil again—purveyors of a unique game, a soccer of grace and gesture and theater founded in the ceaseless stream of dreamers spilling from the poverty of the *favelas* onto the streets and the beaches, boys in ragged shorts seeking to shine more brilliantly than the host of other stars already blazing in a firmament of fever and fanaticism . . . Pele was seventeen, Garrincha was the Little Bird on the wing, and Sweden 1958 was Brazil time.

It was also 4-4-2 time, because that was the way Brazil came to play—though in their case it was mostly 4-2-4. When they're on song, Brazil don't greatly worry about defence—you'll see them play dainty stuff to feet even in their own penalty area, which any other side would consider wildly dangerous and irresponsible—but with players like Garrincha, weaving, vertiginous, electrically fast, they just figure however many goals you get, at the other end they'll get more.

And it was Sweden time too; the conservative Swedes had at last accepted professionalism. Their high-earning exiles in Italy, among them players who'd beaten Italy in São Paulo eight years before, could now be called upon; so they called on George Raynor too, the Englishman who'd managed them to the last four in 1950, to come back and try again. They were not much fancied, but they were, of course, at home.

Among the rest, England were sadly out of kilter. After 1954,

Winterbottom had got some way out from under the dead hand of the selection committee, and laid meticulous plans. But at Munich, he lost the spine of the side—Roger Byrne, Tommy Taylor, and Duncan Edwards. Edwards, an international at eighteen, at twenty-one a big man, was the brightest prospect among the Busby Babes; with injuries that would have killed most men instantly, he fought for fifteen days before he went. Stirring into consciousness when Jimmy Murphy was at his bedside he asked, "What time's kickoff on Saturday?" He would not play in a World Cup; England had not lost as many as Italy had in 1949, but they were much diminished.

Otherwise, the Soviet Union came for the first time, and for the only time all four British teams were there. The West German champions were there—and the French came, with a striker called Just Fontaine.

In their group games they cantered past Paraguay 7-3, and Fontaine got three of them; they were undone 3-2 by Yugoslavia, but Fontaine got both those goals too. They then advanced to the quarter-finals, squeezing 2-1 past Scotland, and again Fontaine was on the scorecard with his sixth goal in three games. There would be more.

Bobby Robson managed England at Italia '90; in Sweden he played for England in the first of two World Cups, and he would later describe the leap from club to World Cup soccer as "prodigious." He said, "It was way above what I'd ever, ever imagined. I thought the game was so difficult, so demanding, playing against bright players, quick players—quick not just physically, you take that as accepted, but quick up here [he tapped his temple]. People saw things, did things in a second."

In their first game the Russians put two goals past England; outplayed but stubborn as ever, England pulled two back to tie. They then faced Brazil, and were the only side Brazil failed to score against. Without Pele or Garrincha, they'd beaten Austria 3-0; obstinate again, England dourly held them 0-0.

So Brazil brought in the stars. Pele was an international at sixteen; one hundred fifty pounds, five foot eight, and pure genius every inch of it. As for the Little Bird, he was picked because the other players demanded it. The Russians were left chasing shadows for ninety minutes; the 2-0 scoreline was a poor reflection of a bewildering reality.

England, meanwhile, battled to another glum stalemate, 2-2 with Austria; forced to play off against the Russians, they lost 1-0. They were unlucky—they twice hit the post—but they were uninspiring and unimaginative too. Vittorio Pozzo had summed up their problem succinctly years before: "Continental teams can read English teams like an open book: your players behave in international games absolutely the same as in league games. Same moves, same tactics, same tendencies—all in one pattern." Still some way from making that prodigious leap, once again the English went home.

Gone too were Scotland, Paraguay, and Austria; but Wales and Northern Ireland had other ideas. After scrapping their way like England to three draws in their group, Wales—managed by United's Jimmy Murphy—beat Hungary in a play-off, and went through with the hosts. Hungary, a ghost of a side, joined Mexico at the exit—but the Northern Irish achievement was the greater. In a topsy-turvy group they beat the Czechs, drew with the Germans, and fell 3-1 to Argentina. The Czechs, however, then served notice that their prewar form was returning; they wiped out Argentina 6-1. Argentina went home, to be met at the airport by an enraged and baying mob, a fate they would in future go to any lengths to avoid; the Czechs went to a play-off with the Ulstermen and, astoundingly, lost to them again.

It was not the first time that a team of undying heart from that troubled and lovely province would upset grander opponents, but in Sweden they'd reached their limit. In the quarter-finals they met France, who beat them 4-0; Fontaine scored two more, and his tally was now eight. Wales, also, had pushed out too far into the game's hardest terrain; they resisted bravely, but the luck was with Pele. Elsewhere, Germany were too strong for Yugoslavia, as they had been at the same stage four years earlier, while the hosts went past Russia 2-0, before a crowd who were having trouble believing it.

When they beat the Germans 3-1 in the semifinals, absolutely no one at all could believe it. But the ordinarily tranquil and mannerly Swedes now succumbed to soccer's demon fevers, the crowd bawling in the stands while, on the pitch, punctuated by niggling and sometimes brutish fouls, not a little cheating, and two expulsions, the game swung Sweden's way. Not that it could possibly matter—in Stockholm, after the French had held Brazil for forty-five minutes (and Fontaine had scored yet again), Pele, Didi, the Little Bird and the rest let rip. The game ended 5-2; Pele had three of them, and the final now was surely as imbalanced as any there had ever been.

First, however, there was the play-off for third place. The French beat the Germans 6-3, but more to the point is that Fontaine scored four of them and took his total to thirteen, a feat never matched in any World Cup before or since.

Four years earlier, Sandor Kocsis had eleven for Hungary; in 1970, Gerd Muller got ten for the Germans. It'll give you an idea of how much harder it is to score goals today when you realize that the leading scorers at all of the last four World Cups—Argentina's Mario Kempes, Italy's Paolo Rossi, England's Gary Lineker, and Salvatore "Toto" Schillaci before his home crowd last time—all won the Golden Boot with six goals apiece, less than half the number scored by Just Fontaine.

In the fabric of our lives, Part 4: I went for a beer at the Glyn Valley Hotel, and met Alan the Marxist Plumber at the bar. I told him I'd got as far as 1958 and he said, "Didn't Sweden get one early?"

They did—after four minutes—and it did them no good whatsoever. The Little Bird left Swedish defenders standing around like gateposts, the gate swaying on its hinges behind him as if he were no more than a breath of wind. At halftime it was 2-1, in the second half Pele scored twice, the game ended 5-2—and at last the magicians, the masters, the finest soccer players in the world could take the Jules Rimet trophy home. They would, eventually, come to own it forever—and Pele would still be with them when they did.

11

Defenders

Mark Morris:	Goalkeeper
Age:	24
Height:	5' 11"
Hometown:	Broughton, Cheshire

He was fourteen, playing for North Wales Schoolboys; a scout from Burnley followed him home. Signed as an apprentice he spent every holiday, every half-term for a year traveling a hundred miles into Lancashire to train there. Then they wrote him a letter to say they were letting him go; no phone call, no word, just a letter—to a fourteen-year-old.

He went back to Wrexham. Since he was thirteen he'd trained there with other schoolboys on the potholed parking lot behind the stadium; today, he's the longest-serving member of the squad.

Of his job he says simply, "You're the last line of defence. Any way you can, no matter what part of your body you use, you keep the ball out of the net." And to do that, he concedes there's truth in the old saw that all keepers are nuts. "You've got to be, to be throwing your head in where the boots are flying, week in, week out. I've got scars all over my face; I've had broken ribs coming out for crosses where a lad's kneed me in the back, and I've broken my toes. My thumbs, they're loose in the joints, they'll pop out—I have to strap them up every game. You get kicked more than anyone else."

The most wince-inducing injury I've heard of involved the

keeper who caught his wedding ring on a nail in the crossbar as he jumped for a high ball. Watching the Argentinian Pumpido break his leg against the Russians in Italy was pretty grisly too. It leaves you wondering, where's the pleasure in this?

"Keeping the ball out. There's no greater feeling than coming off with a clean sheet, because that's your job done."

But there are two types of clean sheet. The team in front of you plays a blinder and you're idle all game—or your opponents make you work for it.

"There aren't many games you'll go ninety minutes and not make a save—and it's harder making a save in the last minute than the first. The first minute you're on your toes, you're sharp, whereas if you go eighty-nine minutes and you've nothing to do, your mind tends to wander. So you've got to keep your concentration. That last-minute save might be the one thing you do all game, you might be 4-0 up—but there's just as much pleasure in the clean sheet then as there is if you've saved shot after shot. Because people don't remember the saves, do they? They remember the goals you let in."

Does that bother him?

"You can't let it. You've got to be thick-skinned to be a keeper. You're closer to the crowd, so if the team are playing badly, you're the one that gets it. Especially here; if we have a bad time here, you'll get slaughtered. They get on you, 'C'mon, you're *crap*'—you'd be surprised."

I wouldn't, actually—and you get more than curses thrown at you, too. Liverpool's Bruce Grobbelaar was hit in the head with a piece of concrete during a game for Zimbabwe against Egypt in Cairo. And sharpened coins come in and out of vogue as missiles—but the projectiles you worry about aren't the ones from the terraces. When you let a shot in, said Morris, you just want to get your shovel out of your bag and dig a dirty great hole for yourself.

"I'm the world's worst loser—I think you've got to be. At Crewe in the FA Cup, they got six, and I was shell-shocked all weekend. Every time I shut my eyes there was a ball going in the back of the net. We got mauled . . . horrible feeling."

I asked what the feeling was in the club now, and he said, "I've been here when we've been bottom. It's a drag—there's no enjoyment, nothing to look forward to, and you can't go out in the town. I got beaten up then, I was with a few of the

lads, and fifteen of them followed us out of the pub. It gets a
bit hairy. But now, you can't wait for every game. The crowds
are picking up, we're playing good stuff; everyone's bubbling."

But, he said, "No one's thinking about promotion. We've
achieved nothing yet—not until the last game of the season."

Oh, c'mon . . .

"It's in the back of your mind, obviously. I'm confident; the
way we're playing, we're not scared of anybody. And to get
promoted would be a fantastic feeling, a great lift for the town.
A club this size doesn't belong in the Third Division."

Tony Humes:	Center Half
Age:	26
Height:	5' 11"
Hometown:	Blyth, Northumberland

Mel Pejic:	Center Half
Age:	33
Height:	5' 10"
Hometown:	Newcastle-under-Lyme, Staffordshire

Humes signed for Ipswich when he was sixteen, and stayed
nine years; as a teenager there he had an example to look up
to: Terry Butcher, center half for England seventy-eight times
through the eighties. Humes is a slighter man, and shorter,
but they're similar characters—quiet and courteous off the
pitch, hard on it.

He came to Wrexham at the start of the season. He'd spent
ten months on a week-to-week contract before that, trying to
get away; it wasn't pleasant. He said, "I was disappointed. I'd
been there a long time, I felt I'd done a good job, and to be
turned round and more or less kicked out—you know it always
happens, but when it's you it happens to, it's hard to take.
But I've come here, and I've not regretted it for a minute."

It was a drop in status and money, and it was a wrench for
his wife, an Ipswich girl. But it was first-team football again,
and if we get promoted, it would also be the first honor he'd
have won in his career. Asked if we'd go up, he said, "I've said
we would from the start of the season."

But they're competitive people, center halves; asked what
being captain meant he said, "You never drop your head."
Pejic talks a lot about "the will to win"; ask him if we're going
up, and he just looks at you like you're stupid. When I asked

Flynn to pick the most important players on the side as the last decisive games came upon us, he named Pejic and Humes.

Humes said, "The main job's to keep the side stable. Everything goalbound's coming through you, so you stay tight on their forwards, and keep the ball away from goal. And then, a lot depends on where you defend. If you defend deep in your half, you've less chance of scoring yourself; when the ball goes up front, you can't support your forwards."

So you only defend deep when you're forced to. You can choose to do it—the Continentals do, sucking you in, catching you on the break—but not many in Britain have the players to do that, and most British sides push up. Pejic also points out that against the lump-and-slam soccer of the Third Division, another reason Wrexham's back line pushes up is they're not very tall; squeezing up the field keeps the monsters out of Morris's airspace. But either way, pushing up or hanging back, how do they work together? What was the difference between Tony Humes and Mel Pejic?

Humes smiled and said, "Mel's older." And he's quicker, and that's it. They're center halves, stoppers—they hold the middle, read the game, see what's coming, break it up, and move it on out again. If one attacks the ball, the other drops off and covers. They don't need to talk about it; they just do it. Morris said, "You see them go off after training together—they're good mates."

"When I was a kid," said Humes, "people said to me, you want to see center halves play, you watch Terry Butcher and Russell Osman. They'd not speak to each other; one would just shout the other's name, and he would know what was happening. But I think wherever you go you'll find center halves get on well. We're easygoing, but as soon as we get out on the park, we change."

" 'Course they stick together." Alan grinned. "They're like policemen. Nobody else likes them."

Pejic's mother is English; his father's a Serb who came to Britain after World War II. He has a brother nine years his senior who played left back for Stoke and Everton, and several times for England, but he never made it to that level himself; he is instead the model pro, a Third Division workhorse.

He was initially a right back, but as the pace of the games increased, with full backs getting more involved offensively, the switch to center half's suited him. A full back, often, will be isolated, one-on-one with a winger; Pejic's happier in the thick of it with another man by his side—and it gets pretty thick.

In the heat of the game, said Humes, "You'll get as physical as you have to. You'll avoid confrontation, especially with the likes of Lincoln, because that's their game—trying to get you in a scrap, so you forget how you want to be playing. But if you've got to be physical, you will be. It's your job."

So he's hurt people?

"Probably, yeah. Not purposefully, but by going in strong— and when you're losing, when you don't know what's going on, when there's players running past you left, right, and center, sometimes you'll stick a leg out. And then you've caught someone so late it's untrue—but if you're getting beat, it happens. When you're getting beat you get so wound up, you just . . . you don't mean to do it, but you can't stop yourself."

He was smiling when he said that. And he added, "You don't want to hurt people; you're a professional, and you don't want to put people out of the game. But you want to win the tackles, don't you? And if someone's gone past you, it makes you feel a bit of a fool, and I suppose you want retribution. You think, I'm not a fool—you're not doing that again. So maybe then you whack somebody."

In the Coca-Cola Cup early this season, said Pejic, Bury hit a purple patch—scored three in twenty minutes. So then, "One of their forwards got the ball, he had his back to me, and he was going to lay it off to his left back. And as he's knocked it [Pejic made an expressive, sweeping, upending kind of movement with his hand], I just caught him from behind— tried to play the ball, but caught the back of his calf. And that, unfortunately, was the end of him for the day."

And you'd never say you've done that intentionally? . . .

"Not intentionally. It's just one of those things, where you try and get the ball—but possibly you try and get the man too. It's not the nicest thing to do, but situations happen every game. Like, the elbow's come in a lot more; when you go up to head a ball, you've got to be careful when the striker's going up that his elbow's not coming across in your face. There's a lot of things go on . . . it's not a nice thing to talk about. But it's a hard game, it's a competitive game. And if it wasn't, people wouldn't come and watch it."

*   *   *

Wrexham went to Cardiff for the first leg of the Welsh Cup semifinal, and lost 2-0. I listened on the radio and we shouldn't have lost; the commentators kept saying there was no way there was two goals' difference between the teams—but having more chances doesn't mean a thing if you don't take them. Cardiff had two, and they did.

Flynn said it'd do his side good, they'd learn a lesson. He said when they'd lost before this season, they'd deserved to—but now, he said, they'd learn you can also lose when you've played well.

Pejic said it was only halftime. "Two goals down sounds a lot, but the way we're playing at home, if we can get one back early in the second leg there's still ninety minutes, and extra time if need be. There's still a lot of football to be played."

Meantime, it's back to the league. Pejic said, "When we've been beaten before, we've always come back and put a run together. So we've two more away games now—and it's important to get four or six points out of that."

And get promoted?

"Yes. Because the teams we've got to play, the last ten games, I wouldn't say it was an easy run-in but we're capable of winning our last five at home, and picking up a couple of wins away. And if we do that, we could go up as champions."

And that's a center half. They're not people inclined to have doubts, so I asked what promotion would mean and Pejic said, "It would mean a lot. Not having had the most successful of careers, this now—this is what's it all about, isn't it?"

Wrexham drew 0-0 at Scunthorpe, the strikers firing on empty again. But it was a point away from home, and with York losing, we went back to third.

Flynn took the squad to the coast for three days, to get in some recuperative golf and some time on the beach. Training? After five games in fifteen days, he said, no one's going to get any fitter than they are now.

While Wrexham were on the beach, other results saw Halifax dumped to last place, the relegation spot where the Vauxhall Conference yawns beneath you—and Halifax on a Friday night was where we played next.

Cross fired over the bar from six yards. Bennett headed over it too, and glanced another shot wide. Watkin dragged the ball across the face of the goal; on either side of halftime, Bennett missed again. It was now 225 minutes of football away from home, we'd made chances by the hatful, and still we were goalless—until Watkin scored in the fifty-sixth. So we shut up shop; the game ended 1-0. Three points took us level with Barnet—and with three more goals than they'd got, we went second in the table.

Second for a day—because the next afternoon Barnet went to Cardiff and, before 16,078 people in an all-action table-topper, were unlucky to leave with a 1-1 draw. It was their first point in four games, and we were third again. And from a partisan point of view, sure, at Wrexham we'd not mind if Barnet imploded into bankruptcy and got out of our road. But love of the underdog is breaking out all over for Barnet's manager and his players; even at Wrexham we feel for them.

Last time he was sacked, Barry Fry came back to find his salary had been halved. The players' paychecks have bounced; in Cardiff they had to pay for their bed and breakfast themselves. The League will inspect their books again next month, if the bank doesn't get to them first; they tried to sell a striker to get out of this mess, but the deal fell through and now the transfer deadline's passed. The club's for sale, the chairman's in bed after a stroke, and Fry's blunt: "We're at the end of the tunnel, and we've had enough."

After the match, Cardiff's chairman went to their dressing room and gave them a cheque for $1,500. He told them to have a drink on the way home; he said they deserved to go up as champions.

We have eight games to play.

Phil Hardy: Left Back
Age: 19
Height: 5' 7"
Hometown: Ellesmere Port, Cheshire

Barry Jones: Right Back
Age: 22
Height: 5' 9"
Hometown: Prescot, Liverpool

Phil Hardy didn't go to Anglesey. While the rest of the squad were on the beach, he was with the Irish Under-21's, playing Germany in Frankfurt.

"Christ," he said. "I knew this'd come up."

It was his first international. The Irish had called on him before (he has a grandfather from Dundalk) but Flynn told him to wait, see if the English came. After all, he's widely considered the best left back in the division; a month shy of twenty, he's played 130 league games already. But the English didn't come, and he wasn't going to wait for the rest of his life, so he took up with Ireland—they got beaten 8-0.

He said, "They were different class. Their running off the ball, their control—you can only learn from a game like that. But it was destroying, especially on your debut."

The balance between attack and defence in a full back's play depends, obviously, on how many problems the other lot set you. Hardy said, "If you've got a winger to mark and he's giving you a tough time, obviously you can't get forward so much. You've got to sort him out first. But as soon as you've done that, then you can push up."

So how do you sort him out?

"Get a challenge in right at the start of the game. The object is to stop him getting crosses in, and if you do a good job on him, he'll be thinking twice. He'll be looking out for where you're coming from next."

"If he gets the ball," said Jones, "he'll be thinking, God, is he coming in on me again? And he'll want to get rid of it. He'll just pass it, won't he? He'll stand back."

"You get a great buzz from it. And the crowd lifts you—you get in hard, they'll cheer you. That'll get you going."

"And you've the confidence to go forward then. You're thinking, right, I can leave him now, he doesn't want it. He's out of the game." And once you're on top like that, "it just brings a smile to your face, you're just smiling all the time. You get the ball and you give it, you're laughing—you say, go on, you have a go. And everyone on the side's saying, look at him laughing his head off. But you're just enjoying it."

Hardy said, "If we don't go up now we want our backsides kicking."

Premier League clubs are watching Wrexham's every game. *Wales on Sunday* say one of them's offered $900,000 for Gareth Owen; they quote the chairman claiming the club could have banked twice that much if they'd taken all the offers coming in. Flynn concedes there's been one big bid, but he won't say for whom, and he says it was easy not to take it; he won't have the fans saying Wrexham's not ambitious. "But most important for me, if I'd have sold that player the others would have said, I thought he was sticking by us, I thought we were in this together. And I'm not letting them down like that, not now."

And he said that if we won promotion, there'd be four moments he'd look back on that made the difference: The first was getting beat 6-1 in November by Crewe in the FA Cup—and they thought, no one's doing that to us again. Three weeks later, we went back there and beat them 3-0; we've been climbing ever since.

The second was signing Mike Lake.

The third was losing to Cardiff in the Welsh Cup, and not being bothered, because we came off still knowing we were better than they were.

And the fourth was not selling that player.

April 2, 1993
Wrexham v. Darlington

Brian Flynn: "It'll probably be one of our hardest matches for a while, because we really are expected to turn them over. People think, Bah, it's only Darlington—who's next? But we won't think that. I'll make sure the players don't think that."

Phil Hardy: "We'll hammer them."

It was a glorious evening, mild, the pale sky swimming with mauve and lilac cloud. We made the Turf End turnstiles with time to spare, and the lines were still long—the Friday-night crowd, 6,972, was the biggest yet—so I stopped at the stall for a deathburger. British soccer grounds serve these things without shame, greasy pads of ground ear and nostrils, and they can dish you one out in a nanosecond. But Alan's a vegetarian, and there's not much call at the Racecourse for veggy burgers; frying one of them takes a little bit longer.

The lines slithered in through the gates; the crowd noise soared as the game began. And you could tell we were up their end straight away. Alan's green patty sat sizzling on the hot plate. My feet were doing a twitchy dance on their own, trying to pull me away into the ground. And then the roar . . .

What had happened was that Bennett charged down a dud clearance from their keeper, Watkin swooped on it, fired, after ninety seconds we were 1-0 up—and for the sake of a veggy burger we'd missed it. Other late arrivals scurried past me, cursing. One said, "I bet it was a cracker too."

We went in consoling ourselves that at least we'd witness a rampage, and we couldn't have been more wrong; we'd missed the best thing Wrexham did all night. Unfazed by the early setback, Darlington started well and got better. On twelve minutes Morris spread himself like a starfish to block a hard low shot; their No. 11 was quicksilver, darting in to give Humes and Sertori (Pejic was on a one-game suspension) a torrid time of it.

And, certainly, we were still trying to play football. It's a way of playing that deceives, that depends on patience, on waiting to make the pass that arrives where you are and they aren't—so after moments of quick grace where the ball goes here and there, and it's pretty but it doesn't look like much'll come of it, suddenly the opening's there; constructed and revealed.

But it's in the nature of things that it can't always work. Keep carving away, and enough times it will; for all the moves that don't come off, there's always the one that does. It's that last ball you're looking for that isn't a yard too long, a yard too short, a yard too tight by their defender—and some days you can't make that ball. Some days every corner is a dud, every cross is soft and slow, every lob, every chip, every nudge and little dink has the wrong sort of weight on it, so then they've always got a body in the way, and the game turns up its toes and the crowd gets glum, sure in the knowledge that it isn't going to go for us. And Darlington scored. They had a corner, we didn't clear it properly, and the guy's drilled it in from the edge of the area. It's 1-1, on the edge of halftime.

"I hope," says Alan, "they're not going stale on us." But he says it's all right. He says Flynn'll give them a rubbing down with the old verbal sandpaper in the dressing room, and they'll come back out all shiny and sparkling.

Lake spins it wide to Cross; the winger snaps the ball over instantly—and the header drops wide. The scoreboard says THAT WAS CLOSE! Not close enough . . .

We go again. Bennett lays it off to Cross, he cuts in, has a poke at it; it bounces out to Hardy, he crosses back in, they head away for a corner. We waste it, hit it straight at their nearest man; he skies it away. We collect it, knock in a far post flyer—and there's no one there. Bennett picks it up, tears in; the keeper throws himself on the ball at his feet. The chant's now urgently straightforward:

Come on Wrexham
Come on Wrexham

Hardy's got lovely distribution. And he keeps pushing up—but Darlington's defence is brave and precise, and they break out quick to that dangerous No. 11—so when they do, Hardy's not there. And is this it? Is this where the season ends? Is this where the pressure tells and the confidence crumbles, and the last ball leaves us forever? You stand there seeing seven more games ahead of you, points slipping away, hope drying up.

We win another corner. Barry Jones climbs, puts meat on the header—and it's wide. Then Watkin gets it on the right side of the area, and his shot's explosive. Oh, man, we thought that was the one. We thought the season was saved right there. In the sudden vast silence we waited for the net to bulge—and the ball flew behind like a rocket into the stand.

People drift away, peeved and disconsolate. As they move across the terrace they keep stopping to watch, muttering and swearing. I say to Alan, it's not going to happen, is it?

"No. I gave up when Watkin hit the stand. I was thinking that net's going to billow, and all we got was twizzling seat backs."

In the dying moments we drop in another free kick, and head it straight to their keeper. That about sums it up. We go round and round, passing here, passing there, camped in their half but boxed out of their area, no way past the bodies.

So we go gloomy to the car. Alan says, "If it's any consolation, the veggy burger was delicious." And I've been home five minutes when he phones me from the pub. "York," he says. "They won 4-1 at Gillingham." So now we're fourth again, back in the bloody play-offs.

Flynn said we were due an off day—and Darlington gave us more problems than most. "They anticipated better than us. And they seemed more relaxed than us."

What? We weren't relaxed?

"No. They were *more* relaxed. Because they've got nothing to play for. And OK, that word'll come around—pressure. People outside saying we've not been scoring. But I'm not concerned about that. I'll only be concerned if we don't create chances—I'll be deeply concerned then."

But we've only scored two in the last four games . . .

"Yes, but there was a phase earlier when we got nineteen goals in five games, and you can't do that all the time. And chances are going to be at a premium now, aren't they?"

What did he say at halftime?

"Not to panic. Just to relax a little." He corrected himself. "To relax a little bit *more*." And he was fiddling about in his seat; he wasn't sitting still. I know for sure, *I'm* not relaxed—and it's going to get more difficult now, isn't it?

"It's not going to get any easier."

So I asked what he'd do at Scarborough on Tuesday night, and he dropped his bombshell.

"Well, Gary Bennett's broken his toe. Their keeper stood on his foot, so he's out for four to six weeks. The rest of the season, basically."

That's a bit upsetting.

"Yes. But we're all in it together. The next one steps in; I've got options. I've got Paskin, I can play Connolly up front, I've got Taylor, Pugh—I've got options. Whether they come off or not's another matter. But I have got options."

I went out to the parking lot and banged my head on the steering wheel. Sure, he's got options. Just none of them feature the leading scorer any more. In the Glyn Valley Hotel I told Alan the bad news and he said, "Oh, well. At least we've avoided relegation."

Round-Up

On hearing that one of his players has taken a knock on the head and doesn't know who he is any more, Partick Thistle's manager says, "Brilliant. Tell him he's Pele."

Norwich go to Nottingham Forest, win 3-0, and go top of the Premier League. Forest manager Brian Clough, staring relegation in the face, says, "Can't avoid the truth. Can't make it look better than it is. Only one thing to be said. We're in the shit."

At the other end of the table, there's no club quite like Manchester United. They've not won the championship since 1967, when they went on to win the European Cup; in twenty-six years they've been second four times, third three times, fourth three times, and once, in 1974, they were relegated. But every year the biggest crowd in the country still poured into Old Trafford, a crowd topping 40,000 even now, when seats have replaced terraces and the capacity's tumbled—a crowd roaring them on to take that title again, a crowd still roaring, still believing, after twenty-six years. I met a man once who went to every game the season they'd gone down; he said simply, "You had to be there, didn't you? You had to help them back up."

Last year they came second. They had had the championship in the bag, but in the last few games they had a fit of the vapors, and let Leeds United slip past them. So they bought a Frenchman called Eric Cantona from Leeds, a gifted stroller who'll spend eighty minutes doing nothing whatsoever in a Gallic reverie, then wake up and win you the game. Leeds fell apart; United are back up there. And in the best traditions of the club, their football is dramatic and dashing; they sometimes seem to be playing five forwards—Cantona, Brian McClair of Scotland, the Ukrainian Andrei Kanchelskis, Ryan Giggs and Mark Hughes of Wales. In the heart of midfield, Paul Ince will soon be the first black player to captain England; all the back line bar one are internationals too, and their keeper, the Dane Peter Schmeichel, is the best in the world. So can they do it this time? After twenty-six years?

Leapfrog: United play Manchester City at Maine Road. It ends 1-1; the point takes United back on top over Norwich. Then, while Wimbledon are bashing Norwich about and winning 3-0, Aston Villa beat Sheffield Wednesday—so now Villa go top. And anyone could win this—but the feeling grows that United are getting the vapors again.

Alan remembers a season years back when Wrexham were near the top of the table all through; from the last two games, they needed just one point to go up. But they lost them both, and he remembers watching the players from the Kop on their knees, weeping.

Soccer gives us an alternative history, an alternative geography. In place of laws and wars and inaugurations, there are record books and fixture lists. In place of kings and politicians are players and managers. In place of capitals and countries are stadia and clubs. We look to England–Hungary '53, the day we learnt we'd given the world a game, and the world had got better at it than us. We look to Glasgow '60, when Real Madrid beat Eintracht Frankfurt 7-3 to lift the European Cup for the fifth time—the day we watched and wondered, can we ever be that good? We look to Wembley '66 and Turin '90, when we were. And then, the geography: summits of desire, plains of desolation. The capitals are the San Siro, the Bernabeu, the Nou Camp; the stands rise around you screaming, roaring, weeping, burning with color and noise. They make a whole other world, a whole other life. On the front pages there's news—but the sports pages are a better planet altogether.

Out of this fevered terrain the World Cup rises like Everest on the horizon each fourth year—and without the base camp of a league to prepare in, you'll never make the peak. That's why Wrexham matter, and United and Villa and all the rest. From the Racecourse to Old Trafford, we feed, we learn, we sing, we *breathe*.

In Sydney, Brazil beats Ghana 2-1 to lift the World Youth Cup. The Brazilian coach says afterward that at least three of his teenagers might be good enough for the real thing in 1994. They have, in other words, moved up to the first ridge.

In Italy Milan lose again, 1-0 to Parma, and their record run in *Serie A* is over. Asked if they mightn't play more freely now the weight of history's off their back, Milan's manager Fabio Capello replies tersely, "Defeat is never a liberation."

Villa go to Norwich and lose 1-0; Norwich go top again. Wimbledon—the Crazy Gang, the Bruise Brothers, the Bash Street Kids—go to Sheffield Wednesday, and make such a boxing match out of it that after the game Wednesday's chairman bars them from the club lounge. Wimbledon's manager says, "Deep down, people don't want to play us." Too right.

In the qualifiers for USA '94, in Wales's group, Czechoslovakia draw in Cyprus—and Czechoslovakia may have ceased to exist, but for the moment their soccer team plays on. There's alternative geography for you.

Every season, the nation's footballers vote on who are the best players among them—the best overall, and the best in each position in each division. Player of the Year: center half Paul McGrath of Aston Villa and Ireland, thirty-three now, his knees so bad he doesn't bother training any more, but he's a defender on a par with Baresi (and, given the nature of the British game, he's better in the air). The *Independent* calls him "the ambling alp"—and like Bobby Robson said, it's not just speed of foot, it's speed of mind. So if you're playing McGrath, it doesn't matter if you're faster over ten or twenty yards. McGrath knows in his head what's happening before it happens: you sprint twenty yards and when you stop, he's there waiting for you.

Young Player of the Year: Ryan Giggs.

Gareth Owen wins a slot in the Third Division's Team of the Year. Barnet have three players nominated, but they've more pressing matters to worry about. Their squad goes to Stan Flashman's house to protest about getting no pay for two weeks. Flashman fines them two weeks' pay for protesting (handy way out, that), then changes his mind. Two days later he sacks Barry Fry again, and team captain Duncan Horton as well. A few hours after that it's announced that Flashman's resigning (on grounds of ill health) and a new chairman reinstates Fry and Horton. So does this mean they can concentrate on football now? With Barnet, who knows?

And the World Cup rolls on. Algeria, Cameroon, Morocco, Nigeria, Zambia, Senegal, Guinea, and the Ivory Coast make the final qualifiers in Africa—three groups of three, the winner of each booking a ticket to America. The identity of the ninth contender remains uncertain, after missiles flung from a crowd of 120,000 in Cairo hit five of Zimbabwe's team. Zimbabwe protests, and Egypt's win is declared void; the match will be replayed on neutral territory in France.

In Dublin, Paul McGrath's Republic of Ireland thump Northern Ireland 3-0, after a minute's silence for the latest victims of the terrorists. Republic manager Jack Charlton (center half for England in 1966) says they could win the World Cup. People laugh, and he tells them not to. "You never know with us."

England travel to Izmir in Turkey. They have nine players unavailable through injury, and the Turkish try hard to make the sick list longer. Ian Wright's punched in the stomach, Gazza's bitten on the shoulder, right back Lee Dixon gets elbowed in the throat, and after the third time they deck him, he has to leave the field with a badly bruised shin. A crowd of 60,000 shower the pitch with coins, cans, rocks, bottles, boiled eggs, fireworks, whatever's to hand. An English fan gets a brick in the face, and may lose an eye. A firecracker in the press box ignites a Turkish journalist's hair. England win 2-0. Lee Dixon says pointedly that if an English crowd behaved like that, we'd be banned from internationals for ten years. Given England's reputation, however—and a general inclination to keep stiff upper lips all round—the English manager is diplomatic. "In different parts of the world," he says, "football is played in different ways."

Belgium, winners six times in six outings, come to Cardiff Arms Park. Ryan Giggs has played as a substitute five times before, Wales's youngest-ever player; now nineteen years old, he starts his first international, scores the opening goal with a searing free kick, and has the Belgians pegged back every time he gets the ball. They end up setting two men to shut him down, which means more space for the rest; Liverpool's Ian Rush gets Wales's second, his twenty-fourth for his country, and becomes the number one Welsh goalscorer of all time. Wales 2, Belgium 0.

Bewildered after trying to mark Giggs in training, one of the Welsh coaching staff says, "One moment he's twenty yards away with the ball. Next thing you know he's on top of you, coming like an express train." After the match, Wales's captain and sweeper Kevin Ratcliffe, a player with fifty-nine internationals behind him, says: "Now I can tell my children I've played with Ryan Giggs."

Brian Flynn watched the game on a monitor in a studio in London, summarizing for BBC Radio 5. When I asked him about Giggs he said simply, "Best player I've ever seen." So I looked at him hard, and he said it again. He said, "I dealt with him in the Welsh youth squad two, three years ago—and when I first saw him in a training session, I could tell. I called Terry [Yorath, the Welsh manager] that night. I told him Giggs would be in the national squad in two years." So I asked what it is, what he's got, and Flynn said, "The lot. Balance, pace, timing, temperament, the lot." He said, "I think he'll take us to the World Cup. We needed something to spark us—and he's the one."

At Barnet, after Stan Flashman quits, Barry Fry meets the new board, decides it's new faces papering over old cracks, and finally resigns after an epic of long-suffering loyalty to become the manager of First Division Southend. It's the worst blow for Barnet's luckless players yet.

In America, a private sale of World Cup first-round tickets to the United States Soccer Federation's "soccer family"—two million registered coaches, referees, and administrators—is wildly oversubscribed. More than a year before kickoff in Chicago, three months before tickets go on general release, over $10 million has been taken already.

It's estimated that economic activity generated around USA '94 will exceed $4 billion.

12

Under the Twin Towers

> "You *want* us to lose."
> —England captain Johnny Haynes
> to an English journalist in Chile

Chile 1962

Nothing was different; England were glum, Italy were a mess, Brazil were magnificent, and the Eastern Europeans were in the army. Aside from the Russians, Bulgaria, Hungary, and Czechoslovakia all qualified; the Bulgarians weren't up to much but the Hungarians had rebuilt and the Czechs, with a side based on the army's Dukla Prague team, were known to be capable. But with Pele and Garrincha around, so what? These were men who could beat four with a shrug, leopards among cattle; there would surely be no holding them.

The Italians made few friends. Their domestic game was as ever the richest in the world, it was more than a little corrupt, and they were in the habit of naturalizing every player they could get; the squad they brought to Chile included several South Americans clutching shiny new passports. The Spanish did the same—Puskas was now a Spaniard—but the Italians compounded the offence when their papers said rude things about Chile, and their scouts started loitering with beady eyes around other peoples' training camps. Their squad, meanwhile, had the usual roster of schismatic egomaniacs, while their soccer had fallen into a dismal, paranoically defensive mindset.

They played a dull, goalless draw with the Germans, turned the team upside down with new faces to play Chile, and promptly found themselves in a war with their much-offended hosts. Amid flying fists and spittle two men were sent off, one nose was broken, and two goals were scored by Chile; Italy went home in a red mist of rancor.

Switzerland went out too, though not before the Germans had broken a Swiss player's leg. Yugoslavia were more chivalrous; when one of their men broke a Russian player's leg, they sent the offender home. But both these sides advanced over a weakened Uruguay and a bold Colombia; they went with Chile and the Germans to the knockout.

Meanwhile, Brazil and England faithfully followed their very different scripts. As ever, England expected; as ever, Brazil delivered. Both sides had fine players, but Brazil had more of them, and knew how to use them.

For England there was Bobby Charlton, one of Busby's Babes who survived the disaster at Munich, and went on to become the country's number one all-time goalscorer, and from London's East End there were Jimmy Greaves and Bobby Moore. Moore was twenty-one, shaping up already as a world-class defender of unflappable poise; as for Greaves, he was the most electric finisher the English game ever saw, an irreverent Cockney full of sly cheek and dash. Before Chile, there were days when it seemed England couldn't stop scoring goals; four against Spain, five against Wales, eight against Mexico, nine against Scotland. In Chile, there were days when it seemed they couldn't start.

As Pozzo had said, the dish England brought to the top table was from a recipe everyone knew; in Rancagua, in a stadium belonging to a mining company, Hungary unpicked all the ingredients and beat them 2-1. England shook themselves together to defeat a melodramatic Argentina 3-1, then subsided to a 0-0 tie with Bulgaria—as dreary as any game in the tournament. So while Hungary had sparkled, trouncing the Bulgarians 6-1, England scraped through behind them on goal difference; they would meet Brazil in the quarter-finals.

In Brazil's group, Mexico had made a game of it, but lost 2-0 anyhow; Pele scored one, and made the other. Spain had pushed them hard too, a fat little Spaniard called Puskas setting up a goal that gave Spain the lead until the seventy-second minute. But with four minutes left the match was decided by the Little Bird, racing down the wing to supply Amarildo with the winner.

Amarildo was in for Pele, who had torn a muscle against Czechoslovakia. Pele was still only twenty-one, but now unquestionably a player of unique and timeless gifts. There were no substitutes in those days; he had spent the last hour of the game in which he was injured standing lame on the sideline while Brazil's ten fit men packed their defence, holding the Czechs for a goalless draw worth a point apiece. For any other country, the loss would have been catastrophic; for Brazil it was bad, but, being Brazil, when Pele limped out, come the next game, Amarildo glided in—a player who'd have walked into any other team anyhow. And, of course, they still had the Little Bird.

Fifty miles from the capital at Viña del Mar, in a pretty little stadium with salt in the air from the craggy shore, Garrincha flew with yet more swooping, twisting grace than he had in Sweden and try what they could, England were nonplussed. He scored twice, made the third, and England's solitary reply was sand blown among the pines on the sea wind. What use Moore, Greaves, Charlton in this company? Once more the game's founders trudged away from the World Cup; as one of them would remark, "Nobody could say an adoring public scattered roses in our path when we returned." The FA, as usual, wrote a report saying Must Do Better; but who could believe they ever would?

For the third time running, Yugoslavia met Germany in a World Cup quarter-final. It was a European equivalent of England–Brazil, Teuton muscle tackling Balkan skill, and though the game was much closer than England's had been, skill prevailed here too; at the third time of asking, Yugoslavia won 1-0. Meanwhile, infused with desire in their backyard as Sweden had been, Chile upset the Russians 2-0—and the fourth game was an upset too, the strong, patient, methodical Czechs beating Hungary by one goal after surviving a barrage of missed chances.

Pele or no Pele, there could now be no doubt about the outcome. In the semifinal Chile fought, at first manfully, and then dirtily, but Garrincha was uncontainable. By the end, he'd been kicked from pillar to post; when he retaliated he was sent off, and was hit in the head with a bottle hurled from the crowd as he went—but by then it was 4-2, and two of them were his.

In the final Brazil met the Czechs, who had again defied expectation when they outthought Yugoslavia and outgunned them 3-1. But fine tactical intelligence is no answer to genius; the score was the same in the final, and the Czechs were on the wrong end of it.

Eight of the Brazilian side had played in Sweden; among the three who hadn't, Amarildo scored one goal, and made a second. Brazil collected the World Cup again, and the world could only acknowledge that there was no one else like them—could only wonder, indeed, how they could possibly be beaten.

Changing the Rules

By the time the 7th World Cup went to Chile, the competition had settled into its ideal format. Sixteen teams played in four groups of four; each team played the others in each group, the top two went through, and the bottom two didn't. The last and defining change to this formula, made since Sweden, was that if two sides finished a group level on points, then goal difference settled the placings; a good move, because it meant there was no need any more for play-offs that could, potentially, make a nonsense of results in group games already played. So you went into the thing knowing you had three games, and you did well and scored goals or bust.

Twenty years later, the expansion of the tournament from sixteen to twenty-four teams made everything complicated again. To fill a knockout "round of sixteen" after the first phase, we've ended up with the cumbersome and arithmetically arcane business of the four best third-placed teams going through with the rest—four teams going through, when they didn't actually do very well. So could we run this thing better?

Mutterings sometimes surface about increasing the number of finalists yet again, from twenty-four to thirty-two this time. You'd then have eight four-team pools; you'd be back to the top two making it, the bottom two making for the airport, and the sixteen who play on in the knockout all more clearly deserving to do so. Proponents of this further expansion argue that it restores a greater measure of lucidity to proceedings, while also being democratic—it opens up the field for more of the little guys to have a go.

But two years' worth of qualifiers seems democratic enough to me; the argument is mostly a smoke screen for people trying to make the World Cup an even more gargantuan corporate cashfest than it already is. Even on its present scale, it's grown far too big for more than a handful of countries to contemplate holding it seriously, and what's democratic about that? So we have to find other ways of making it work better with the twenty-four teams we've got.

If the American organizers had any say in the matter, they'd have improved the World Cup in two ways—starting, in the first phase, with three points for a win instead of two.

Two things stifle much of modern international soccer. The increasing efficiency of defensive play means goals are harder to come by—at Italia '90 there was an average of 2.21 goals per game, the lowest ever, compared to an average over fourteen World Cups of 3.22, or an all-time high of 5.38 at Switzerland '54. So no one's ever going to do a Just Fontaine again. But with more specific reference to the World Cup's opening phase, there's also a psychological problem.

The deranged and extensive passions attendant on this game (basically, the nationalist hysteria) mean that not losing becomes more important than winning for far too many teams. So group matches are often sterile affairs, in which one or both sides opt to shut down and play for a draw; in the first round as it stands, after all, three draws mean three points, and that'll most likely see you through. As a result, at Italia '90 in particular, we saw a lot of negative early games, teams meandering around in a state of tension-throttled somnambulism.

Three points for a win would do away with this; it would unhitch the arithmetical stranglehold, and with it the stonewalling mentality. Go out strong for a win in your first game, put three points in the bag, and you're up and running—and the evidence that this would work is in the English league. Because we play like muscled speed freaks, our game is often more exciting than the more cultured, leisurely stuff you get elsewhere anyhow—and three points for a win really encourages that. So the Americans wanted to make this change—

but it isn't America's tournament, it's FIFA's, and it remains two points for a win.

Secondly, in the knockout phase, USA '94 wanted to do away with penalty shoot-outs, and play sudden death after ninety minutes instead—the next scorer wins. As for the final, they wanted to go the whole hog and have a replay.

This is interesting, because since the tournament was first awarded to the U.S.A. in 1988, there's been derision around the world, with people saying Americans didn't know a free kick from a free lunch, and in general just weren't "soccer people." Yet the suggestions above are precisely what a soccer person would like to see happen to make the World Cup a more wonderful thing. But when I asked a senior official of USA '94 what FIFA had done about these suggestions he could only say, "To the best of my knowledge, they took no action on it."

I saw a cartoon once in which a man stands in a room labeled FIFA IMPRACTICAL IDEAS THINK TANK. He's holding a square ball.

We've already come across Sepp Blatter's calamitous notion of kick-ins replacing throw-ins, whereby we'll end up with the goalmouth under bombardment, and a lot less football. A few years ago, however, when FIFA were growing alarmed that they'd put the World Cup in America and no one would turn up (it will, in fact, be a sellout), they floated some other crackpot ideas. There was talk of making the goals bigger—while FIFA president João Havelange of Brazil suggested playing the game in four quarters.

Coming from the man supposed to be the senior custodian of a sport whose whole essence is flow, this latter notion is execrable—especially as its motive can only have been to pursue the favors of your commercial-raddled networks.

As to having a bigger goal so the ball can go in it more often, that's pathetic. If scoring goals was easy, what would be the point? Three points encouraging teams to play more positively is one thing, but marooning the keeper in an aircraft hangar while people run up basketball scores is something else entirely.

In floating these dismal ideas, it seems FIFA thought for the most part the world would blame the Americans, and for the most part, predictably, it did. Happily, however, there's no present chance they'll be implemented, and thus soccer will be served up to you in uncorrupted form—live on ABC and ESPN in games of two halves, without commercials, with goals the size they're supposed to be.

Enjoy.

England 1966

If England couldn't win the trophy under Wembley's twin towers, they never could—but for a while, it looked as if neither they nor any other team would get to lift it up anyhow. Nine pounds of gold seraph on an onyx base, the Jules Rimet trophy was put on display at an exhibition in Central Hall, Westminster, and on March 20 it was stolen.

The FA and the Flying Squad ran round in a red-faced panic for a week, until a dog named Pickles found it under a bush in South London. Pickles got a year's supply of free chow from a pet-food company, there was talk of a film part—and the Jules Rimet trophy wasn't seen again until the winners raised it overhead four months later.

When England kicked off the tournament against Uruguay before 87,000 at Wembley, it looked as if their performance would be as embarrassing on the field as this incident was off it. Uruguay set their minds on defence; England, stale and nervous, were unable to breach them, and left the pitch when it ended 0-0 in an echoing silence. They went on to beat Mexico and France, 2-0 each, but neither win was convincing, Jimmy Greaves was injured, and away from the capital the action in the other groups was so much better that England's prospects looked as mediocre as ever.

In the northeast, where games were played at Sunderland's Roker Park and at Ayresome Park in Middlesbrough, Italy self-destructed again. Internecine club politics influenced baffling selection policies, and that in turn produced uncertain form; from politics to panic, in Italy, is no great distance. They began well enough, putting the horror show of four years earlier behind them with a 2-0 defeat of Chile; then they changed the team all round, and lost limply by a goal to the Russians. Still, the third game was against North Korea, the tournament's rank outsiders; adored by the crowd, fast, sporting, spirited, exotic, and a million miles out of their depth.

Just before halftime, one Pak Doo Ik scored a goal as memorable as that of Joe Gaetjens for the U.S.A. against England; the Italians, fractious and demoralized, had no answer to it. The Koreans went through with the Russians; while they were cheered to the rafters, the Italians said miserably that they'd get home "at an unannounced hour between midnight and dawn at an unannounced airport." Like the English, for all the power and talent in their league, when it came to the highest test it seemed the Italians couldn't shape a national team; while the English failed for want of invention, the Italians succumbed again to disorder and neurosis.

In the Midlands, at Aston Villa's Villa Park and Sheffield Wednesday's Hillsborough, the Germans announced their intentions with a 5-0 demolition of the Swiss. In a powerful side, Franz Beckenbauer was, at twenty-one, already patently blessed with composed and dangerous class and he scored twice. Muscle then tackled meanness; they scrapped to an ugly 0-0 with Argentina, who had a man sent off. Both these sides went through, over Switzerland and Spain; one of the English would say later of Argentina, "They had so much talent they could have given any side trouble, if they had just concentrated on playing football."

The pick of the groups, meanwhile, was at Old Trafford in Manchester, and at Everton's Goodison Park on Merseyside. It had Brazil, Hungary, and Portugal, with Bulgaria to make up the numbers, so one great team would have to fall at the first. In Florian Albert, Hungary had a worthy successor to the Galloping Major; in Eusebio, Portugal had Europe's answer to Pele. They had had to go to Africa to find him—Eusebio was from the Portuguese colony of Mozambique—but he was at the peak of his powers, twenty-four years old, for five years the star of a Benfica side that had four times made the final of the European Cup, and twice won it. In 1962, Puskas gave Eusebio his shirt after Benfica beat Real Madrid; now, the best player in Europe would face the best player in the world. It's what the World Cup is all about—and if some group games are dull, they certainly weren't here.

Pele and Garrincha took a goal each against Bulgaria. The Little Bird was aging, but even so Bulgaria could hardly cope. Down the road in Manchester, Portugal beat Hungary 3-1, a scoreline that belied the brilliant soccer surging back and forth in a sparkling game. Back at Goodison Park, Hungary and Brazil then laid out a feast even more spectacular, one of the games of all time, making amends a thousand times over for the violence in Berne twelve years earlier; a game without an injured Pele in which Albert took charge until the crowd roared his name in the rain. Hungary won 3-1; they then put out Bulgaria, so it came down now to Brazil or Portugal—to Pele or Eusebio.

Sadly, Pele still wasn't fit. Unforgivably, Morais of Portugal fouled him needlessly when Portugal were already two up. They won 3-1 and Pele, who'd been kicked all round the pitch before he was taken down for the last time, said he'd never play in a World Cup again. Happily, he changed his mind; the question the world had asked four years ago—how could this Brazil ever be beaten?—now had its elegiac answer. To beat this Brazil, you waited for time to pass and let age beat them for you.

In the quarter-finals, West Germany put four past a spitting, kicking Uruguay who had two men sent off. In Sunderland, Russia overpowered Hungary, who'd shot their bolt against Brazil—while at Goodison Park they were treated to another astounding piece of theater. North Korea scored against Portugal in the opening minute; spilling forward fast and sprightly, in minutes they added two more. North Korea 3, Portugal 0— how could this be? Eusebio stirred; he scored four times, two of them penalties after the despairing Koreans began knocking men down. Portugal got a fifth—and after their bighearted incursion into world sport's fiercest terrain, North Korea vanished from the scene, a mystifying memory, a puff of scented Asian smoke. We'd not see another side from that continent until Iran went to Argentina twelve years later.

Argentina, meanwhile, were disgracing themselves at Wembley; with a bad taste in their mouths, England went to the semifinals of the World Cup for the first time.

But England, of course, could kick with the best of them. As well as the magisterial Bobby Moore and the lean, mean Jack Charlton in a rugged defence, they had the toothless terrier Nobby Stiles, a gap-grinned urchin who seemed to have no ability of any kind with a football whatsoever—but he wouldn't let you past him, and he'd be as hard as it took in the process. In the group game with France he committed a nasty foul, nasty enough that two of the FA's upright citizens went to England's manager to demand that Stiles be dropped.

The manager refused; when he'd taken the job he told them that he picked the team and he alone, and he stood by that. He was going to win the World Cup, and sometimes the World Cup got brutal—and when it did you needed a man like Nobby Stiles.

The manager's name was Alf Ramsey; he'd played thirty-two times for his country at right back. He knew humiliation—he played in Brazil when the U.S.A. won, and at Wembley when Hungary came, and he wouldn't have it happen again. When he was appointed in 1963 he said straight out, "England will win the World Cup"; the words would haunt him, but he always believed it. Now he'd put together Banks in goal, Cohen, Wilson, Moore, Jack Charlton at the back; he had Stiles fighting every inch of the midfield, while beside him Jack's younger brother Bobby directed the attack, with a shimmering swerve and a shot like a rocket. Martin Peters played on the left, first selected only nine weeks before the tournament, and wide on the right, Alan Ball, young, tiny, a yapping bundle of energy— a man who would run and run long beyond the time when his legs would scream at him to stop. And finally, up front, there were Roger Hunt and Geoff Hurst, neither of whom could hold a candle to Jimmy Greaves for dash or panache, and were preferred over him anyhow. They had skill, of course, but as an all-round team they were quintessentially English; they had heart and passion pushed to a point where skill could go to hell. And Ramsey always said he believed in wingers getting behind people to supply the likes of Greaves, but in the end he left Greaves out, shaded 4-4-2 into 4-3-3, and went flying in the other lot's face.

In the semifinals the Germans put out the Russians 2-1 in a filthy scrap on Merseyside, while England and Portugal played a clean and gripping epic at Wembley—Portugal, in fact, didn't commit a foul in the whole first half. In the slicing maelstrom of the Portuguese attack, Stiles marked Eusebio into oblivion; at the other end, Bobby Charlton scored. Portugal rallied; Banks, Moore, and Jack Charlton denied them, and Bobby Charlton scored a second. There were eleven minutes left; three minutes later Eusebio pulled one back from the penalty spot. It was the first time England had been scored against—and as the clock ran out, Portugal poured forward. At both ends, the keepers were forced into lunging saves— then it was over, and England were there.

The semifinals are often the best games; people make the final, and then freeze. But this time it didn't happen; England–West Germany 1966 ranks with Brazil–Uruguay 1950 among the finest of the fine.

In sixty-five years the Germans had never beaten England; they knew it and, nervous, they set Beckenbauer to mark Bobby Charlton. Would it have been different if they'd freed him from that task and allowed him to play? It's one of those tactical decisions still discussed with airy knowledge decades later; Beckenbauer himself has said that in 1966 he was still too young. But all the same, it was the Germans who went ahead, after thirteen minutes; six minutes later it was 1-1, Geoff Hurst rising to head home Bobby Moore's free kick.

The score was balanced, so was the game; by halftime there could have been more goals at either end, but neither keeper could be beaten. Strong, driving, committed, much alike, both sides attacked and both refused to buckle—until, with thirteen minutes left, Alan Ball won a corner. He took it himself, and in the goalmouth melee Martin Peters drove home. English defenders looked to the sideline; how long must they hold on?

They held on to the final minute, when a frantic Germany equalized. There would be an extra period for the first time since 1934; the players collapsed on the turf, and Ramsey strode out to speak to his men. He said, "Look at them. They're finished." And he told them, "If you pass the ball to each other, you'll beat them."

They did, and they won, in high drama and controversy. Ten minutes into the extra period Alan Ball, still running and running (he'd say later he "died twice" in this game) crossed a ball to Geoff Hurst; Hurst pelted it against the crossbar, and the ball dropped down. On the line? Over it? No one knows to this day; the Swiss referee didn't know then. He went to his Russian linesman, they talked, and the goal was declared good. The Germans were appalled, enraged—nor could they pull it back, try all that they might. Then, in the dying seconds, mercifully (since otherwise the disputed goal would have been a sour shadow forever) Moore lofted a pass forty yards from his penalty area, inch perfect, to Hurst just beyond the halfway line. With the Germans committed to desperate attack, he was alone; so he sucked air and ran, one final effort beyond the far side of exhaustion. People were spilling onto the pitch in a chaos of ecstasy; the man on the BBC was screaming, "They think it's all over!" In the tumult Hurst looked up, and fired. "It is now!"

He had scored the first and, so far, the only hat trick in a World Cup final. Grown men wept in the streets; the queen gave Bobby Moore the Jules Rimet trophy. Alf Ramsey would be knighted—while from South America came accusatory howls of conspiracy, because England had played all their games under the twin towers of Wembley.

It was, in fact, the first time the home side had won since 1934. Home advantage is a double-edged sword; the crowd can either roar you on, or you can crumble beneath their too-great desire, the weight of it too pressing on your shoulders. But England didn't crumble—and 103 years after the FA was founded in the Freemason's Tavern in Lincoln's Inn Fields, the 8th World Cup was played on the grounds of the world's first soccer clubs, and won and brought home by the people who made them.

13

Midfielders

Gareth Owen: Midfielder
Age: 21
Height: 5′ 8″
Hometown: Connah's Quay, Clwyd

At sixteen he left school with nothing, no qualifications at all; but he knew by then he was going to Wrexham, and the game was all he wanted. He remembers his trial vividly; thirty lads on the training field on a freezing, snowy December day. "It was frightening."

Five of them made it, but only Owen came through. He got his debut at eighteen; he's played 120 games, and he's near double figures for Wales Under-21. He's been to Poland, Romania, Cyprus, Denmark—and could he have imagined this at fifteen, playing that trial in the snow? He said, "Not really. Running out for your country—I never dreamed, not in my wildest dreams. . . . Running out now, I still get as much buzz as I did on my debut. It's still brilliant every time."

So what does a midfielder do? He smiled, and asked if we had all day. Then he said, "You score goals. You've got to tackle, have determination and strength, good passing ability, be good in the air; you've got to be up and down, up and down, getting the ball, helping your defenders, supporting your forwards, scoring yourself—it's the hardest position on the pitch. You've got to be a complete player, basically."

Owen's highly valued, and I don't mean the half-million price tag the papers have set on him, or the fifteen scouts watching Wrexham's every game. I mean, instead, what his captain thinks: "Gareth's a good player. If he slowed himself down a bit he'd be an excellent player, he'd be world class. He's great with the ball at his feet, he's got so much ability to get past people, his acceleration's unbelievable. There are times, if he just thought a bit more first . . . sometimes he runs with the ball when he should pass it. But he's got so much ability it's frightening."

Owen concedes he's not the best short passer; he says it'll come. Meantime, "The first thing I'll look to do is go at someone. Maybe in the last third you'll get rid of it, you don't want to be caught with it there; but in the mid-third I'll look to do something with it. Then in the last third, the boss has told us we've got licence to do what we like—to try things, because something might always come off. Different bosses might tell you to get crosses in, if you've got a big man in the team, or to play it behind defences, if you've got a quick one. But here, it's down to us what we do."

And what a midfielder does, in some ways, resembles traffic control. The greatest of them, like France's Michel Platini in the eighties, are the playmakers—men who rule the middle, and everything flows through them. That means knowing the strengths of the people around you, and serving those strengths —so Owen plays different passes for different players.

For example: Karl Connolly's not the quickest, so he likes the ball to his feet. He doesn't want it behind the full back, because then he's got to get in a race with the guy; he's tricky, so he'd rather take the ball past the man himself. Gary Bennett, by contrast, goes more into the channels, hunting down the lane between center half and full back; being quicker, he likes it played where he can chase it. But Benno won't be chasing any balls for a while—so are we going up?

Owen said, "There wouldn't be any point playing if we didn't think so."

Romania away was his best experience so far. "There was everything in that game—they tried to get us turned, they tried to play the short stuff. Then they were diving, spitting, elbowing. But we won, 3-2. It was my first trip away; you get in the airport and you think, bloody hell, what's this place? Armed guards everywhere . . . it was an experience all right."

So I asked him, if he had to explain why all the world is so much in love with this game, from Connah's Quay on the Dee to scary, weaponed-up Bucharest, how would he do it?

He grinned. "Couldn't tell you. You look at it, it's just a bag of air being kicked between two sticks—but every lad, when they're ten, they want to be footballers, that's their dream. And playing well in front of a lot of people, there's no better feeling in the world; I wouldn't want to do anything else. And where I play—goalscorers get a buzz out of scoring goals, everybody does—but for me, there's nothing better than a defence-splitting pass, or a defence-splitting run. Something that excites the crowd."

He said, "I'd love to be Ryan Giggs. He must feel it every time he gets the ball." He added, "People that don't like their jobs . . . I know people that work in chicken factories. Or my brother, he works nights. That'd kill me." But I don't think he need worry about it. I think Gareth Owen's going up, whether Wrexham do or not.

Mike Lake:	Midfielder
Age:	26
Height:	6′ 1″
Hometown:	Manchester

Wrexham went to Scarborough; the pitch was a mud bath, and the stand looked like a garden shed. We drew 1-1; with York also drawing, we stayed behind them in fourth.

Two days later, I asked Lake what the difference was between the Premier League he left, and the Third Division he joined. He said, "Obviously, you're playing against better players in the Premier. I wouldn't say there's a gulf, exactly, there are individuals here who could make the jump—but having said that, you tell a Premier side to go to Scarborough and play football on a pitch like that. You can't do it—and that's the difference. Playing in front of 35,000 at Anfield, or playing Tuesday night at Scarborough in a mud bath."

He was four years at Sheffield United; between injuries and them playing the long ball, it wasn't the best of times. Then being put on the transfer list was a blow—but Wrexham was a good place to come. For a midfielder the long ball's boring, the thing's flying over your head all the time; here, the game goes through him and Owen, and it's much more about control and distribution.

Of their partnership Owen said simply, "If Lakey's not there, I am. And if I'm not there, he is." But since Lake had come, he tended to "sit" more—to hold the middle—because Lake was a more forward-minded player. So I asked Lake if he knew why he played that way.

"It's just what you're good at. Defending . . . if I were to say what my bad point was, it would be my marking. I'm more creative, I like to score goals. And Gareth's a lot quicker, he can get back quicker, and that helps me; he's a good foil, and you need that right mix in midfield. You can't have two players the same, you can't both be wanting to get in the box all the time—because if the ball comes out you're leaving yourself open, you're leaving a hole.

"So we both watch what the other's doing, and talk; I don't think you can communicate enough, especially if you're work- ing with just two of you. Some teams play three in midfield, or four, they tuck in, and it's easier for them. Darlington had four, so it was harder for us to win possession; they could make little triangles, and play around us. So the teams that tend to do well against Wrexham—make sure no one else gets hold of this—are the ones that pack midfield and overrun us. But then, a good team dictates the style of play; us, if we get it wide, we'll pull their midfield out. We didn't do that against Darlington—so I'd say midfield was where we lost hold of that game."

Lake comes sixty miles each way from Manchester every day, sharing rides with big back-up defender Mark "Carlo" Sertori. In the empty dressing room after training, Sertori was anxious to get away—but when I asked who Lake looked up to, Carlo joined in, and forgot getting home in no time.

Lake named Platini, and then Glenn Hoddle, a player of delightful vision who played some fifty games for England, and should have played a hundred. But his work rate was suspect; he was the kind of player England doesn't trust.

"Platini was the best," Carlo said. "He could put a ball wher- ever he wanted, he could give it and that was it. Bingo."

"He was a step above," said Lake. "And the attitude of some people . . . why we didn't build a team round Hoddle I don't know. France did, with Platini, but a player like that's classed as a liability here, because he doesn't work box to box. Which is stupid, because you've got to have the player who can unlock defences. It's like with Gascoigne—everyone's saying he's not fit, he's got to get up and down more, but why? Why can't he concentrate on the creative things, and let other players do the defending? You've got to have the mix."

But no—in Britain we've all got to pound up and down, heroes with hairy arses.

Lake shook his head. "If it weren't for Gascoigne . . ."

England would be void of finesse altogether. And, said Carlo, "People say we're fast and strong. But the Continentals have got lads just as quick, quicker, and they're better technically— and they go in just as hard, too. So we're getting really well behind. I mean, Des Walker's gone over there [to Italy] and he's supposed to be one of our quickest defenders—and he's been shown a clean pair of heels a few times, hasn't he? But we don't work over here. You hear Walker, he'll go nine till one, have dinner, then go till five again. They'll work on things for hours and hours and hours."

"They'll work on the cross," said Lake, "pinpoint, pinpoint every time. Or the ball with the outside of your foot. Or the free kicks, they've all got specialists."

"We do far too much stamina training," said Carlo. "Abroad, they're all thin as anything. And *fast* . . . unless we change it here, technically, I'm telling you, we're going to get left miles behind."

It's the old British debate, and you'll hear it more from mid-fielders than anyone, because they're the guys who do the pounding up and down. Mind you, what Lake and Sertori might say if Flynn turned round and said, Right, we're training seven hours a day from now on . . .

The first eleven European Cups were won by Real Madrid, Eusebio's Benfica, and the Milanese clubs AC and Inter. Glasgow Celtic and Manchester United won it in 1967 and 1968, then the crown passed in the seventies to the Dutch and the Germans, to Franz Beckenbauer's Bayern Munich, and Johan Cruyff's Ajax. Then this happened:

1977:	Liverpool
1978:	Liverpool
1979:	Nottingham Forest
1980:	Nottingham Forest
1981:	Liverpool

1982: Aston Villa
1983: Hamburg
1984: Liverpool

In 1985, Liverpool went to the Heysel Stadium in Brussels to defend their title against Juventus. On the terraces before the game, English fans charged the Italians; in the panicked crush that ensued a mass of Italians tried to get away, a wall collapsed, and thirty-nine died.

I remember getting home late from work and rushing to turn on the TV. I remember thinking, just a minute—should be halftime by now . . . and then the piles of bodies, men and boys dead with purple faces, or alive among them trying to rescuscitate brothers and sons, fathers and friends, and so many weeping, weeping.

English clubs were banned from Europe for five years.

Before the ban we'd have a team in the European Cup, another in the Cup-Winner's Cup, and a couple more in the UEFA Cup. We'd have eighty-some players going into Europe every season, learning on the park and watching from the bench how they do it in Italy and Spain, in Germany and Holland, in Poland and Portugal and Romania and Greece.

Then we were away for five years. We stopped playing with the best and the learning process stopped, and while we trod the stagnant waters of our insularity here, over there they pulled away into the future.

But there's more to it. We've also fallen behind on the field for the same reason we produce these knots of fearsome idiots in the stands—as a society, we're all run out of verve and imagination. On the field we thump the ball, and on the street we thump each other. And thus the crudity of our soccer is a metaphor for the mean conservatism of our country.

So at the World Cup you'll see midfielders of great power, but they'll also have vision and grace. You'll see, perhaps, the German Lothar Matthaus, the motive force for their victory in Italy. Or you'll see the dazzling sudden surges of the Italian Roberto Baggio, or the deft paintwork of the Belgian Enzo Scifo, or the muscular charges of Holland's Frank Rijkaard—and these are the players Mike Lake looks up to.

And it was interesting, to find Lake and Sertori in the Third Division ready so bluntly to pin down our malaise, but then, it's interesting to find a team in the Third Division who can play football, and a manager who lets them. Because although we may have given this game to the world, in the game—as in so many other things—we remain tardy beyond belief in acknowledging that anyone else might have improved on it.

April 10, 1993
Wrexham v. Crewe Alexandra

> "This'll be a good game. They like to knock it about, and it's attractive. It'll be enjoyable to play in."
>
> —Mike Lake

Crewe Alexandra was founded in 1877 by railway workers from Crewe Junction; the Alexandra was the hotel where they met when the club was formed. In recent years, under manager Dario Gradi, they've earned a reputation as something of a farm club, producing a steady string of talent for the bigger clubs. David Platt, let go as a teenager by Manchester United, was shaped as a player by Crewe; they sold him to Aston Villa for $300,000. After Italia '90, the Italian club Bari bought him from Villa for precisely twenty-two and a half times that amount.

So Crewe play football—play it well enough, indeed, that while we were scuffling with Darlington and Scarborough last week, they snuck past Bury into fifth right behind us. So the nerves are jangling; we can't let York get away from us, and we can't let the pack in our wake catch up. We're 8,164, a new season's high, sunlit and buzzing; we watch the names roll out on the scoreboard, we study the program, we read the runes. In place of Bennett Flynn puts Connolly alongside Watkin up front, Mark Taylor on the wing . . .

We're unbeaten at home for six months; they're unbeaten away all this year. In the opening seconds they're in our box already; Humes makes the stop. We go down their end, Owen fires, and their keeper Dean Greygoose saves under the bar. Morris saves twice; Greygoose saves from Connolly in his midriff; Connolly tries again, hitting the woodwork with a spectacular bicycle kick. Then Lake plays a terrible bobbler back to Humes; Humes has a striker hovering on his shoulder as the ball comes over his head. Composed, he takes it on his knee, drops it to his right foot, turns, lets the striker go past him wrong side, then lobs an instant diagonal out wide to Cross. That's a center half.

But for a long while now we're under pressure, the crowd nervous and angry . . . then Owen slings it up into the area, Taylor swivels, it's dropping thigh-high when he latches on and slams it in, he's wheeling away, arms raised—and by God we really needed that to happen.

Crewe didn't—and their boisterous fans are angry now, out of their seats, leaning round the corner of the stand to spit and snarl at the Wrexham stand running away along the side of the pitch next to them. A few police get in there, trying to settle things down—and on the field we hold firm while Crewe comes back. Seven minutes pass, then Greygoose fumbles a header from Lake, Watkin pounces on the loose ball, and he walks it in a stabbing little stumble through the keeper's arms into the net. 2-0.

When halftime came, the announcer on the PA asked Crewe's lot to stay in their seats for five minutes after the end of the game. Someone behind me muttered, "Right. It'll take us five minutes to get over there."

But we weren't long into the second half when I started thinking the venom would fade. We'd scored twice, but I'd still rated the first half evens, and that was where the friction lay— whereas now Lake and Owen grabbed the game by the neck, and for the next thirty minutes it was exhibition time again. So we stood in the sun and enjoyed it and the fear and the angst bled away, and you could feel a great collective smile breaking out like the sunshine all over us.

How we didn't score again I don't know. Greygoose barely got his fingertips to one delicious long chip under the bar from Lake—but otherwise the flowing freedom of it, the sweet swapping back and forth of passes along the ground, the happy surges of noise as full backs, midfielders, wingers, even Pejic one time all took turns to have a run at them—and Crewe were chasing shadows the whole time.

There was a message for Steven Jenkins of Summerhill that his wife had had a boy. Now there's a man with his priorities all straight.

Then, with nine minutes remaining, a Crewe defender played an ill-advised back pass to Greygoose. Watkin was after it like a barracuda, and the keeper was committed—if he didn't get to it, he'd have had Watkin right there in his face. So they arrived at the same time, both crashing in feet first to win it . . . it was a fifty-fifty ball, the type you have to go for every game. The bodies clattered together, sliding fast and hard—and Greygoose didn't get up. The ref was showing Watkin the yellow card, which seemed harsh, but Crewe's captain was standing by his prone keeper looking badly anxious, gesturing frantically to the ambulance people on the far side of the pitch. Other players gathered round, and the medics, and still Greygoose didn't get up. Then they called for a stretcher.

We heard later he'd snapped his ankle, but it was obvious enough something was broken. It took an age, but when they finally carried him away the ground rang full with warm and worried applause.

During the delay Pejic and Humes went slowly among the other Wrexham players, talking quietly, keeping them calmed down. In the attempt to contain us, Crewe had used both their subs, so they were down to ten men; their sweeper went in goal, but though we had all the possession in the last minutes, we didn't bother testing him. Players took turns to take the ball to Crewe's corner flags and stand on it there, so the game could go away peacefully and not give us more incident. We had three points; all we wanted now was for the thing to finish.

In the players' lounge afterward everyone said it was a fifty-fifty ball. They told Watkin not to worry and he said he wouldn't, but he did look troubled. He said, "I had to go for it." And people told him he never deserved to get booked—which, in truth, he didn't. It was just one of those things.

Benno and Paskin pulled beers from the fridge; we watched the day's results coming in on TV. When it came to our turn they showed the goals, and they showed Watkin and Greygoose crashing together. The presenter called the challenge "very reckless"; Benno vociferously disagreed. But there you go—shit happens, and we had three points.

I asked Pejic if he was feeling any pressure; he said he'd be feeling some if we'd lost. And York won as well, they beat Cardiff 3-1, so they were still that one point out in front of us—but he said the pressure was on them now. They had three games left, two of them away, but we had five, three of them at home. "So they've got to win everything, haven't they?"

And the next stop's Chesterfield on Easter Monday. Humes said they were long-ball merchants, said he'd wear his tin hat—but, he said, it was easier to deal with the long ball away from home. "At their place they've got to come at you, haven't they? So you soak it up, then you hit them on the break." He smiled. "Hopefully."

Behind us the chasing pack are out of it, eleven points adrift; they keep drawing with each other, scrapping for places in the play-offs. As for York, with three games left, the most they can get to is 78 points. We've got 68—so to be sure of promotion, we need eleven points from five games to go past them; four wins, or three and two draws. If York, on the other hand, were to fluff just one of their games . . .

On Easter Monday they won at Halifax—and 2,500 Wrexham fans went to Chesterfield. The road over the Pennines jammed; the kickoff was delayed fifteen minutes to let them in. Then Chesterfield scored after twelve minutes. 0-1. Two minutes later Connolly gave it to Owen, and flew away down the middle. Owen gave it back as he went through, a thirty-yard pass, and Connolly scored. 1-1.

Second half: Barry Jones was knocked unconscious. When he recovered he tried to play on, but after a few concussed minutes, Flynn sent Jimmy Case on in his place. Then Chesterfield scored again. 1-2. Three minutes later, Cross sneaked a ball through to Lake; he slipped his defender, and pelted it home. 2-2. And four minutes after that, Taylor went one-two with Lake, got to the goal line, pulled a sharp cross back for Watkin . . . 3-2.

The ten minutes added on by the referee for injury time must have felt like an eternity. Flynn said, "I've got a habit, a superstition, of not looking at my watch. And Barry'd had a bad knock, so who knows how long it took to see to him? And they were bombarding us—but," he said wryly, "we like to entertain, don't we? Like to keep you on the edge of your seat."

And from four games we now needed eight points. Three wins would do it, or two and two draws—assuming, I said, that York would win both their last games.

Flynn said, "I'm not assuming anything. Our destiny's in our own hands."

Round-Up

One of the FA Cup semifinals is a Steel City clash between Sheffield United and Sheffield Wednesday. England's veteran winger Chris Waddle scores for Wednesday with a fulminating free kick in the opening minute, then weaves a spell over proceedings so profound, with his feints and his shimmies, his dancing through the tackles and his pinpoint passes, that United seem surely to be doomed—yet somehow they scramble an equalizer. The game goes to extra time, and when Wednesday finally wins it's with the simplest goal of all, a header from a corner. The corner's floated in by an American midfielder named John Harkes—so at the final whistle, as the United players fall in tears to their knees, John Harkes becomes the first American to book a place in the FA Cup final, the oldest game of them all.

Glasgow Rangers play Olympique Marseille in the European Cup, and the game throws up an oddity: the French keeper wears a short-sleeved shirt. This isn't just unusual, it's illegal; the keeper's jersey has to have long sleeves so if there's a ruck of bodies in the area, and the ref sees hands going for the ball in the thick of it, he can tell whether it's the keeper or not by the sleeves those hands are coming from. When this Gallic misdemeanor is pointed out to the London studio by enraged pedants hitting the phone lines, Jimmy Greaves, now a commentator, responds with poetic opacity: "Send him off. Ban the fish. Shut the tunnel."

On the other side of the world, USA '94 gets under way in Asia. The Japanese beat Thailand 1-0; the United Arab Emirates stick four past Sri Lanka. Oil states like the UAE have pumped money into soccer for a couple of decades now, but so, in an odd little way, have we. One of the FA's roles is to act as a missionary for the game, spreading the sacred word far and wide around the globe, and for the most part well and good—but when it comes to the sheiks, the deal gets more complex. One of the FA's sponsors in recent times has been British Aerospace, purveyors of death-dealing gizmology to undemocrats of all stripes—and the tangled deals they like to strike include commitments to recycle some of the profit as development aid. Under the heading of "development" comes teaching them to play soccer—so when England toddle off to play friendlies in the desert, I'm afraid the marketing subtext involves the promotion of items packing a lot more punch than a can of Coke or a Snickers bar.

Concerning a different brand of coke: Roma's Argentinian striker Claudio Caniggia is suspended indefinitely by the Italian authorities after testing positive for the white powdery stuff. Argentina's captain at Italia '90, Diego Maradona, has already spent a year suspended for the same offence—and maybe this explains the way they play. Maybe they've all just got fizzing white lines behind the eyes.

In Britain, we fuel our boys on beer—and they'll be sinking a few in Manchester. While Coventry hold Villa to a draw, United go a goal down to Wednesday at Old Trafford. So they attack and attack, and with four minutes remaining they equalize. And then—in the sixth minute of injury time, before 40,000 souls in a state of advanced hyperventilation—they nick a winner, and climb back to the top of the table.

Pele called it simply "the beautiful game," which it surely is. But games like that, if you're a United fan—well, it's like spending Saturday afternoon having the emotional equivalent of a heart attack. And at the end of it the doctor says you'll live . . . till next Saturday, anyhow.

14

Total Football

Felix
Carlos Alberto, Brito, Piazza, Everaldo
Clodoaldo, Gerson
Jairzinho, Tostao, Pele, Rivelino

Mexico 1970

Brazil brought the best team there's ever been. You can pick holes if you want: the keeper was wobbly, and the defence could be broken if you went at them. But they had so much in attack that defence was an afterthought; managed by Zagalo, the controlling heart of their midfield in Sweden and Chile, they also came better prepared than anyone, and with better PR. They sang Mexico's praises so tenderly, and were anyway so wonderful to watch, that in the end, to all intents and purposes, they were playing at home.

These previous champions met the present champions in the first round in Guadalajara; the classic confrontation of effervescence and effort. But the effort England could make was feared all the same; they'd lost only once in nineteen games before the tournament. In matches in Bogotá and Quito, played as preparation for the altitudes in Mexico, they briskly disposed of their hosts—but in other ways, their preparations were as woeful as Brazil's were diplomatic.

That Bobby Moore should be arrested in Bogotá on trumped-up charges of shoplifting in a jewelry store was hardly their fault; Moore coped with the same aplomb he displayed on the field, and went on to a warm embrace with Pele in mutual recognition of their very different talents. That England otherwise should offend their Mexican hosts at every turn was less impressive altogether.

The qualities that worked for Ramsey at home didn't travel well; English to his bones, he was dogged, deeply private, hopeless with the media, didn't think much of foreigners, and didn't do a good job of hiding it. England grumbled about the heat, the crowd, the press, the food; the Mexicans took umbrage, one of their papers called England "a team of thieves and drunks," and on the evening before the game with Brazil a large crowd assembled round England's hotel. They then chanted, sang, played music, honked horns, and exploded fireworks all night—and that'll teach you to turn up your nose at the tacos.

Even so, a bleary England and a bubbling Brazil gave soccer one of its landmark games, and if chances counted England might have won it. But they missed them; when Pele set up Jairzinho, he didn't. It ended 1-0, Moore and Pele smiled and swapped shirts, both teams beat Romania and the Czechs to go through anyway—and the only reason it didn't end 2-0 was because Gordon Banks made the greatest save of all time.

England has always produced fine keepers. The goalkeeper with the record number of appearances for his or any country is English keeper Peter Shilton, who played for the 125th time at Italia '90—and he'd have played more often than that, but there was competition for places. But Banks was best among the best, and in Guadalajara he proved it.

The game was still scoreless when Jairzinho crossed for Pele at the far post; Banks was stranded at the other post as Pele's header punched down hard, perfectly placed to bounce up inside the woodwork. Pele knew he'd scored and turned away, celebrating already—but behind him, from a standing start, Banks covered the best part of an Olympic long jump, one hand outstretched, and scooped the ball up and away over the bar from bare inches before the line. Neither Pele nor anyone else could believe it—and when Banks later fell ill, England would suffer.

* * *

In Mexico's group, crowds of well over 100,000 in the capital's giant Azteca Stadium, great cliffs of screaming people, produced the most intimidating atmosphere yet seen in a World Cup; opponents and referees alike were howled into submission. Russia clung to a 0-0 draw; a feeble El Salvador were helped to a 4-0 trouncing by a referee who let the Mexicans get away with taking a free kick he'd given to their opponents—and a fancied Belgian side fell to an equally suspicious penalty award. Mexico and Russia advanced.

To the north, in León, the Germans had a scare when Morocco had a go at them and scored, and they didn't pull it back until the second half. Then Uwe Seeler got one, appearing in his fourth World Cup, and Gerd Muller got another; he would take ten in the tournament. A colleague of Beckenbauer at Bayern Munich, Muller was one of the greats. In his career, he scored 628 goals—and he'd say later of keepers, "God help them. Often I didn't know where the ball was going, so how could they?" He got three against Bulgaria, three more against Peru, and the Germans went through.

So did Peru who, despite that defeat, were a sparkling team. Managed by Didi, another Brazilian veteran of '58 and '62, they played like Brazil in a whirlingly positive 4-2-4. Numbingly negative, by contrast, were Italy, who brought wonderful players, and played them all as defenders. In a grim group they beat Sweden 1-0, drew 0-0 with Uruguay and Israel, and went through with Uruguay looking no more likely to do well than in previous years.

In the quarter-finals, Uruguay scraped past Russia 1-0 in the Azteca. In Guadalajara, Peru had the courage to take it to Brazil, and in a flowing game were rewarded with two goals; Brazil, however, got four, athletic, impulsive, joyous, incomparably gifted. And in Toluca, at last, after years of fear-raddled fumbling, Italy woke up and played; Mexico's feverish progress hit the buffers with a resounding 4-1 crash.

Meanwhile, in the broiling heat of León, England went 2-0 up over Germany after an hour, looking powerful and intelligent—but the Germans made good substitutions, Ramsey made bad ones, and his players wilted in ninety-eight degrees as the Germans came strong. Gordon Banks was sick and his replacement, Peter Bonetti, was too slow to stop Beckenbauer's shot and in the wrong place to stop Seeler's header. In extra time Muller completed an extraordinary recovery—

one of the great World Cup comebacks—and England, stunned, was out. At Wembley they'd made it to the top of the mountain; now they fell off it altogether. They wouldn't even qualify in the next two World Cups.

But Germany's time had not yet come. While Brazil outplayed Uruguay 3-1 in one semifinal, the best and the worst of Italy was on display in the other—and for the Germans, drained from León, the best and the worst added up to too much. The worst was the premeditated foul that left Beckenbauer playing encumbered with an injured arm; the best was Gianni Rivera of Milan, European Footballer of the Year, and Luigi Riva, a prodigious goalscorer from the Sardinian club Cagliari.

The Italians scored early, after eight minutes. Timid and dour, they foolishly tried to sit on it for eighty-two minutes more. They came under the cosh for their pains, but it nearly worked; the game was three minutes into injury time before Germany equalized, and won themselves another extra period. So now Beckenbauer was brought down, and the game went crazy. In fifteen minutes the wolfish Muller first gave Germany the lead, before the Italian center half Burgnich and then Riva took it back again, 3-2; in the second fifteen minutes Muller then equalized yet again, only for Rivera to make it safe at 4-3.

But it was still some years before the Italians would grow confident enough to play with the brio that's native to them. After showing what they could do in the two previous matches, in the final they fell back into paralyzed caution, and were given a lesson; it was as one-sided an exhibition as there's ever been. At halftime, when it was still 1-1 after a glaring defensive lapse had let the Italians back in, they might have fought for it; instead they collapsed, and Brazil ran riot. It ended 4-1—and Pele's Brazil, deservedly the first nation to win the World Cup three times, took the Jules Rimet trophy home for good.

I've seen Brazil play three times: at Wembley, in the Stadium of the Alps in 1990, and at the Robert F. Kennedy Memorial Stadium in D.C. three years later. On paper it doesn't look good; they lost two and drew one of those games—but on the field, they showed me soccer like I've never seen it played by anyone else.

In the RFK, for forty-five minutes before the Germans got a hold of them, they were quick, sharp, bold, constantly surprising; the ball was caressed, perfectly controlled, athletically distributed. For those forty-five minutes, they made the world champions look like schoolboys; an experienced writer next to me said simply, "If Brazil ever stop playing this way, then the magic will go out of the game."

In Turin too, in a titanic clash with Argentina, they were brilliant, and so unlucky to lose that it defied belief, but that's another story—and then there was Wembley. It was one of those first-time things—the first time you have sex, the first time you get drunk, the first time you see Brazil, the first time you walk out under the twin towers from the players' tunnel at Wembley . . .

In an echoing concrete vault the teams jogged on the spot in two lines, studs clacking, doors banging, TV men and officials scurrying in a lather of officialdom. England were muscular and imposing, stern, expressionless—but I knew them, and Brazil I didn't know. So for a fan, right there, I was in heaven; close to the demigods in the gold and green, men many shades of color with brown gleaming eyes, men serene and entrancing from a country ennobled by the grace and daring of their football. And I remember walking out and understanding Wembley—the enormity of it, the great bowl looming wide beneath a pink and velvet dusk, the pitch radiant under the lights, the sweeping banks of humanity ebullient and ferocious in their noise, the old palace, the high temple of the people's game full to the rafters because Brazil had come . . . and England beat them 1-0, but that's not what I remember.

I remember that from the kickoff, Brazil played a dozen passes before any Englishman even touched the ball. There's simply no one else like them, and they're my tip for USA '94.

Offside

Among the chances spurned by England when they played Brazil in Guadalajara was a moment when Hurst broke through Brazil's defence and received the ball—and then, fatally, hesitated before he shot. He paused because he thought he was offside. He should have carried on—but it got in his mind and he paused, and he fluffed it.

Offside is the only complicated rule in soccer. It only applies in your opponent's half of the pitch—and the idea is that *at the moment when the ball is played to you*, there should be at least two of your opponents either between you and the goal line you're attacking, or level with you. But since, in practice, the keeper will always be one of those two, look at it this way instead: when in their half, to be legally in play, you should always have at least one defender to beat—but you don't have to beat him with the ball at your feet. Nice if you do, obviously—but another of soccer's key skills is the timing of runs so that when the pass is made to you you're onside (i.e., you've got one or more defenders between you and the goal), but when the ball arrives you've slipped them, got behind that defence, and met the ball in clear space.

The offside rule means you'll most likely see two things at USA '94. Somebody, somewhere, will put the ball in the net, and have the goal disallowed for offside—cue rage while the linesman's flag flutters, and the scorer, thus deprived, gnaws the turf in despair.

And secondly, you'll see a team or two playing an "offside trap." This is dull stuff, but they can't all be Brazil, and if it works it's a sure way to snarl up the other team's traffic. In essence, when your defence breaks up an attack, takes possession, and reroutes the ball forward, what then happens is your defenders all quickly push up in a line, as one. Thus, if the attack they've initiated breaks down and the ball comes straight back, forward players on the other team are either stranded offside behind them, or back-pedaling with them to stay onside. So a well-oiled offside trap's hard to beat; you simply drain the play away from your goal.

The reason for the offside rule is obvious. Without it, you could just send a striker to go stand on the keeper's toes all game. With it, if you want to score, you've got to beat people. And if you're as boldly gracious as Pele's Brazil, or as quick and smart as Johan Cruyff's Holland, you will.

West Germany 1974

Brazil had showed the world in 1970 that the way to win was to attack. Italy couldn't get it in their heads—but Germany, Holland, and Poland all could and did, the Dutch in particular. The way they did it was to play something called "total football." Under this rubric there were, in theory, no such things as defenders, midfielders, or forwards any more. Cruyff, Neeskens, Johnny Rep, and the rest were instead a swirling, fluid, unreadable side whose players switched positions until you never knew who was where, and all you knew was that they were attacking you again. They were the best thing in Europe, the Hungary of the seventies—and would share a similar fate.

With Beckenbauer now an attacking sweeper—a reinvention of the role from the original, Italian conception of it as a purely defensive position—the Germans played this way too, if not so deftly. As for Poland, they knocked the English out in the qualifiers after their keeper Tomaszewski locked the door on them at Wembley; but in Germany they'd prove to have plenty more about them than just a good keeper.

Another good keeper, an amazing keeper, was Italy's Dino Zoff—a man unbeaten in a dozen games, bringing a clean sheet to Germany that stretched over eighteen hours of soccer. Being unbeaten, however, is only halfway to winning—something they'd not learnt from Brazil, and which Brazil themselves now forgot. Without Pele, Gerson, Tostao, and Clodoaldo, the miracle team was a memory already; Brazil were shaky, and it was down to Europe to pick up the torch.

Before they did, FIFA's World Cup Committee changed the structure of the tournament again. After the opening round, the remaining eight teams, instead of going into quarterfinals, now went into two further groups of four and the winners of these second-round pools would contest the final. It meant six more games, so I suppose it looked good at the bank—but whatever happened to the World Cup being a knockout competition?

Today, there are no easy games. Soccer's a global sport and, on the field at least, it's democratic—but twenty years ago, Europe and South America still traveled haughty first class. As for the passengers down in steerage, in 1974 these were Australia, Haiti, and Zaire. Among these, it was known that the Africans could play individually (as early as 1962, Walter Winterbottom predicted that an African side would win the World Cup before the year 2000), but collectively they were tactical innocence incarnate.

Zaire's crazed and crooked President Mobuto rewarded each of his players with a car, a holiday for two anywhere in the world, and a house "built of durable material" for qualifying. Ju-ju men claimed to have helped qualification along by casting jinxes on opponents, or conjuring visions of naked girls in their dressing rooms. Asked how he coped, their Yugoslavian manager said, "I'm the witch doctor here. I touch them on one leg and say, 'You score with him.' "

But Zaire could conjure no magic in Germany. Scotland were vexed when they could only score two against them, and admitted they'd underestimated them ("where the devil had this lot come from, playing stuff like that?"), and Brazil only got three. But Yugoslavia ran up nine—the highest winning margin in World Cup history.

Australia made a better fist of it; they drew with Chile, and gave stiff resistance and not a few frights to both East and West Germany, before losing to both. As for Haiti, they should never have been there in the first place; in the qualifiers Trinidad and Tobago scored against them four times, and four times the Salvadorian referee disallowed the goals—which sounds, I think, like taking the offside rule just a touch too far.

Haiti went to the World Cup, and when they got there they beat Dino Zoff—a clean sheet for 1,147 minutes, and you go and lose it to Haiti. With the shades of North Korea hanging over their heads, Italy pulled themselves together and won 3-1; one of the Haitians then tested positive in a dope test, was hauled off and beaten by his own officials, and flown home in fear. The rest of his team soon followed, in shreds after conceding eleven to Argentina and Poland.

Argentina looked good. They had men who could score, among them Mario Kempes, coming into the squad at nineteen; they were playing football, too, not street fighting, but against a rakishly rapid Poland their defence was porous, and they lost 3-2. Italy then totally misread them; for once, it was Argentina who took a kicking as the Italians grew desperate, and the 1-1 scoreline was a travesty. It also left Italy still needing to beat Poland, and they couldn't do it; again they were overrun, and again the 2-1 scoreline gives little hint of Polish élan, Italian disarray. Once more they went home, talent blighted by an apparently incurable stage fright.

Elsewhere, Scotland made the first of five appearances running: a series of performances varying wildly from gritty epic to ignominious farce. This was one of their better ones; stout hearts and endless running held the plainly more talented Brazil and Yugoslavia to draws, but their paradoxical failure to run in goals against Zaire saw the better teams go past them on goal difference anyhow. In more extreme forms, Scotland's long-suffering fans would be obliged to read this script again and again—their team reaching noble heights against good sides, plumbing horrible depths against bad ones.

But the place to be in the opening round was Hanover, where the Dutch were putting on a show. They couldn't finish against a resourceful Swedish side, but a hapless Bulgaria and a nasty Uruguay were blown away. Uruguay were reaching a nadir; they weren't even any good at kicking people any more. Or, maybe, Cruyff was just too good to be kicked; you stuck out a boot, and found your studs clawing air. Uruguay went home; the next two World Cups would proceed without them.

And, for sensitive souls, the place not to be in the opening round was Hamburg. After the massacre of the Israeli athletes two years earlier at Munich, the tournament was thick with security—but when East Germany played West, we got the Cold War live. We also got an upset; East Germany won. This doubtless did the morale of the socialist man no end of good; but it also did West Germany a favor, because it meant they fell into an easier group in the second round. East Germany got Holland, Brazil, Argentina; West Germany got Poland, Sweden, Yugoslavia. So maybe losing in Hamburg hadn't been a bad idea at all . . .

Holland swept all before them. Argentina never knew what hit them; 4-0, two of them for Cruyff. Brazil, taking nervous note, tried like Uruguay to kick them; at least they were good enough to have the boots and blows land, and they managed to knock Neeskens flat out. But when he recovered he scored, and so did Cruyff; they did what Brazil were supposed to do, fast and spectacular—but Brazil had forgotten themselves. As for East Germany, they merely expired; the Dutch were in the final by then anyhow, the best team around.

The other group was more of a dogfight. West Germany were worth two goals over Yugoslavia, but they were pushed to the limit by Sweden before taking them 4-2; then they faced the Poles. Poland had won their two games as well; they were unquestionably dangerous, and on a different day what was now effectively a semifinal might well have been theirs—but it rained. As with Honved at Wolves, Poland's game was about pace and touch—and you can't play that way when you're up to the ears in mud. They did surely have a go at it (given the historical connotations, everybody wants to beat Germany) but power's a better ally in the ooze than panache, and though Tomaszewski saved a penalty, he couldn't keep Gerd Muller out—so Germany would play Holland.

In Munich's Olympic Stadium the Dutch kicked off, idly passed the ball to each other with impertinent ease, and then Cruyff took off. He beat one man, was tripped by the next, Holland had a penalty in the opening minute, and Neeskens made no mistake with it. It was the most dramatic opening a World Cup final has seen—and it was Holland's undoing.

Like Brazil, their attack was so good that weaknesses at the back went unseen; now, however, when they toyed smugly with the Germans instead of killing them off, the Germans—unlike the Italians four years ago—refused to roll over. Before half an hour had gone, obdurate persistence was dragging them back into the game, and another penalty pulled them level; now they attacked, and the Dutch on the defensive weren't the same team. Two minutes before halftime, Gerd Muller made it 2-1, and while the second half saw chances at both ends, and a second goal from Muller disallowed for offside, 2-1 is how it ended. The hosts hung on, and, for the second time, greater power and tenacity, a steelier nerve, and plain remorseless efficiency took the Germans to the title over what had seemed to be the better team.

The winner was Muller's fourteenth goal in his two World Cups; no one else has scored that many. It was also his sixty-eighth for his country and, as it would turn out, his last. (For comparison, Bobby Charlton holds the English record with forty-nine.) They called him "Der Bomber"; he was five foot nine, all muscle from stud to scalp, and the most remarkable stat is that those sixty-eight goals came in sixty-two appearances—an astounding strike rate.

So was Muller the difference between Holland and Germany? Cesar Luis Menotti, who managed Argentina four years later, said it was a case of "one specialist beating ten all-rounders," but Muller wouldn't have seen it that way. Instead, he sent the credit in another direction; both at Bayern Munich and for Germany, he said of Franz Beckenbauer, "I was the instrument for turning his genius into goals."

And then there was Berti Vogts, the fierce little full back who dogged Cruyff's every step; a man who was Beckenbauer's understudy at Italia '90 and who now, twenty years after tying down Johan Cruyff, will manage the Germans at USA '94.

In the past twenty years, Germany have appeared in four out of five World Cup finals; not as pretty as other teams, maybe, but harder, stronger, always more organized. They have a tactical and managerial continuity, a driving efficiency both on and off the pitch, that makes them the hardest team to beat in the world—so if anyone in America can take it over Brazil, Germany can.

15

Wingers

Karl Connolly:	Winger
Age:	23
Height:	5′ 10″
Hometown:	Prescot, Liverpool

When he was fourteen he started training at Tranmere Rovers, and he went there for two years. Then his mother died, his life fell to pieces, and he stopped playing. In his own words: "Couldn't be arsed. Couldn't be arsed with anything really. Didn't work, nothing. Signed on the dole, did odd days in the fish-and-chip shop. That was it." Three years later he met his girlfriend, and things came back together. He didn't get work—not in Liverpool—but he did start playing again, Sunday morning football.

A referee who saw him tipped off Wrexham; he played five reserve games, scored seven goals, and he's been here ever since. He said, "It's all I wanted to do, play football. Can't do anything else." He'd left school with nothing.

He was a striker when he came; he'd never played wide. When they moved him, he said, "It took a while to get used to it. In the middle you're more involved; wide, you're only involved when the ball comes to you. So at first I'd be going off looking for the ball, instead of staying out there."

But they've done the right thing. When I asked what it was like to score a goal he said, "Doesn't bother me. Benno, he loves scoring goals, it's a different feeling for him—but I'd just

as soon set one up as score one. I'll be just as happy with that."
And that's a winger.

Otherwise, this one, he talks best with his feet—and, places
like Liverpool, for a lot of people your feet are the only way out.

Mark Taylor: Winger
Age: 28
Height: 5' 9"
Hometown: Hartlepool, Cleveland

Taylor'd been at Blackpool six years when Flynn came for
him. He said, "I'd been dropped, I'd had an up-and-down season; I fancied a change. It seemed an ambitious club here,
very ambitious; no one I spoke to had a bad word for it."

So I asked what made a good club, and he said of Flynn
and his staff, "They create an atmosphere of pure football. It
shocked me when I first came. I was used to managers and
players who were footballers, yes, but there were always rules,
on the pitch and off it, and here there don't seem to be; I've
never had freedom to play like you get here. And maybe if I'd
had it when I was nineteen I'd have been a better player,
because it makes young players, this place. We've got twenty-
odd pros, and only six or seven are seniors—you'll not find
many clubs like that, it'd be the other way round. And it means
the kids are experienced here, they're not naive; they've played
games."

Whereas other clubs . . .

"When I started at Hartlepool, the team in the paper Friday
night was the team that played. You didn't find out if you were
playing off the boss, it was off the press; that gets up your
nose. Or take what's happening at Preston North End. New
manager's come in and he's treated everybody like robots, like
pieces of shit; from an environment where football was played
he's gone to the long ball, and you just can't do that overnight.
So I think he talked to eight or nine players before the transfer
deadline, and nobody wanted to know—everybody in the Football League knows the atmosphere there." And Preston, in
fact, would be relegated.

Taylor has fifteen appearances this season, six as a substitute; before the goal against Crewe, he'd scored only twice. It's
not what he came for—so what's it like, being in the reserves?

"Depends what age you are—my age, it's terrible. I've had a

few injuries, which hasn't helped, but then again when I've had a chance, I've had a few bad games. But it's not as bad here as other clubs. Other clubs, if you're in the reserves you're not wanted, you're not part of the team—you're treated like a foreigner, you're scum, you're not doing your job properly, you've let people down. But here, you're treated with respect. Everyone's in the same boat here."

Flynn told Taylor he'd be starting against Crewe two days before the game. Taylor said wryly, "Not putting any pressure on me, he said he expected me to do something. But he's stuck his neck out for me a few times before, so I think he was just saying, you stick your neck out for me now."

Flynn said later he told Taylor before the game that he'd score. Then he grinned and said, "But I probably tell them that every time. Probably tell them without thinking."

Taylor said, about getting your chance, "Sometimes you can try too hard. You try to take players on, and you lose it; you try to do things in the wrong areas, and make yourself look silly. So I'm glad he told me a couple of days before; I could get my thoughts together. Sounds a bit deep, but things hadn't been going too well, and I had to relax. I had to go out and do what I normally do, what I do in training—not try and force everything."

So how did he feel when he scored?

"Unbelievable. Thought I was going to run out of the ground. It's the best feeling in the world, best feeling I've ever had. It's better than sex—lasts longer, too. Initially it's the *relief*—then you're on a high for a couple of days. And everybody knows about it, your family know—but that one on Saturday," he said . . . then he smiled. "I was pleased."

Gareth Owen came by, so I asked him, too, what it felt like to score. He grinned wolfishly and said, "A good tackle's better than a goal." But that's a midfielder.

"A winger's expected to provide goals for his midfielders and his forwards, and to score goals himself. He's expected to be creative, to make things happen—and he's expected to give options, for defenders and midfielders to find him. He's an outlet. And then he's expected to defend—to protect his full back from their winger, or their overlapping full back. But first of all, he's there to create—to run at people with the ball, to get to the goal line and get in the cross."

Taylor's played other positions; the biggest difference is that, out on the wing, "You've got to rely on other players to provide you with the ball, in the areas where you can do some damage—wide, deep in their half. Other positions, midfield or defence, you can dictate your own game—you're supplying people, people are making runs for you, giving you options. But as a winger, you've got to make your own options."

Unlike a striker, forever on the move from one side of the pitch to the other, you might also see a winger standing still for a while, waiting, pondering. "Because you can't go any further out, can you? Go any further, you're out of the ground. So you get as wide as possible, where you're easy to find—then you loiter with intent."

And this is what we go to see: the man wide gets the ball, and he goes. He feints, leans, accelerates; the full back's left for dead, kicking air. And then?

"You can't pick people out. You've got to just *know* where you're going to put that ball. So you get to the line, and you're looking to keep it away from the keeper—anywhere away from the keeper's a good ball. And your front two men will be making runs, near post and far, and there's a fifty-fifty chance they'll get it, or their defenders'll get it. And if you play with them a certain amount of time, you just *know* they'll be timing their runs right, for you to cross it without lifting your head up. If you lift your head up to see where they are, you've delayed too long, they'll be marked. So once you get a chance to put a cross in, you put it in first time."

And the striker swoops, the net bulges, the crowd roars and sings. . . . I asked Taylor why it was such a great game and he said, "Because it only takes a second to score a goal, so you can never determine the outcome. It's not over until the referee blows his whistle."

Jonathan Cross:	Winger
Age:	18
Height:	5′ 10″
Hometown:	Wallasey, Merseyside

Jonathan Cross turned eighteen a month ago, but Taylor doesn't believe it. "He's got to be thirty-five. I want to see his passport."

Taylor also said, if the full back was kicking you, that meant you were having a good game; Cross agreed: "Most defenders

think wingers are the softies of the team. So if they can't get
the ball off you, they'll get frustrated, and they'll kick you. But
you've just got to get on with it. At the end of the day you'll
come off smiling, and they'll come off on a downer."

Retaliation, in other words, is for idiots; the way Cross
paused carefully before answering each question suggested he
wasn't one. And relations between press and players in the
British game are often rancid; the loutish hysteria that passes
for reporting in the tabloids doesn't incline players to say
much, and they become adept in the deployment of noncom-
mittal clichés. Barely into the edge of the spotlight in the Third
Division, Cross had already mastered the art; talking like a
much older man, he gave nothing away. Asked if we were
going up, he smiled and said quietly, "We hope so."

When I asked him about tomorrow's table-topper with
Cardiff, North Wales against South, a big crowd expected, he
said, "We're buzzing, we're really fired up. I'm really looking
forward to it." Then he smiled again and said, "If selected."

April 17, 1993
Wrexham v. Cardiff City

> "I don't think they'll freeze. It'll be something different
> for Cross, it'll be interesting to see how he handles it—
> but I think he will. He's being carried along. On the tidal
> wave."
>
> —Brian Flynn

For three short years at the end of the seventies, Wrexham
were in what's now the First Division, one rung down from
the top flight; the club drew seventeen, eighteen thousand.
The captain was a big striker named Eddie May, once a porter
at Smithfield meat market in London; he's now the manager
of Cardiff City, and there's not been a game like today's since
he played here. Big clubs have come in the knockouts—last
season, astoundingly, Wrexham beat Arsenal in the FA Cup—
but it's been long, barren years since 10,852 came to see us
in the league, and many years, too, since two Welsh sides were
in a promotion struggle like this.

Two hours before kickoff, a police helicopter hovered over
the Racecourse in a warm, cloud-flecked blue sky. Around the

ground and the train station behind it, pairs of mounted police watched the Cardiff fans gather.

> *Blue Army!*
> *Blue Army!*

By the station entrance, police-dog handlers held German
shepherds tight on their leashes. There were police in pairs
on foot, police on motorbikes, police in cars, police in vans.
On the bridge over the tracks where the road leads into town,
one officer on his horse said with weary patience to a group
of blue-shirted fans, "I'm not going to argue with you. I'm just
asking you—and next time I'll be telling you—to go back down
the road. You're not wanted in the town."

Away from the center, on the far side of the ground, outside
a pub that had shut because the landlord evidently figured
the risk of the place getting trashed outweighed the value of
the trade he could have done, they sat and waited on the verges
in the sun. Knowing what to expect, they'd brought their own
beer; they were jovial, and they were loud.

> *We're barmy*
> *We're barmy*
> *We're off our fuckin' heads*

Forty minutes before time we got in the ground, stomachs
knotted with fretful expectation. Phil Collins belted out, indis-
tinct and hissing, from the ramshackle PA; the police chopper
hummed and clattered above the floodlight towers. The noise
behind us in the Kop was a sea of sound, answered by the Blue
Army in kind from the packed and heaving visitors' stand.

On the field the players had their kickabout, warming up.
Cross, absorbed, stood in the corner beneath us, curling balls
over to Morris in the goalmouth. Other players made triangles
in the middle of the pack, or laid balls off for someone to sprint
onto. At the far end, Cardiff were in a pack, working out,
stretching, greeting their fans—then Gary Bennett ran out.
They'd had him in a hyperbaric chamber all week, pumping
him full of oxygen to accelerate the healing process—and he
was on the substitute's bench. The talisman, the genie . . .

> *Psycho! Psycho! Psycho!*

> *There's only one Gary Bennett*
> *Only one Gary Beeeehhhh—eh—nnett*

So the Blue Army roared back, referring to our Welsh Cup defeat at their place last month,

> *Where were you*
> *Where were you*
> *Where were you at Ninian Park?*

Alan said, "I want to win so *desperately.*"

Right away their No. 11 comes charging through, knocks Pejic over, goes free on goal—and gets called back for the foul. Morris hoofs it out, we win a corner; no outcome. It comes back our end, Taylor makes a fine sliding tackle, Lake cannons it away. Jones breaks upfield, then Owen—but the tackles are crunching in. Cardiff's defence is big and burly, built round two canny old Welsh internationals—Kevin Ratcliffe at center half, Robbie James at full back. Take on these guys, it's like running into a wall.

And I'm too tense to write this; I'm having breathing difficulties here. They get a corner; Owen hoists it out. Back they come, and back again; Pejic clears, then Humes, then Taylor. They get another corner; Cross is back in the area now, heading it away. Corner No. 3. Jesus. Lake clears. Get it OUT . . . corner No. 4. They're all over us. "Lot of big tall bastards," mutters Alan. And this is five minutes of *hell* right here . . . someone fouls Barry Jones, and we get a second to draw breath. We kick it upfield—*bang*, it's back in our faces. Morris falls to save at the incoming striker's feet. They're fired up, this Cardiff lot . . .

Cross wastes a corner. And they've got an offside trap, we're not cute enough to crack it—so we never get through, and it feels like we're defending all game; it is, to tell the truth, a horrible experience. The Kop's writhing, helpless; Cross misjudges another ball and the guy behind me boils over. "FUCK he annoys me, it's so fucking FRUSTRATING." At the far end they reach for the ultimate insult:

> *Are you English*
> *Are you English*
> *Are you English in disguise?*

Cross goes away down the line. Two men close on him, and he has the beating of them. He leans infield, sways, nudges

it, the ball's gone past them and he's shimmying through—
so they sandwich him, both stepping forward and crunch, no
through road, *kid*; the foul blatant, the sneering disdain of
older men for a whippersnapper writ large all over it—and the
ref doesn't give it. The Kop's rage grows exponentially: What
are you looking at YOU BLIND BASTARD—by which time the
ball's back at our end. Pejic bodychecks one of their guys,
twenty-five yards out—and the ref sees that all right.

We make a wall, and they hit the free kick straight at it. The
ball ricochets away, wide left; they've got a man out there, he
crosses it back in—and Cohen Griffith gets on the end of it to
poke home from six yards. A dreadful silence falls on us as the
Blue Army erupts.

From the restart Griffith comes streaking our way again;
Humes decks him, and gets booked. If Humes is losing it, what
are the young ones feeling? On the sideline, Gary Bennett's
warming up—and Cardiff get a second. We give away another
dumb free kick—so Robbie James curls in a floater, and Na-
than Blake climbs high to greet it. He hangs in the air; the
marking's abject, the header's a bullet, 2-0. The far end's a
storm cloud of raised arms, a thunderclap of noise—but the
truth is, they deserve it. The truth is, we've never been in it.
The truth is, this is the most depressing time I've had since
John Major got elected. We're talking heart-in-the-boots time,
disbelief and emptiness—months of Saturdays full of hope
suddenly taking a wrong turn, pitching you face-first down
the blackest well of disappointment.

And there's worse. I'm depressed enough now to bring up a
thing I've avoided, game after game, in shame and disgust—
but you should know that Cardiff's scorers, Griffith and Blake,
are black. And you should know that every time they power
through, these two, every time they get the ball as Cardiff's
dominance mounts, there are men all round the Kop, some of
them with children, for Christ's sake, yelling BLACK BAS-
TARD, and GET THE NIGGER, and going OOH OOH OOH—
a base foul grunting.

When the whistle goes, we slump to the concrete in stunned
dismay. Alan says, "I don't know what's more depressing. The
football or the racism."

You don't want to know about the second half. We played
better, but we could hardly have played worse. Bennett came

on and surged about a bit, Taylor leaving the field a sorry figure after an indifferent performance—but their defence locked up Bennett just as tight as the rest. As for Cross, blocked and checked and shut down, he lost it.

We had a free kick, and it rebounded uselessly off their wall, so Cross chased back for it, tangling over the running ball with one of Cardiff's men. As they ran together the tangle intensified, and finally Cross swung his fists. He hadn't proved, today, quite such a wise young man after all.

Connolly jostled with Robbie James too, not that he was going to see any change from it. Five foot ten's nothing; this was a lion cub trying to knock down an elephant.

> And it's Cardiff City
> Cardiff City FC
> You're by far the greatest team
> The world has ever seen

When it was over, while the silenced Kop glumly emptied, I stayed on the terrace and scratched down my last notes beneath the circling racket of the police helicopter. At the far end they were having a promotion party; they still needed one point to be sure, but they had two games left to get it, and on that form they'd get six. Eddie May went out with his coaching staff to applaud them for their support—and some Wrexham fans spat on him.

The Cardiff team watched the results on TV in the players' lounge. When the table came up and they were top of it, they cheered. To cap the afternoon, York had won—so we have three games left, and we need to win them all.

CONNOLLY: "First twenty minutes, didn't even get started. I'm going home to get drunk. Work it out on Monday."

MORRIS: "Crap. We were crap. You don't mind if you've lost fair and square—but we were *crap*."

HUMES: "You can't analyze why a game went wrong on you, not right after it, you're still in it. I'll think about it over the weekend. And we'll see what we're made of now."

At the bar of the Glyn Valley Hotel, Delbert—an Arsenal fan—says he knows we've lost. But, he grins, he's not going to wind us up.

Alan growls in his beer, says he *wants* to be wound up, says he's *angry*.

But getting it in perspective, says Delbert, beaming, all the terrible things that happen in the world, Somalia . . .

"Somalia," snarls Alan, "didn't *lose*."

Next Saturday in the league we have Carlisle to deal with—but if we're to get our heads back on straight, we need to do it before Saturday. We need to do it by Tuesday evening, three short days after this dreadful afternoon, when we play the second leg of the Welsh Cup semifinal—a game in which we must, somehow, pull back a two-goal deficit against that same Cardiff City.

On Monday, Cross said, "We've just got to try and get our form back. Cardiff, to be honest, played out of their skins—and we seemed to sit back, we just never got started. So tomorrow we've got to get our revenge."

I said he'd lost it; he'd hit out at that guy . . .

"I did. But he's thrown a punch at me. So as I've gone down I've just . . . I've got a bit aggressive. I've ripped his shirt, I've lost my temper—but when you're 2-0 down like that, you're bound to flare up a bit. And you shouldn't, I know, I was out of order; I was lucky I didn't get booked. But we've just got to stick it out now. Get back on winning ways."

Flynn's assistant Kevin Reeves said, "Cardiff were more wound up for it, they're more experienced—and they're a very organized, hard-working side, they grind you down; they're strong, they're powerful. And four or five of the youngsters here, it was new to them, that buildup. We've played big games before, but not as favorites—the form team, playing at home—and that got to them. But the only way you get experience is by going through those things, so they'll gain from it. Hopefully, they'll gain from it quickly."

Like, by tomorrow evening.

He said, "We have to get the ball wide. We have to get at their full backs—and then, we've said to the lads, that's the first time we've lost in ten games. Those boys haven't suddenly become bad players overnight."

All the same, the team will be changed. Someone trod on Benno's toe again . . . Reeves said, "Benno's one of those lads who wants to play. If he's fifty, sixty percent fit, he'll play. There's a pain threshold some players can go through and others can't, and he's one who can. But the danger now . . . obviously we want to win the Welsh Cup, and it's Cardiff, there's a bit of a thing there—but we've got to be realistic. The three league games are vital; they're more important than Benno playing half a game tomorrow and coming off injured, and being a doubt for next Saturday."

So who plays?

"We'll give a run out to a young lad called Stephen Pugh. It's a big game for him, but if he plays like he has been playing, he's a handful. He came on against Belgium for the Welsh Under-21's, he changed the game. And he's a confident lad, he's hungry for it; he's itching to play."

So Connolly goes back wide where they like him, and Taylor gets dropped, and we come up against the realities of life in the Third Division. Wrexham may be better off than most—but we're not Manchester United, we don't have internationals to spare hanging around in the reserves. You take a few knocks, and the barrel's empty in no time—so Flynn may talk bravely about "having options," but what he has in reality is kids. It was, he admitted later, "the last throw of the dice."

On a gorgeous spring evening, the sun slanting through a veil of pastel cloud as it fell into the hills, in a ground bright and floodlit and filled with an electricity of joy, Wrexham played the best football they'd played all season—football that swayed and flowed, surged and thundered like the ocean striking the shore, football that shone like the sun on the green mountains after rain. For ninety minutes we swarmed all over them, and the Racecourse rocked and sang—and why? Because in this game in the end it's not tactics or formations, it's the fire in your soul—and Wrexham were ablaze.

We won 1-0, Stevie Watkin scoring from Phil Hardy's cross after twenty-four minutes. And it might have been five, and it should surely have been two—but Cardiff's keeper made a save on the brink of halftime that defied belief. Connolly's header was all the way in, hard and fast, and the keeper was horizontal in the air, low, the ball way above him—so the hand that got to it, out of purest reflex, must have been reaching up on an arm made of rubber and elastic. But he got to it, somehow; he saved the goal, and he saved the game for Cardiff.

They went through to the final, 2-1 on aggregate, and all

power to their elbow. On a Tuesday night they brought a thousand souls up the winding border roads, and those thousand through all their last desperate fifteen minutes kept up an insistent drumbeat chant, *Eddie May's barmy army, Eddie May's barmy army*, clinging to the game for their team with stubborn tenacity while we poured in waves round their goal, and the Kop moaned and keened, pleaded and yearned, screamed and cried out as chance upon chance was made and shaved wide, made and beaten out.

Stephen Pugh? Invisible at first, out of his depth, he soon learnt to swim; he did bravely and well—until he was stretchered off with his knee ligaments torn. And what could we do then, with Pugh, Paskin, Bennett all injured? Flynn sent on Carlo Sertori—a man signed as a striker two years ago, converted by Flynn into a center half, and suddenly now obliged to be a striker again.

He'd not been on sixty seconds when he introduced himself; he went crashing full pelt into their net, bundling keeper and ball all together over the line in a great bruising heap. So then one of theirs flared up at him, and they were pushing and shoving and squaring up, and Pejic was into the ruckus with flame in his eyes . . . but it was that sort of night. The game is violence regulated into art by the simple matter of a round ball and a few rules, so what you get is something unstoppably fast and intricately beautiful all at once, fueled up and veined through with passion and desire. What you get, sometimes, is supercharged . . .

I asked Flynn how a manager could turn a team around so dramatically, and he said he only saw them for thirty seconds before they went out to that second game. But in the papers after Saturday there'd been a lot of crowing from Cardiff; Eddie May was quoted saying Cardiff were so much better it was embarrassing. So Flynn took the cuttings and photocopied them together onto one sheet; then he blew that up, and he hung it on the dressing-room wall.

He said, "I can criticize them; Kevin can criticize them— but nobody else can. Nobody outside of here can criticize my team."

Round-Up

In the Premier League's Easter Monday program, Manchester United beat Coventry, and Aston Villa beat Arsenal. Four games to go, United on top, one point in it.

In the First Division, Birmingham City lead Swindon Town 4-1 with thirty minutes to go—and the game ends 6-4 to Swindon. Swindon's manager, the peerless Glenn Hoddle, says, "We threw caution to the wind and came back from the dead . . . it *is* Easter Monday."

England didn't know what to do with Glenn Hoddle, and they don't know what to do with Chris Waddle either. Waddle's the best player in the country—a winger in his early thirties playing out of his skin for Sheffield Wednesday. He's "The Shuffling One," ungainly, stoop-shouldered and bowlegged—but as he drifts though defences up and down the land his subtle promptings help make Wednesday the most purely attractive side of the season. So the England manager names his squad for a World Cup qualifier against Holland, and Waddle isn't in it.

A few days later I meet Marcel the Underpantless Dutchman—I think of him this way because during Italia '90 all his luggage went AWOL in the bowels of an Italian airline, leaving him stranded in Sardinia with nothing to wear. He's been sent by his paper to try and find out why Waddle isn't playing; in Holland, he says, they're grinning all over their faces in mystified relief. But there you go—can't pick someone with a mind of his own, can we?

Wednesday are in the FA Cup Final against Arsenal, and—this has never happened before—they're in the Coca-Cola Cup Final with them too. And if there's a charge against Waddle, it's inconsistency—so, fortunately for the England manager, in the Coca-Cola game Waddle has an off day, and Arsenal win 2-1. But more noteworthy here is the fact that Wednesday's goal is scored by John Harkes—a collector's item, the first goal scored at Wembley by an American.

A letter to *The Independent* a few days later says the first goal scored by an American at Wembley should, in fact, be credited to Mike Masters. Masters played briefly for Colchester United in the Vauxhall Conference; on May 10, 1992, they contested the FA Trophy (a kind of nonleague FA Cup) at Wembley against Witton Albion, and Masters scored the opening goal in a 3-1 win. There's always a stat hound somewhere.

From the safety of Southend, Barry Fry sues Barnet for $150,000 in unpaid wages. Barnet, meanwhile, go on winning regardless—and we've given up wondering what can stop them because, evidently, nothing can.

In the Premier League, Manchester United beat Chelsea 3-0; Aston Villa beat Manchester City 3-1. Three games to go, United on top, one point in it—and how can I describe a run-in like this? It's a pennant race *ad extremis*.

16

Corporation Time

"Football sells products all over the world.
All this is due to my work."
—João Havelange

Argentina 1978

In 1976 the generals took over. During their "Dirty War," thousands disappeared; torture, rape, and murder were standard practice. Unabashed, FIFA let the World Cup go ahead in Argentina, giving welcome legitimacy to one of the Western world's nastiest regimes. Unabashed, Coca-Cola underwrote them while they did it to the tune of $8,000,000. It was squalid on the pitch, too—but in the circumstances, who won a game of soccer seems neither here nor there.

Light relief was provided by Scotland. Managed by Ally MacLeod, eccentric to the point of unhinged, they declared they were going to win the World Cup, and promptly lost their first game in it 3-1 to Peru. A player was sent home after failing a dope test. Lurching from one calamity to the next, they drew 1-1 with Iran, and only managed that after a fumbling Iranian put the ball through his own net. The Scottish press fell from wild hopes into foam-flecked rage; one report's opening paragraph on MacLeod consisted of four words: "Is the man mad?"

Scotland were left needing to score three goals against Holland to stay in the tournament. Taking their fans on another vertiginous emotional bender, they proceeded to play magnificently, and did indeed score three goals; unfortunately, they also let the Dutch score two. Holland squeaked through on goal difference; Scotland went home.

Without Cruyff, the Dutch didn't look like the team of 1974. The Germans had lost key men too; Muller had retired from international soccer, and Beckenbauer had joined Pele at the New York Cosmos. Both teams advanced—the Germans via the contradictory achievements of a goalless draw with an impressive Tunisia, and a 6-0 rout of Mexico—but neither convinced. The form teams looked instead to be Brazil, Italy, and France—and Argentina, of course, were at home.

After 1974, however, Brazil were trying foolishly to be more European—more vigorous, less fancy. The players didn't like it, and an ill-sorted side were lucky to scrape through. They drew with Spain and Sweden; it wasn't what was expected, and their fans burnt images of the manager in the street.

As for Italy, France, and Argentina, they were drawn in the same group. Italy had two men who would at last bring them out of their shell; the manager Enzo Bearzot, and the lean little striker Paolo Rossi. France had found Michel Platini, still only twenty-one, but plainly a great player, while Argentina had Mario Kempes, now twenty-three and scoring goals by the boatload in Spain. Then they had the crowd, leaning on referees in a partisan fever.

At the River Plate Stadium in Buenos Aires, where the fans greeted them with a huge cloudburst of shredded paper fluttering away over their heads from the packed and screaming stands, they beat Hungary 2-1 in an ugly game. The Hungarians scored first, but tried unwisely to get their retaliation in first too; Argentina rode the tackles, hit back, got on with the job, and Hungary ended up playing with nine men.

Two hundred miles down the coast at Mar del Plata, a resilient Italy beat France 2-1 after going behind in the thirty-eighth second. They'd arrived in Argentina off the back of some poor results, amid a torrent of gloomy criticism; the Italian press were banished from their training base and, urged by Bearzot to prove the doom merchants wrong, they did so—leaving France needing a result against Argentina.

They should have got one; in Buenos Aires they played brilliantly. But while the crowd yelled and seethed the Swiss referee gave Argentina a penalty that was dubious at best, then denied France a penalty that was plain as day. Funny, that.

Italy then beat Hungary—so when they met in Buenos Aires, they and Argentina were already both through. The result, however, would determine which groups they entered in the second phase; Argentina, obviously, wanted to remain in the capital, rather than shifting two hundred miles up the Paraná to Rosario. But a firmer referee made no mistakes, Dino Zoff worked wonders to keep out Kempes, and a fair game ended 1-0 to Italy; they stayed put, and Argentina went up the river.

Argentina faced Brazil, Poland, and Peru; Italy faced Austria, Holland, and West Germany. Compared to past World Cups, neither field looked impressive, a replay of the game Italy had just won seeming the best bet for the final—then Holland woke up. They oiled the wheels of the total football machine with a couple of fresh young players, and ran over Austria 5-1. When the Germans, in an unseemly role reversal, then played an abjectly unambitious game to lock out Italy 0-0, the advantage went to the Dutch.

The Germans stirred themselves. German games with Holland always have a private edge, as German games with England do, or Brazilian games with Argentina. This time, one of the tournament's better matches ended 2-2, the Dutch twice coming from behind. So when Italy beat Austria, their game with Holland was the decider—but while the Dutch were waking up, the Italians were nodding off.

Against Holland they couldn't score. They did take the lead, Dutch defender Erny Brandts sticking the ball in his own net—but after halftime Brandts scored again, in Italy's goal this time, and by then the Dutch looked stronger. A second goal was enough to decide it; a tiring and dispirited Italy fell back. Holland went to the final again; as for Italy, it was clear Bearzot still had work to do, if they were ever to stay the distance after all the empty years.

Meanwhile, Argentina struggled past Poland, Kempes scoring twice, and Brazil put Peru aside 3-0; paralyzed with tension, they then kicked lumps out of each other for ninety minutes and nobody scored, because most of the time nobody attacked. But if that was dull, what happened next was plain grubby.

Brazil had scored one more goal than Argentina—so if they could beat Poland by the same number of goals by which

Argentina beat Peru, or by more, they'd advance on that superior goal difference. But the schedule dictated that Brazil play in the afternoon, while the hosts didn't play until the evening; in other words, Argentina would know what they had to do. Brazil said the games should be played simultaneously, that they should both go out to do their best ignorant of the other's performance; fat chance. Brazil beat Poland 3-1—so Argentina took the field knowing they needed four goals.

Peru—the same Peru that had held Poland 1-0, drawn with Holland, beaten Scotland—then sat on their hands and let Argentina wander through them at will. They were supine, listless, they simply didn't play; Argentina scored six. It has, of course, never been proved that inducements were offered, or threats made; Brazil could only rage, while the Peruvians unconvincingly defended themselves, and Argentina slunk into the stained final of the 11th World Cup.

So the result loses its meaning somewhat. Argentina won 3-1 after extra time, in a game littered with rank fouls by both sides—nearly a foul every other minute, with an intimidated referee inclined to see Dutch fouls rather quicker than Argentinian ones. For the record, amid this unilluminating exercise, Mario Kempes was the difference, a great striker taking two goals, making the third—but if Argentina cried conspiracy when England won at Wembley, it wasn't surprising now if the luckless Dutch said grimly that in any other place in the world, Argentina would not have won.

It should, of course, have been held in any other place in the world to begin with—in any place not so smeared with its own people's blood. But in Argentina, no one could hear you scream—least of all FIFA, their ears by now filled with the fizz and bubble of the corporate dollar.

Gargantua

Argentina was the last competition with sixteen entrants; next time there would be twenty-four. Political promises had been made—and to pay for them the World Cup now ballooned into a monster, a sponsorship orgy, a corporate carnival so gargantuan that you can't move around it without stubbing toes on a logo at every turn.

In 1961, Sir Stanley Rous of the FA became FIFA's sixth

president; a schoolteacher, a referee, a football man. Back then, like any other sporting organization in a world not yet sucked into the great maw of TV, FIFA was an amateurish body, bumbling along on a moderate sufficiency of mostly straightforward funds. From a private house in Zurich with a receptionist and a pair of snoozing dogs, Rous—being English—ran a dull, conservative ship; you had the World Cup every four years, sold the tickets, took the money, and that was pretty much that. What you certainly didn't do was go about the place glad-handing foreigners.

In 1974, after the first seriously globewide election campaign undertaken by a sports administrator, Rous lost his job to Jean Marie Faustin Godefroid Havelange, João for short—a businessman from Rio who'd mostly made his money in insurance. He'd also represented Brazil in the swimming pool at the 1936 Berlin Olympics; sixteen years later at Helsinki he was in the pool for them again, this time playing water polo. In 1963, he got onto the International Olympic Committee; in 1970, as president of the Brazilian Sports Association, he saw to it that Brazil's team had funds and facilities to prepare for Mexico for three thorough months. Then, with the Jules Rimet trophy on the shelf for good, Havelange went campaigning.

Soccer was on the rise around the world; smarter than the complacent Europeans, Havelange hit the flight paths to go out and take charge of it. Traveling in a cloud of Brazilian glamour, Pele and others at his side, in Asia and Africa and Central America he promised that if they voted for him he'd give them a bigger World Cup, and that they'd get their due slice of it. But more than that, they'd get a new, pro-active FIFA; they'd get coaching programs, money for facilities, training for sports medics and referees—and they'd get new competitions to play in, too.

In 1977, three years after Havelange was elected, the first World Youth Cup, for players under twenty, was held in Tunisia. It was called the FIFA Coca-Cola Cup.

Adolph "Adi" Dassler made his first shoe in 1920; in the little town of Herzogenaurach a few miles north of Nuremberg, he built the company he called Adidas. On the other side of town, after a bitter family rift, his brother Rudolph founded Puma; in 1956, Adolph's son Horst would be in Melbourne,

persuading Australian dockers not to unload his uncle's Puma
kit sent out for the Olympics.

Horst Dassler would become the most powerful man in
world sport. He was the kingmaker behind Juan Antonio Sa-
maranch, a member of Franco's fascist *Movimiento* who's now
president of the International Olympic Committee—and, after
1974, he became the money-raiser for Havelange's FIFA. It was
Dassler who moved in Blatter to be Havelange's adjutant; it
was Dassler who founded the marketing company that con-
trols the World Cup.

Coca-Cola were the first on board. They'd been around the
Olympics for years, but what they got into now with soccer
was, in effect, the first globally conceived marketing program;
it was sponsorship reborn as a perpetual-motion machine,
the Real Thing circling in a four-year orbit round the turning
circle of the biggest competition in the world's biggest sport.
Soccer, TV, Coke—it was a lucrative trinity, and it paid for
the new king-size World Cup.

By the time Spain '82 came round, FIFA had blossomed
from a few filing cabinets in Zurich into a cavalcade of be-
suited bigwigs, salesmen, and flunkies whose expenses, as
they toured in splendor round their fabulously enriched new
terrain, all but matched the costs of the twenty-four teams.
Eight years later, at Italia '90, the price at the door for a
company wanting in—wanting to sponsor soccer's quadrennial round to its climax at the FIFA World Cup—was around
$20,000,000.

The gatekeeper—the company that says whether you get to
have your logo, your signage, your brand exclusively attached
to a media product reaching half of all humanity—is called
ISL Marketing. Based in Lucerne, ISL was founded in the
early eighties by Horst Dassler; despite having no past and no
record, it acquired exclusive rights to the World Cup immediately, and to the Olympics within a year. It's now the joint
property of the Dassler family and the humungous Japanese
ad agency Dentsu; it's got the honeypot locked up, and it
determines the names you'll be seeing all over USA '94.

Official Partners: Canon, Coca-Cola, Energizer, Fuji film,
General Motors, Gillette, JVC, MasterCard, McDonald's, Phil-
ips, Snickers.

Marketing Partners: Adidas, American Airlines, Budweiser,
EDS Information Technology Services, ITT Sheraton, U.S.
Sprint, Sun Microsystems, Upper Deck Trading Cards.

The first lot are FIFA's; the second tier go in with the local organizers to provide cash and/or services to support the tournament on the ground. Then there's a third batch of outfits buying licenses to attach the World Cup logo to their products; in Italy there were forty-seven of them, so everywhere you went you ate the official pasta, drank the official mineral water, sipped the official coffee, snacked on the official cheese. The cheese wasn't bad, either—but what the hell has this got to do with soccer?

If Havelange hadn't done it, someone else would have; it would be turning your face against reality to suppose that the World Cup, in a world ruled by television and multinationals, could ever really be much different from the giant promotional free-for-all it's become.

Much of what he promised has materialized, too. Older purists mightn't like it, but a twenty-four-team World Cup is terrific; we get more soccer, and we get to see guys we've never heard of playing it. When Cameroon got to the quarter-finals of Italia '90, and scared the pants off England when they did, the faith placed in Africa's fast-improving game was richly rewarded; the little guys should have these slots, and they don't look so little these days either. At the World Youth Cup in Australia in 1993, Africa was well represented again, a bright Ghanaian side knocking out England in the semifinals—so FIFA's corporate money has gone out to these places, and a happy crop is being harvested.

But the downside leaves a bad taste in the mouth. When they say USA '94 will sell out, they're almost certainly right—but the fact is, of the 3,600,000 tickets, a goodly chunk of them will never be sold to you or me in the first place.

A year before USA '94, tickets for the first forty-four games, for the opening groups and the "Round of 16," were arriving on the market. In round numbers that was nearly three million tickets, of which a million sold out in the U.S.A. like gold dust. Another million was reserved for sale to the public in the participating nations come New Year 1994, once qualification was over and the draw had been made. So, I asked, where's the third million?

A small number may be canceled; in some or all of the stadia, a few rows pitchside will probably be taken out, or covered over, for security reasons. Another small number will be kept aside; they'll be sold at stratospheric prices as part of hospitality packages, so the likes of Jack Nicholson can get valet parking, canapés, and a tall blonde in a short skirt to pour him champagne in his front-row seat. A larger number will be accounted for by media overspill; press boxes in American stadia, designed for domestic coverage of your domestic sports, aren't big enough for the global media herd that descends on the World Cup, and every game will have several hundred journalists spilling out into the stands.

And the rest, the bulk of those tickets, go to sponsors. In return for funding and promoting João Havelange's New Model World Cup, their contracts allocate literally hundreds of thousands of tickets to the corporations. So if you see an empty seat—an empty seat a soccer fan would give blood to be sitting in—it's most likely because some multinational creep in a suit who doesn't actually give a fuck about football is taking his girlfriend out to dinner instead.

A year before USA '94, the World Cup organizers laid on US Cup '93; England, Germany, and Brazil came to play with the U.S.A., and a successful dry run for the main event was enjoyed by all concerned. So on June 13, 1993, at Soldier Field, Chicago, the U.S.A. played world champions Germany; it was the first time the two nations had ever met on a soccer field, and with the World Cup set to leave its traditional shores for the first time a year later, it was a historic overture. Fifty-three thousand went, and were richly entertained—but I did meet one guy who didn't bother.

In my hotel, the night before the game, I was joined at my table by a man who'd brought his girlfriend from Columbus, Ohio, for the weekend. I said I was there for the soccer and she told me ingenuously, "Do you know he had two tickets for that game just sitting on his dresser, and he didn't even tell me?"

The guy had some piece of the food-and-drink franchise at Soldier Field; somewhere down the line he'd picked up his company tickets. "I didn't tell her," he said, "because I wasn't going to use them." So I told him that in a fan's eyes he was committing a sin, a gross abuse of privilege. Taken aback, he said, "Well. I suppose I might go see a half."

Spain 1982

Under the new dispensation, this time we got Cameroon, Algeria, Honduras, El Salvador, New Zealand, and Kuwait. El Salvador and New Zealand took a pounding, Honduras did better, Kuwait lost their temper, Cameroon put down a marker for the future with three draws, and the Algerians were robbed.

The formula FIFA settled on was different from today's. From six groups of four, twelve went through to four more pools of three teams, the winners of these to be the semifinalists—a scheme guaranteed to create mind-searing gridlock. Still, there comes a point where griping over the formula gets silly; if you win your games you go through, right? Unfortunately, if you're Algeria, maybe not.

The Germans were fancied. They had a zippy winger named Pierre Littbarski, and Karl-Heinz Rummenigge, a shark of a finisher who was European Footballer of the Year. So the Algerians went and beat them 3-2. They couldn't keep it up against Austria and were squarely beaten 2-0, but in their last game they raised themselves again, and beat Chile. Everyone beat Chile—so Algeria and Austria had four points each. The Austrians were through, with a better goal difference; the Germans had only two points.

In the group's last game, the Germans and the Austrians therefore played out a deliberate, tepid 1-0 win to Germany; an act of collusion as shamefully blatant as Argentina—Peru four years earlier. It was so obvious what had happened—that they had calculated what score would see the two of them through, and then gently arrived at it—that they should have both been shown the door on the spot. But FIFA looked away.

Other larcenies, meanwhile, were being perpetrated by the Spanish. As in Argentina, if the hosts did well, that had more than a little bearing on the tournament's bottom line—and it looked as if a referee or two knew it. The Spanish weren't a strong side, but an indulgent draw gave them Northern Ireland and Honduras, so progress seemed assured; an assurance which disintegrated when Honduras scored after seven minutes. Finding themselves contained by able opponents, Spain were then obliged to fall over a lot in the Honduran penalty area, this tactic eventually paying off as they crept to a 1-1 tie.

They then beat Yugoslavia 2-1 with the aid of another penalty, awarded for a palpable foul—a foul that, however, had equally palpably not been committed in the penalty area. Still, there was only Northern Ireland left.

Not so easy. A motley of players from up and down the Football League, with a Manchester United striker who was the youngest-ever player to appear in a World Cup—a big, fearless man of a boy named Norman Whiteside, just lately turned seventeen—the Ulstermen had held the other teams in the group to draws. So Spain now kicked, pulled, and pushed them round the park while the referee looked amiably the other way; his attention was caught, however, when an Irishman pushed back, and off he went. Yet, wonderfully, the Irish won 2-1, and came top of the group. Humiliated, Spain slid through with them over Yugoslavia by the merest split of a numerical hair. Like Yugoslavia they had three points, and they both had the same goal difference; Spain, however, had scored three, Yugoslavia only two. This was deemed the necessary difference, which would have been fair enough—only Spain shouldn't have had that penalty against Yugoslavia in the first place.

So what can I say? That they were lucky? The fact is that in the modern World Cup, home advantage has seemed twice in this chapter to have a bit more about it than just a crowd on your side—but happily there was nothing quite so queasily favorable to Italy last time. To an extent, perhaps, the sponsorship machine is now so churning with dollars that hoping for maximized ticket revenue from a successful home run is less of an issue—while the particular American situation, which we'll come to later, suggests that tickets will sell to an avid public whoever's playing.

All the same, FIFA's deal with the organizers of USA '94 does stipulate that FIFA shall receive a guaranteed minimum revenue from ticket sales of 105 million Swiss francs. When I asked my source how much that was in dollars he smiled and said "Less and less"—by which I fear he meant "More and more," as your currency like mine turns into international rubber—but give or take, it's $70 million.

So I'll be watching with interest to see who the U.S.A. gets drawn with in the opening round, and how the games are handled when you play them. Not, of course, that I'm suggesting for one minute that the good honest American—or indeed the noble manly Spaniard, or the proud upright Argentine, or above all the democratic and open FIFA of João Havelange—would dream of permitting anything the weeniest bit sneaky to interfere with the conduct of this most morally uplifting of sports.

In the other opening groups, England scored the fastest goal in World Cup history, twenty-seven seconds after kickoff against France. Elsewhere Brazil were wonderful, Argentina stumbled, Italy were dire, and Kuwait had a brainstorm.

England's goal seemed to set all to rights; they went on to win 3-1 after years in the slough of despond. Twice they'd failed to qualify; the previous manager had broken both contract and faith for the lure of the petrodollar, and run away to the United Arab Emirates. At the European Championship in 1980, fans fought on the terraces in Turin in clouds of tear gas, while on the pitch England flailed about and flopped. The qualifiers for Spain had been no more edifying, featuring a riot in Switzerland, and England's first-ever defeat by Norway in Oslo—a result that brought from a Norwegian radio commentator the memorably deranged exultation "We are the best in the world! We have beaten England! Lord Nelson, Lord Beaverbrook, Sir Winston Churchill, Sir Anthony Eden, Clement Attlee, Henry Cooper, Lady Diana, we have beaten them all! Maggie Thatcher, can you hear me? Maggie Thatcher, your boys took a hell of a beating!"

Still, England skidded through—then found themselves at war with Argentina in the South Atlantic. Should the British teams now withdraw? While the FA agonized, FIFA said if they did, they'd fine them—there's tact—but the war was won and lost, in fact, the day before England played France. Some were relieved, all too many waved flags and forgot the body count, Thatcher settled in for a long and crazy decade (and would be a malign and ignorant shadow over the game along the way), and in the halo of the moment, England won a game of soccer again.

The instant goal—kickoff, throw-in, near post header flicked on, far post volley, 1-0—was scored by a midfielder named Bryan Robson, a player of boundless power and spirit who, it seemed, was the perfect foil for Glenn Hoddle. In the next game—a 2-0 win over the Czechs—he was injured; with other key players injured already, a more familiar England stuttered falteringly to a 1-0 win over Kuwait. They went through, so did France, and Kuwait lost their marbles.

Sheik Fahd al-Ahmad al-Jaber al-Sabah, a brother of the emir, had spent several million dollars getting his team ready. He was president of the Asian Football Federation and, coincidentally, his side played all their qualifiers bar one at home. In Spain they drew with the Czechs—then Platini's France took them to bits. As Giresse went through to score the fourth, the Kuwaiti defence pulled up; someone had blown a whistle in the crowd. Fahd then tried to take his team off the pitch, stomping down there in a vehement pique. FIFA fined Kuwait $10,500—and I'll bet that really made a dent in their finances.

Greatly more pleasing, meanwhile, was another exuberant side from Brazil. In a stirring opener with a strong Russian team, they edged it 2-1; Scotland, in much better form than four years ago, then had the gall to score against them first, so they shifted a gear, and scored four back. They didn't need to shift many gears to get four more against New Zealand, and advanced looking easily the best side in it.

Whether Argentina could trouble them seemed uncertain. They had Diego Maradona, at twenty-one as outstanding a player as any since Pele. But they slipped up against Belgium, losing 1-0, while Hungary ran up the highest World Cup score of all time, 10-1 over El Salvador. Maradona then woke up and made the same Hungary look like nobodies in a 4-1 walkover— so the question was, in the second round, would Maradona show up?

As for Italy, it didn't look like they'd trouble anyone. From a dismal group, with every game drawn bar Poland's 5-1 thumping of Peru, they squeaked through over an unlucky Cameroon; whoever won the World Cup, it wouldn't be this bunch. As ever, they were in bitter conflict with a sniping press, and Paolo Rossi was miles out of form. He'd been banned for two years after a match-fixing scandal, on his return he'd played only a few games for Juventus before going to Spain—and what Enzo Bearzot had started building four years ago now looked set to fall apart any minute. After all, in the next round they were grouped with Brazil and Argentina.

England played Germany. The Germans dropped Littbarski, England dropped Hoddle, and a 0-0 result was predictably sterile. Now both played Spain, and it was win or go home. The Germans picked Littbarski and won, 2-1; England got in a lather over the arcana of the rules, fretting about what would happen if they won by the same score—but it was immaterial. They didn't pick Hoddle, and they didn't win; bye-bye.

Northern Ireland went home as well, but only after an altogether more spirited display against the Austrians; they drew 2-2. Drained by their great efforts and the heat, they were then unpicked by a magisterial Platini; the French went on to meet the Germans, looking dangerously clever and incisive.

By contrast, Poland-Belgium-Russia was dullsville. It started well enough, Poland dismantling Belgium with three goals. Belgium tried harder against an uneasy Russia, who could only beat them 1-0—but the dim business of these groups of three now showed at its worst, since Poland's better goal difference meant a draw with the Russians would suit them fine. They packed the defence, wasted time, and got one.

But in the fourth group, the first twenty-four-team World Cup at last caught magnificent light. Italy played Argentina—and compared to the fretful dullards of the first round, were unrecognizable. By the end, so was Maradona, brutally extinguished by the remorseless defender Claudio Gentile; but once that task had been alarmingly accomplished, in the second half Italy played football. Rossi's key still wouldn't turn in the ignition—he missed a sitter—but the winger Bruno Conti caused all kinds of problems, and Italy scored twice. Argentina could only get one back, and now faced Brazil.

Brazil had Zico, Eder, Junior, Falcao, Cerezo, Socrates; this was not 1970, they had no Pele to lead the line, but the midfield was so packed with blazing talent it seemed they'd manage without. They went ahead after eleven minutes; Argentina wrestled well and bravely, but couldn't find a way back in. Brazil got a second, and a third, and as with Gentile for Italy, the dark side was on offer here too; Brazil showed Maradona their studs on and off all game, and when they sent on Batista as a substitute he had a gleam in his eye—as in, now it's my turn. So sure enough, he kicked Maradona—and for the twenty-one-year-old, it was a kick too far. He kicked Batista back, in the balls, and in his red mist was shown the red card. Argentina managed a goal at the death, but it meant nothing. This time more sinned against than sinning, their title was gone, Maradona had failed, snuffed out harshly by older, harder men, and Brazil looked winners more than ever.

There followed in Barcelona the game which some think the greatest of all. Beforehand, Brazil's keeper said he worried Rossi might wake up; five minutes into the game, he did. Ghosting into the area, the slim little striker materialized on the end of a cross, and headed home. Six minutes later Brazil were back in it, Socrates rifling in a wonderful shot from the tightest of angles. He'd been released into space by Zico, whom Gentile would pursue with only sporadic effectiveness, and increasing vengefulness; but the Brazilians were not so tight in defence as the Italians, and a woeful, elementary lapse was now pounced on—by Rossi. 2-1 Italy.

The game surged and swayed, bursting with skill and speed in every corner of the pitch. The Brazilians pressed harder and harder; at last, with twenty-two minutes remaining, Falcao came drifting through the area to finish with venomous accuracy. 2-2, and Brazil were in the semifinals again. They had the better goal difference, a draw would see them through, but still they attacked. Only Dino Zoff stood between them and the last killer strike—and when it came, it came at the other end from Paolo Rossi. Again invisible in the area, he leapt on his chance with the acceleration of a cheetah, and Italy were 3-2 ahead. Thanks to Zoff it stayed that way, whatever Brazil could do—and Bearzot's Italy were hot.

In the semis they disposed of Poland 2-0; Rossi got both, one a deft, opportunistic little nudge through a crowd, the other a spectacular header on the end of a dashing run by Conti—but they were hardly pressed. In Seville, France and Germany, on the other hand, pressed every button on the console.

The French had hit their stride, but the German camp was full of malcontents and Rummenigge was injured. So it was artistry rampant tackling pulled muscle—but pulled or not, the Germans now put in some muscle as nasty as their deal with Austria was cheap. Early in the second half, with the score 1-1, Patrick Battiston was released clear on goal by a sweet through ball—so the German keeper Schumacher ran out and jumped at him, his hip smashed into his face at full speed, knocking out two teeth and breaking his jaw. It ranks high on the list of all-time brutal fouls, yet, astoundingly, he wasn't sent off, nor was a penalty awarded.

The French, obviously, were disturbed; only their keeper kept them in it as extra time loomed. Now the Germans sent on Rummenigge—but it was the French who went ahead, and eight minutes into the extra half hour, justly, they made it 3-1.

But the Germans just never give up. Eight minutes of the game remained when they pulled one back; only two minutes remained when they equalized—and a game that should have been France's ten times over went, for the first time in World Cup history, to the horrible, tormenting lottery of a penalty shoot-out.

Germany won it—and everyone in the world now wanted Italy to win the final, and see justice firmly done. But in a vicious first half they missed a penalty, and sad fears rose that again they'd fall apart, that for the third time the German machine, a grinding, destructive machine this time, would snuff out a more attractive opponent to lift the title.

Paolo Rossi had other ideas; Bearzot's Italy did not fall apart. The second half was eleven minutes old when Rossi scored his sixth in three games—and now it was Germany that grew flustered, Italy that played, fast, sweet, sharp as a razor. Twelve minutes later they got the second, and twelve minutes after scored another, when Bruno Conti ran over half the length of the pitch to put a cross on the button for Altobelli. They were three goals up, and worth every one of them.

In the dying minutes the Germans got one back—but this was a game even they could not rescue; in the second half, they'd never really been in it. After what had gone before, the only team anyone could have wanted to win had done so; justice was indeed firmly done, and for the first time since Pozzo's teams of 1934 and 1938, the World Cup went back to Italy—who, when they play the way they can, are the finest footballers in Europe.

And I remember how in central London the streets filled magically from nowhere with hooting, blaring cavalcades of cars all waving from their windows the red, green, and white flag of Italy, all the Italians in the city pouring from their homes and their businesses to launch an impromptu burst of joy across the grimy heart of the capital. I remember how old Sandro Pertini, then Italy's president and much beloved by his people, leapt like a child to his feet in happiness in the royal box beside King Juan Carlos, as his team brought the glory home in style. I remember how they said it was the first time that wonderful, fragmentary country had ever really felt united as one nation, united in the game.

I remember that two years later Michel Platini's Frenchmen went on to become dazzling and rightful champions of Europe.

And I remember watching them do it on television in a café in Morocco—where I also watched local games of soccer on dirt pitches, the terraces bedecked with red banners bearing the Coca-Cola logo.

17

Strikers

Steve Watkin: Striker
Age: 21
Height: 5′ 10″
Hometown: Acrefair, Clwyd

Tony Humes: "Stevie's a great player, he's a lovely player to have on your side. He gives us another dimension, because we can slip the ball to his feet and he's strong, he'll hold it up, and he's intelligent—he knows when to lay it off." As a defender, he said he wouldn't fancy playing against him. "He can turn you one way, turn you the other—he takes you places you don't want to be."

Watkin's the only player on the first team born in Wrexham; Acrefair's ten minutes down the road. He's quiet, and smart; he signed schoolboy forms at fifteen, but when they offered him a place a year later he turned it down, opting to stay in school two years longer. But once he graduated, he signed pro anyhow. "It was always first choice."

He didn't get a game in his first season; when it was over, he went to New Zealand. He said, "I enjoyed it. The standard of football wasn't particularly good, but the experience was." I said Flynn had told me he'd come back bigger and he said, "I'd been on the weights. But if the boss reckons it did me good"—he smiled—"then he must be right."

He got his debut the next season; that game, he only played the first half. "It passed me by. It was so quick, the pace of it.

I was running round like a chicken with no head." So he's learnt a bit since then. He has seventeen goals this season from thirty-six games, a strike rate anyone would settle for. And for a striker, the bottom line is scoring—so what's it like when you do?

"It's hard to describe. You just get a buzz out of it—for ten, fifteen minutes afterward you're on a high out there, your confidence is way up, and you're looking for another. Scoring goals seems easy then, which it isn't—but when you're on a run, you go three or four games scoring, you can't wait to get out there. But if you go seven or eight and you don't score, you get apprehensive in front of goal; you don't do things naturally then. You tend to snatch at things."

I asked which was the best goal he'd scored, and he laughed. "I don't score many good goals, they're all in the six-yard box— but the most important was the winner against Arsenal in the FA Cup last year. There was 13,000 here—and Tony Adams [an England international] went to clear it in the box, and he miskicked it, so I nipped in front of him, slid it in; it was pretty scrappy. But you don't care, so long as it goes in—and I couldn't believe it, I don't think anyone could. 2-1 up against Arsenal, with ten minutes to go. And those ten minutes took forever."

The essence of a striker: "You don't care, so long as it goes in."

Gary Bennett:	Striker
Age:	30
Height:	6′ 0″
Hometown:	Liverpool

I asked what it was that made a person a striker, and he said he didn't know. "I think you're just born one; from when I started, I just loved scoring goals. I couldn't ever play in defence, I got nothing out of it—but once I went up front, started putting it in the net, I knew it was what I was made to do."

And he said, when you're going through on goal, "You can't explain the feeling. I suppose it's just determination. You look up, you pick your spot, and you go for it. But I think if you pick your spot early, and hit your shot early, you'll get better results. Sometimes keepers make your mind up for you, so I've gone round a few—you look up and they're on their way down at you, so you walk the ball round them. But most times if you hit it early, that'll do them; if you speak to any keeper they'll say the more you dither, the more chance they've got of standing up to you. So pick your spot, and hit it early. That gets best results."

Flynn said goalscorers, like goalkeepers, are a different breed. To be a keeper, you've got to be daft—and to be a striker, you've got to be clinical. He said, "Benno's the best one-on-one finisher I've seen for a while. When he's through on goal, he'll score more often than not. And as they say, he's not afraid to miss. That's the old adage, isn't it? Never be afraid to miss—because if you miss and it affects you, you'll never go in there again."

I said I wouldn't want their job, and he smiled. "They get the glory, don't they?"

Benno's strike rate's better than Watkin's: twenty-one in forty games. But he's just turned thirty, he'll not be going to the Premier League—so when he came available at the start of the season, why did Flynn take him?

"Proven goalscorer. Good character. And it's true, he's the worst one for training ever, that's a club joke; if I'd had him on trial for a month, I'd probably never have signed him. But when it matters, he's there."

Pejic said, "I'd never pick him on my five-a-side. He's liable to stay out on the wing and do nothing, absolutely nothing. But then again, he's liable to have one chance—and he'll score."

Benno loves scoring. He said, "It's like having sex. That's the closest thing. 'Cause when you score, all your adrenaline's pumping—and when you go out on the pitch, it's your aim to put that ball in the back of the net. So when you achieve that aim, it's just a really great feeling."

And then you wheel away, hands in the air, eyes wide, mouth open and yelling . . .

"I suppose I do celebrate more than most. Some of the lads have a go at me about it. But I don't know where I am for a couple of seconds, especially in a big game. For a couple of seconds I'm in a different world—and that's the beauty of football, the way people are different. If you get a center half score a goal, he doesn't know what to do. Or Stevie'll score, and he's a quiet one; he'll just put his arms up, grab the nearest player. But me, I'll go on a run to the supporters—

because supporters are what's most important. Players don't matter, managers don't matter, chairmen don't matter. But the guy who sits in the stand, the guy who stands on the terraces—he's the main man."

So Benno comes to the Kop, leaning back from the knees, fists clenched, thumbs up, mouth a rictus of abandon. He said, "Before I was a pro I used to watch Everton a lot, home and away, and it used to annoy me when they'd got beat, the way they'd just trudge off the pitch. So win or lose, I'll always acknowledge the fans. They've paid their money—and I know what it's like to stand there when it's pissing down with rain. See, I always used to think, when I was on the terraces, it was something I'd like to do, to play football—and I know they'd all like to be doing it too. So I'll always acknowledge them."

When he was nine, Benno's family moved ten miles out from Liverpool to Skelmersdale, Skem for short, which they called then the Promised Land. There were green fields, and new factories with jobs in them. "Of course," he said, "the factories are closed now. But that's another issue."

He left school at sixteen, and got an apprenticeship as a clothing cutter. At twenty he was qualified, well paid, and enjoying it, and playing his football on Saturdays for Skem. But he was scoring a lot of goals, so the manager started writing to clubs about him; Wigan Athletic asked him to come on trial, he took a week off, and they signed him. Then Wigan's manager was sacked; he moved to Chester, and took Benno with him. He was there five years, had eighteen months at Southend, two more seasons back at Chester—and then he came here, because he'd had a spot of bother.

His ex-wife's brother came round, asked if he could store some stuff in Benno's spare room, stuff for a new house he was getting; Benno said fine, and left him the key. When he got back he took a look, and the stuff was all antiques; it was, as they say, "bent gear." So he called the guy, told him to get it out of his house; the guy came back, and two minutes after him came the police. Benno was in jail overnight, it was on the front page of the *Liverpool Echo*, he's in court on May 7, the day before our last game—and he seemed sanguine about it. But his manager at Chester wasn't sanguine at all.

"He offered me a new contract—but from what he offered, I think he thought he had me over a barrel. And sometimes you make a stand, and you stick with it. So he put me on the transfer list. I think he wanted me out anyway."

Flynn said he knew Benno'd talked with other clubs—but he wanted him. He said, "I kept chipping away."

Benno said, "I came and had talks here, and the first thing Brian Flynn said to me was, The trouble I hear you're in—is that a problem? And I said, No. Then I started to explain, how it was my brother-in-law brought that stuff—and he said he didn't want to know. He said he'd asked me if it was a problem and I'd said no, and that would do, and I couldn't believe he was like that. And I had to be thankful to him for giving me a chance, because people read the papers, they get wrong impressions . . . maybe he thought I was a gamble. But hopefully I've repaid him with a few goals."

Twenty-one, to be precise.

He said he was a bit disappointed. He'd had the odd injury— but he'd be happier if he'd scored thirty.

He had flu, and with the broken toe, he wasn't one hundred percent. "But we're only three games from promotion. A broken toe won't stop me now."

Some clubs make you play when you're injured . . .

"I always had that at Chester. I've played with so many injuries, I've had cortisone injections—and that's one thing they won't do here. The boss told us at the start of the season, he won't make us play if we can't. But that actually makes you want to play, if you possibly can. And I can."

So I asked how he'd compare Wrexham to clubs he'd played at before, and the answer was prompt.

"This is the best club I've been at. I've had a manager before that was an absolute lunatic—he used to bully people, he used to rant and rave—and after being under that, sometimes I wish the gaffer here *would* give someone a bawling out; I'm not used to this. So you speak to other players, they're unhappy—and I don't think life's about that, is it? You don't want to go to work in them circumstances—and that's why I appreciate being here. Some people think you've got to have that army style in football, and you do need discipline, of course you do. But life here's easygoing, it's comfortable, the manager trusts you, he respects you—and because of that, you don't take the piss. If we come in and we've had a bad game he'll say, If anyone thinks they had a good game, they can take tomorrow off—and all the lads'll come in. It's honesty, and that's why we're doing fairly well. I won't say we're doing *very* well, because we haven't achieved anything yet. But if we get promoted, it couldn't happen to a nicer fellow, or a better club."

I asked him later if he was one of those who, health permitting, would go on playing as long as he could, and he said, "Maybe I wouldn't want to at another club. But at this one I would."

The figures speak for themselves. Benno's career strike rate is one goal per four games. Here, it's a goal every other time he goes out—so this was, as he said, the best time he'd had in his career. He said, "I wish I'd come here a lot sooner. I've never enjoyed my football as much as I do now. And it'll be a shame if we can't cap it with promotion."

If we don't make it into the top three, we're in the play-offs. Fourth plays seventh, fifth plays sixth, over two legs at home and away; the winners go to Wembley to decide it. Benno said, "I've had a dream where I score the winner at Wembley. I don't know if it was a dream or a nightmare. Dreams are mixed up sometimes. I hope that one was."

April 24, 1993
Wrexham v. Carlisle United

Three games left, three wins required.

Kevin Reeves said, "That depends on York's last game at Rochdale, and I've got a feeling Rochdale are going to win. They beat Lincoln 2-1 away last Saturday; that gives them a sniff of the play-offs, which is what we want. We want them to have something to go for."

But we can't be counting on anyone else. Halfway through the time I spent talking with Benno, twenty-four hours before kickoff, Flynn called him away for a word. When he came back, he said, "He's just told me I'm playing. And he says we've got to go for their throats, first twenty minutes; try and get a couple of goals, hopefully set our stall out then. So we won't start the game trying to suss them out, or feel our way in—the ball'll be going straight over the top, to get me in behind them. So if you'll pardon the expression, I'll be absolutely fucked after twenty minutes. But that's what he wants me for."

Carlisle haven't won at the Racecourse since before World War II; they're from way up north in Cumberland by the Scottish border, they're sixteenth with nothing to play for, and the visitors' stand is empty. The game begins, and Benno goes tearing up at their goal, forcing a clearance—and when the ball comes out, suddenly they're all over us. You think, hang on, this wasn't in the script. But they get a corner; the ball loops over, their No. 6 rises far post, *thump*, seven minutes gone, and it's 1-0 Carlisle.

Disbelief. The Kop falls silent in abject, hollow, bewildered disbelief.

Tony Humes: "We'll see what we're made of now."

Twice, he sprays precise long diagonals from defence to the wing; one right for Cross, one left for Connolly. The second time, Connolly comes within a whisker of beating three men, surging into the area before he falls at the last. Then Pejic pushes forward, chips it up to Watkin, he touches it down to Connolly, Connolly cuts in, lobs a floater on to Benno—and the keeper collects. But we win a corner, then another; the ball drops in, the keeper parries Benno's header, in the six-yard area Connolly hacks at the rebound and misses and it's pushed away, and through a flailing of boots Pejic seizes on it, scalps it in, 1-1.

> Shall we tell them, SHALL WE TELL THEM
> Who we are, WHO WE ARE
> We're the barmy Wrexham army
> La la la la la

We're playing now, we're getting it wide. Owen's cross flies inches over Benno's leaping head. Jones takes his turn to chip it in, Benno heads on, and a frantic defender dives to clear off his toes as he turns and streaks through.

> Waah-oh, Waah-woh-oh-oh-oh
> Benno, Benno, he's a-gonna score
> Not one, not two, not three, but four
> Benno, Benno, he's a-gonna score

The goal that follows is the best of the season. Deep in the right-back position Cross dispossesses one man, turns upfield, beats another, and slides the ball on to Lake. Lake skips neatly past the next man as he lunges in, then quickly moves it along the deck to Owen in the center—and the rapidity of the distribution, combined with the beating of those men, has opened sudden acres of space. Owen sets off through the sunny green void; Connolly makes a run for him on the left, Bennett and Watkin spill forward into the area. Owen feeds Connolly; he takes one light touch to control it and *ping*, he sends the deep cross over without breaking stride. At the far post Bennett rises; he heads it into the goalmouth for Watkin, and Watkin in his turn heads it home. 2-1 Wrexham.

It's what you go to see—a defence torn to pieces, wheeling back in panic as men are beaten, passed, turned, as the runs are made and the space carved open; five men taking turns to move the ball on with the deftest precision, at exceptional speed. So we have grins all over our faces, stoned on football. Alan's leaning back, sighing. He says, "Lovely. You'll not see a better goal than that. Ever."

Carlisle don't fold, not a bit of it; the rest of the game is agony. We need another goal to secure it, but Carlisle know they could score again too—so for the rest of the half we play fitfully; they block our chances, and they bring it out fast. The Kop fills with a racked mix of emotions, pregnant with hope and dread, keening when we have it, terrified when we don't. You can't bear to watch, and you can't bear not to . . . Benno hits the crossbar.

> Psycho Psycho
> How's your toe?
> How's your toe?

At halftime, people glued to their radios spread the word round the terrace that Rochdale and York are 0-0. Good, but not good enough . . .

After the interval we're attacking the goal beneath the Kop, playing to the fans—and the opening of the second half's a whirlwind, corner after corner, goalmouth scrambles and last-ditch clearances, shots parried and headers hoiked off the line, Pejic and Benno grinning at each other in the six-yard box while they wait for yet another corner to come in . . . but when it does, the last poke over the line somehow never quite happens. Connolly's playing a firestorm down one wing; Cross on the other, in Alan's word, is as apposite as we've seen him—but still we can't kill the thing off.

And then Carlisle have a hot spell, winning their share of the corners in turn. Time slopes past so slow here you feel pinned to the concrete, bound to a grinding wheel . . . as Morris saves. So it's agony, relief, and then agony again when Benno misses by inches; agony when Owen fires a screamer and the keeper fluffs it, it squirts from his hands under his body, and trickles away just a fraction outside the post.

Huge black rainclouds mass behind the Kop. Owen fires another from range, a bullet—it cannons away off their No. 11's head, and he folds to the ground seeing stars. When the corner's cleared Owen fires again, from twenty-five yards; it shaves a foot or two wide. And the tackles are digging in now; when Carlisle send on a substitute to try and wrestle back into it the Kop scream out

> *You poor bastard*
> *You poor bastard*

But still the anxiety mounts, as the rain now pours down. And still there's no news from Rochdale . . .

Cross tears away down the right; a defender heads the incoming ball off Watkin's nose. From the corner the keeper takes it, hoofs it up our end; Connolly, end to end all game, steals it back, and sends it long again for Benno to chase. Benno goes to the corner with it, trying to find his way round the full back to cut the ball inside—and we're screaming for the whistle now, a piercing racket bearing down on the referee, *end it now, end it now* . . . Benno gets it in to Owen, he's dancing though the middle, and the scoreboard says this:

ROCHDALE 1 YORK 0

The biggest roar of the season lifts the roof off the rafters. Huge booming chants echo to a rhythmic thunder of hands clapping, boots thumping against the tin wall behind us.

> *The Reds are going up*
> *Thackety thack thack thack*
> *The Reds are going up*
> *Thackety thack thack thack*
> *We love you Wrexham, we do*
> *Thackety thack*
> *We love you Wrexham, we do*
> *Thackety thack*

And yet still the agony continues, as Carlisle attack again. We try to break out—and they hobble Steve Watkin. John Paskin comes on, as the tumult of singing and clapping and hammering boots swells and surges, a flood of noise spilling over their keeper as we win a corner. There are two minutes left. Cross dinks it in, at the near post Connolly flicks it on across the goalmouth, and Paskin barges in to head it home. 3-1, safe at last.

> *Going Up*
> *Going Up*
> *Going Up*

On the scoreboard: WE WILL TELL YOU
                    THE FINAL SCORE
                    AS SOON AS
                    WE GET IT

The referee blows his whistle. The players run to applaud the Kop, then go round to do the same for the main Yale Stand. And while the noise thunders all about me I'm dancing, notebook thrown down, shuffling and swaying on the spot with not a thought in my head. So we stay in the rain until confirmation comes that York have been beaten, and then the roar redoubles over the shining grass.

Humes said, "We heard the roar, and we didn't dare look behind us at the scoreboard. Then in the dressing room we still didn't know for sure—and we heard the roar again in there. Then someone told us, and we knew."

The boss came in, said he wanted to say a few words. But he's a small man, and Joey Jones, the reserve team coach behind him, is tall as a house, and Joey's got this great big fat grin on his face. So I don't know whether the boss got to say his few words or not, because the players said they all just fell about laughing.

So it's two games to go, two points needed; Humes said it'd be great if we could do it at Northampton on Tuesday. "Then the last game, all we'd have to do is turn up and enjoy ourselves."

I said it was good, when they'd come to the Kop with their hands raised, applauding, and the people were all chanting and cheering in there, and he said you had to. He remembered early in the season they'd had a terrible run of three games away, lost 4-3 at Bury, 4-0 at York, 4-1 at Gillingham. He said, "You're so angry with yourself, so down, you just want to get in the dressing room, and you forget. Then someone wrote to the paper, complained we hadn't thanked them, and he was right. Because they come so far, and they keep on coming— like Northampton, that'll be a home game. They're part of why we're where we are now."

But mostly, we're where we are now because we've got good players, and a manager who glued them together. Humes said, "He's so confident. When I first came he said, Something big's going to happen here. And you look and you think, Hold on. Then you look again and you think, Yeah, he's right. It is."

Round-Up

AC Milan make the European Cup Final, beating PSV Eindhoven 2-0 in the San Siro—but in *Serie A* they're stuttering. Inter rein them in; a lead of eleven points shrinks to four.

In Italy, to safeguard the development of Italian players, a club can only have three foreigners on the pitch at any one time. But in their squad Milan have six—the Dutchmen Van Basten, Gullit, and Rijkaard, the Montenegrin Dejan Savicevic, the Croat Zvonimir Boban, and Jean-Pierre Papin of France. So when the last of these, Papin, was bought from Marseille, the rest of Europe was enraged; it seemed Milan's owner, malls-to-media magnate Silvio Berlusconi, for an outlay of $60 million was collecting the world's best footballers the way other people do postage stamps. Van Basten is both World and European Footballer of the Year, 1993, and Papin has held the latter title too, and is probably the only striker who comes close to the Dutchman. So how come Inter are reining this lot in? Because all the money in the world doesn't do you any good if the players you buy with it are injured.

Berlusconi's idea is to have, in effect, two A teams, so that he can always turn out a fresh side no matter how many competitions he's in. And he wants victory, not just for the glory or the ego ride, but because it's business. You watch his side play on his TV channel, and in the breaks you watch ads for the products you buy in his malls.

The goal is a Super League—a European League to span the continent as the domestic leagues span the countries. The latest proposal is to merge the European Cup with the UEFA Cup into a regionalized 128-team format, with play-offs heading to a final at the end of it. The idea's shot down, because the European Cup is too sacred, but the last eight in that competition play a mini-league already, not a knockout any more; that way they get more big Euro-games, more big Euro-gates, more big TV Euro-audiences. That way we got, in 1993's competition, the champion clubs of Italy, France, Holland, Scotland, Portugal, Sweden, Belgium, and Russia all playing one another in a sponsor's transcontinental mass-media dream.

So be assured some variety of Super League will soon be upon us. And if you want to understand the importance of soccer, consider this—that between the passion of the fans and the interests of the owners, the advent of such a league would represent a more unified European activity than anything the EC's bickering mandarins in Brussels have ever come up with. Politically and economically, attempts toward European unity seem sometimes to have all the harmony of a pack of cats in a sack—but in soccer, we've been getting there for decades.

Beirut hostage John McCarthy and his partner Jill Morrell publish their autobiography *Some Other Rainbow* to rave reviews. During McCarthy's captivity, Gary Lineker scored six goals for England at Mexico '86; McCarthy reports that this led him for a while to think "lineker" was Arabic for "goal." Trying to reach out to him, a friend of McCarthy's unfurled a banner by the scoreboard in the stadium where England were playing Morocco. It read, JOHN MCCARTHY BEIRUT: TINKER TAYLOR SAYS TTRA. That's "Time to Roll Another," a private joke about roll-your-own cigarettes—and it says worlds about the game that they figured if there was any way to reach him, if there was anything he might be permitted to watch with his captors on TV, it would be soccer.

Manchester United beat Crystal Palace 2-0; Aston Villa lose 3-0 at Blackburn Rovers. Two games left, and United have a lead of four points—so most people conclude that's it. Not Alan; he puts a fiver on Villa to win it at 14-1. His reasoning? Villa's last games are against relegation candidates Oldham at home, and nothing-to-play-for Queen's Park Rangers away. United, on the other hand, must entertain Blackburn, who still have a chance to finish high enough to make next season's UEFA Cup. Then, on the last day of the season, United must go to Wimbledon—and the Crazy Gang like nothing better than mugging the rich folk. So I'd say it'll go to the wire; I'd say 14-1 are good odds.

18

The Hand of God

"I feel no bitterness toward the Argentine captain. He acted
instinctively and got away with it."
—Bobby Robson

Mexico 1986

Mexico's second World Cup was all about one man, a man said
afterward by the press in Argentina to be

omnipresent,
strong as a bull,
fast as a missile,
the star of the century,
passing like the air through narrow spaces—
in his veins doctors will not find blood, but rocket fuel.

He was Diego Armando Maradona; he was twenty-five, he
was five feet six inches of jet-propelled muscle, and he was the
greatest player the world had seen since Pele. He was also,
unfortunately, an arrogant little twerp whose career would
feature petulant farce and peerless genius in equal parts.

He was sixteen when he first played for Argentina; in 1979,
when he was eighteen, Boca Juniors in Buenos Aires made
him the world's first $1.5 million player. After Spain '82, Bar-

celona bought him for $4.5 million; two years later he went to Napoli, and the price was $7.5 million. He won the Italian championship for Naples twice, a notable feat against the northern powers of Turin and Milan—but his finest hour was Mexico.

In their opening group, a zippy South Korea had the gall to score against them, but Argentina scored three. They drew a sour game 1-1 with Italy, beat Bulgaria, and went through top of the group. The format had settled to its present shape, sixteen teams in a knockout once the round-robins were done—so in the Round of 16, Argentina now found themselves head to head with Uruguay.

It was a grisly prospect. Uruguay came through in a third-place spot from "the group of death," and their play was so ugly they made Argentina seem angels by comparison. They kicked their way to a draw with the Germans, had a man sent off against an electric Danish team who annihilated them 6-1, then went out against Scotland so charged up that they had a man sent straight off again for a filthy foul in the very first minute. But, playing ten against eleven all game, grit and spit still saw them to a grim 0-0; Scotland went home bruised, while Uruguay scraped through to a contest in which everyone expected a torrent of red cards. But an excellent Italian referee contained it; Argentina held tight for a 1-0 win, they were in the quarter-finals and the question was, who could stop Diego Maradona?

In the opening groups, only Denmark and Brazil won all three of their games; Russia also looked ominously strong, wiping the floor with Hungary 6-0 despite missing a penalty. But the Italians looked tentative, the Germans unsteady—and while the hosts rolled forward on a wave of crowd noise, when it came to crunch time Mexico surely just weren't big enough. As for England, they were risible.

They arrived unbeaten in a year, in good shape after three weeks' altitude training in Colorado, and they had an easy group. Portugal were weak enough, without a bitter dispute over money to wear them down further; yet England blundered around against this hapless lot for seventy-five minutes, with all of the ball and no notion what to do with it, until the Portuguese decided they might as well attack even if their bonuses were lousy. End result, 1-0 Portugal.

Needing points badly from their next game with Morocco, English wheels now fell off altogether. The captain left the field injured, the man who took over from him threw the ball at the referee and got sent off—so ten men found themselves hanging on against another alarmingly capable side of African "no-hopers." It ended 0-0, with a nation enraged. "Just don't come near me," growled Bobby Robson at the press.

But at the World Cup a team often takes a couple of dour games to find itself, then suddenly emerges looking the pick of the pack. Against Poland, on paper the toughest of their group matches, a reshuffled England were in a different class; by halftime they were 3-0 up and coasting, all three scored by Gary Lineker, a rapier-sharp finisher blessed with pace, stealth, and a temperament so eerily equable that he's never once been booked in his entire career.

England went to Mexico City to face Paraguay in the Round of 16 feeling happier altogether. Paraguay were a good side, too—until they went 1-0 down and saw sparks. It was Lineker who scored, so they elbowed him in the windpipe; while he was off the pitch and the Paraguayans were screaming at the referee, England got a second. When Lineker came back he got a third, and England were in the quarter-finals.

Their opponents were Argentina, and no one could possibly pretend it was only a game. The two countries had been at war only four years earlier; amid intense security, every press conference navigated passages of taut and effortful diplomacy. In the Azteca, the first half was similarly strained—then, in four minutes of the second half, Maradona took off the chains. His first goal was scandalous, his second astonishing; a yard from the TV back home, I remember beating my fists on the floor in rage—and then being defused, left gaping in wonder.

An English midfielder sliced a high, looping back pass to his keeper Peter Shilton; Maradona raced after it. The two men leapt for the ball in the air and, for all his spring-coiled muscle, there was no way Maradona's head could have reached it ahead of Shilton's hands. There was no way it did, either; instead he punched the ball in the net, and everyone saw him do it. A hundred and fifteen thousand in the stadium, millions on TV, millions seeing the pictures in the papers the next day, everyone saw him do it—everyone except a Tunisian referee and a linesman from Costa Rica. Maradona looked, saw that they'd not seen him cheat, and raced in celebration to the corner flag.

Afterward, he evaded the truth with a phrase infamous in soccer history; he said the goal was "A little of the hand of God, a little of the head of Maradona." But by then he'd shown us what else he could do. Collecting the ball in his own half, he set off on a slalom through half the English team, bucking, veering, leaving one player after another tackling air, the run a staggering, turbo-charged display of ferocious speed, vicious swerve, and leonine strength, all capped with the coolest precision as he glided the ball home past a hopelessly wrongfooted Shilton, dumped on his butt as Maradona zoomed by. The English sat on the turf in his wake, mystified; it's the greatest goal I've ever seen. It was 2-0 down, and not a thing you could do about it; he robs you, then he blows you away.

What England did about it was they sent on two wingers, and went back to the way we know best—give it to the wide men and run at the bastards. The wingers were John Barnes, Jamaica-born, lazily graceful, swaying like a magician through the tackles, and Chris Waddle, "The Shuffling One," plucked from a sausage factory in Newcastle. Between them for the last twenty minutes they had Argentina on the rack.

With ten minutes left Barnes crossed, and Lineker was there to take his sixth goal of the tournament; it was 2-1, and now the game was a firestorm. Shots crashed away off bodies, frantic defenders cleared from the mayhem in Argentina's goal—until, with three minutes left, Barnes crossed again. Lineker was diving through the throng, his head an inch off the ball; but somehow he ended up in the net, and the ball didn't. 2-1 it finished, England went home, and Barcelona bought Lineker for $3.3 million. The game goes on—and you say to yourself, we'll be back next time.

Under the canny coaching of a Serb named Bora Milutinovic, Mexico made the quarter-finals for the first time in their history, cruising 2-0 past a leaden Bulgaria. The Germans went through too, but only just; Morocco gave them almighty resistance, and it was the eighty-ninth minute before Lothar Matthaus got the winner. They seemed deeply unconvincing.

The rest of the Round of 16 was more vivid. Against Italy, Platini took control for the French, and sent the champions home with a performance more emphatic than 2-0 would suggest, while in Guadalajara an increasingly sumptuous Brazil destroyed Poland 4-0 without breaking stride. But the best two games featured upsets more exciting yet, from teams no one had fancied at the outset.

Denmark had beaten Scotland, Germany, and Uruguay with a fast, fluid passing game that promised much at their first World Cup. When they went ahead against Spain, it seemed they could only go on—but the Spanish had other ideas, in particular a striker named Butragueno, "the Vulture." After he'd equalized and Denmark were committed to attack, Spain kept catching them on the counter, and the Danes fell to pieces. It ended 5-1, Butragueno getting four.

Belgium's game with Russia was even more surprising, one of the best of all time. Russia scored first after twenty-seven minutes; at halftime it was still 1-0. Early in the second half Enzo Scifo equalized; Russia went ahead again, once more the Belgians equalized, and at full time it was 2-2. Now Belgium took control; in the extra period they took a 4-2 lead, before Russia pegged them back to 4-3—and though the Russians spilt forward, that was how it ended. It was a wonderful two hours, end-to-end all game—and a useful reminder that any game's worth watching, no matter how unglamourous the form book would have it appear.

Away from the Hand of God controversy, the quarter-finals had much that was good about them too. The worst game saw Mexico reach the end of their road against the Germans; both sides had a man sent off, the thing dragged on scoreless through extra time until it tottered to a penalty shoot-out, and then the hosts lost their nerve. From the spot, the Germans couldn't miss, and the Mexicans couldn't score to save their lives. 4-1 Germany.

Sadly, the other two games were much better, but both had to end in a duckshoot as well. Belgium tied Spain 1-1, then beat them 5-4 from the spot; they were into the semis, and it broke English hearts. Bobby Robson wrote later, "Imagine, Belgium in the semifinal. I would have settled gladly for a semifinal against Belgium."

As for France and Brazil, they played a classic; but after Brazil missed a penalty this also ended 1-1, and the French held steady to win the shoot-out 4-3. So in the semis we had France, Germany, Belgium—and Diego Maradona.

The intelligence of Germany's manager Franz Beckenbauer

now became as evident from the dugout as it had been when he played on the field. The Germans had been dull and shaky all tournament, but still they had stubbornly progressed; now they set a man to mark Platini out of the game, and the replay of the '82 semifinal ended in a 2-0 win achieved without incident, French flair all snuffed out.

It hardly seemed to matter. Belgium might have upset Russia, but against Argentina they were doomed; early in the second half Maradona scored twice, the second goal another explosive solo burst that left four men for dead. After that, it might have been five; when another coruscating run ended with the ball sliding narrowly wide of the post, the Belgian keeper just stood and stared for an age, replaying what he'd seen in his disbelieving mind; then he smiled and went to pick up the ball, knowing he'd played on the same pitch as a genius.

In an excellent final, the Germans were tougher; outplayed in every department, they were 2-0 down early in the second half and yet still, somehow, they pulled it back to 2-2 with nine minutes to go. But three minutes after that, Maradona settled it; a deft sweet pass sliced the Germans wide open, and Jorge Burruchaga ran through gladly to take the winner.

Argentina were champions again and this time, though the Hand of God may have helped, there was no denying they were worth it. The Germans, by contrast, had battled to the final on little more than obdurate grit, as better teams fell by the roadside—and four years later, it would be very much the other way around.

Why America?

The 1986 World Cup wasn't originally awarded to Mexico; to start with, Colombia had it, an idea whose deep craziness fast became apparent. When they withdrew, Mexico took over after some unseemly lobbying, and the Europeans weren't pleased. They hadn't fancied going to Mexico sixteen years earlier—the heat and the altitude were bad enough, but the time shift meant Euro-TV wanted early afternoon kickoffs, a time when sane folk barely walked down the street, never mind playing soccer. Just in a training session, English players lost five to eight pounds a man.

But Mexico got it, and the U.S.A. didn't. The floundering North American Soccer League had figured collaring the World Cup might save them, and a bid was written in the NASL's offices; when it failed the NASL folded, and the idea ended where most people thought it belonged, in the bin. So how come, eight years later, the U.S.A. got it anyhow? The reasons are threefold, and simple: because you asked, because FIFA wants your money, and because Adidas does too.

There has, in fact, been soccer in America for as long as the game has been organized anywhere. Immigrant communities brought the sport with them as they poured in through the end of last century, and the American Football Association was founded in 1884 in Newark, New Jersey. Renamed the USFA, it joined FIFA in 1913 and on August 20, 1916, the U.S.A. played its first recognized international in Sweden, winning 3-2 before a crowd of 17,000.

The twenties saw the heyday of the American Soccer League; by 1924, twelve East Coast teams were playing a forty-four game schedule from September through May. Big games, like those between the Fall River Marksmen and the New Bedford Whalers, drew crowds over 10,000; Americans played alongside pros signed from all over Europe, and the league was a definite contributor to the international game. When visiting teams toured, attendances soared; in 1926, the all-Jewish Austrian champions Hakoah of Vienna played a New York team and 46,000 came, a record that stood for fifty years, until Pele arrived. And as we've seen, American players from the ASL made the semifinals of the first World Cup.

It didn't last, for two reasons. First, the game never really broke out from its ethnic bases; America had new games unique to its own culture, and becoming an American meant learning to play baseball as much as it meant learning to speak English. Soccer, by contrast, was an import; if you were Scottish, Irish, Hungarian, Croatian or whatever, you tended to play with your own kind, and the game was a Sunday reminder of your past roots, while your new future was on the mound and at the plate, or padding up for the gridiron.

Second, the game's owners fell into a bout of fractious infighting, with clubs suspended from the ASL forming "outlaw" leagues at exactly the wrong time—the time of the Wall Street crash. So the money dried up, the ASL folded in 1932, and pro soccer in North America died with it.

In the years that followed, a bewildering motley of indoor and outdoor quasi leagues struggled in and out of existence in a fog of mutating acronyms; the diehards played on in college, or vaguely semi-pro, but the stands were bare. When you beat England in 1950, the news went unnoticed; when 107,765 watched Scotland beat you 6-0 in Glasgow two years later, the biggest crowd an American national team has ever played before, I doubt anyone noticed then either.

Still the diehards struggled on. In 1967, the fourth attempt to found a pro league took place when two existing leagues merged to form the NASL. Seven years later, the Chicago Sting became the league's eighteenth team; the next year, 1975, the Cosmos bought Pele for $4.5 million, attendances skyrocketed, and the world caught its breath. Was this it?

In fact, the Pele deal showed everything that was wrong with the NASL. Short-term, it pulled the crowd—but long-term, spending bags of loot on superannuated foreigners while neglecting to develop American players at the grassroots resulted in a top-heavy monster. You had a Manchester United, and no Wrexhams to feed it; the pyramid was upside down, and at the first change in the wind of fashion, the first whiff of recession, it crumbled.

When FIFA picked Mexico to replace Colombia in 1983, the last hope went out of the window; in 1985, the NASL folded. In its wake, another melee of bits-and-pieces leagues swirled around once more, and the rest of the world shrugged. In the land of the hoop and the home run, it seemed soccer was a ball that would never get rolling. So when, on July 4, 1988, the 1994 World Cup was awarded to America at FIFA's congress in Zurich, the rest of the world turned round and said, You *what?*

As I say, you asked; only Brazil and Morocco asked too, and it wasn't a contest. The idea had evolved that the tournament should swap between Old World and New, so after Italia '90 it was the New World's turn—but, struggling toward democracy under intolerable debts, the New World couldn't handle Havelange's gargantua. With stadia crumbling as fast as the cruzeiro was collapsing, Brazil's bidders quietly admitted that their bid was derisory, made only to keep face with the fans back home; of nineteen votes on FIFA's executive, they got two. As for Morocco, it was a political bid; seven votes assured

African pride but, as it was said, the World Cup isn't a development program. So ten votes and the tournament went to the U.S.A., and the rest of us had a derision attack.

But the way *FIFA* see it, their baby's the only thing as big as the Olympics—so if you could all be got to watch it, your TV would have to start bidding the kind of lunatic strings of zeroes NBC pays to screen the five rings. (For Atlanta '96, $450 million.) I think, myself, it's a cockamamie dream; by the time Americans at large get soccermania, if they ever do, the fragmentation of the broadcast universe, along with economic reality, will have put paid to that kind of megadeal for good.

But FIFA aren't dumb; there's a market to be cracked in America in many more ways than selling World Cup TV rights. The NASL may have gone, but it left a legacy—and FIFA know how many millions of American kids play soccer now, they know how only basketball is a bigger participant youth sport, they know how more colleges have soccer programs than American football programs, they know how your women's game is the strongest in the world . . .

You already take part in all FIFA's global competitions; from Under-17 on up, American sides have qualified for every world championship bar one since Italia '90, and only Italy can say the same. So they're bringing you the World Cup so you'll sit up and pay attention; so you'll go pro, basically, pay money to watch week in and week out, and have your media cover you doing so. They think, in short, it's high time you turned a pastime into a business.

And close behind FIFA come Adidas; the more people who play and watch, the more who buy kit and accessories. No company is tighter with the game's rulers worldwide than Adidas—fifteen of the twenty-four teams in Italy wore Adidas gear—but compared to the likes of Nike, for the moment their market share in the biggest market of all is puny. So here they come, riding in on the back of the World Cup to try and change that—riding in with their own creation ISL at the sponsorship wheel, hoping next time you buy boots, those boots will have three stripes on them; hoping next time you buy shorts, shirts, and tracksuits, they'll all sport the trefoil motif. And here we thought it was entertainment.

When the United States Soccer Federation took on the World Cup, they said a pro league would be up and running before the kickfest arrived. The promise was smoke; this and other omens were not auspicious. The president of the USSF was a building contractor named Werner Fricker; he had around him people who were anathema to FIFA, marketing deals welled up and imploded like bubbles in mud, progress was cumbrous on matters like venue selection, and rumor began to float that the Yanks couldn't hack it. No one would show up, no one would watch, no one would even screen it, and FIFA would lose their shirt. So the tournament, it was whispered, would go to Argentina, or to Germany—and if the first idea was implausible, the second might well have been a threat.

In 1990, Fricker was ousted with FIFA's connivance by a lawyer from L.A. named Alan Rothenberg. Rothenberg organized the soccer at the 1984 Olympics, which sold out from the quarter-finals onward, drawing the biggest crowds of the games—and USA '94 got on the rails again.

When I first met Rothenberg in August 1992, I found him hard-edged and forthright. Proposing three points for a win in the opening groups he said, with healthily impolitic bluntness, "You're not going to see any more Argentina crap then. They're going to have to go out and score some goals."

The English columnist Paul Gardner had written in the weekly *Soccer America* that the organizers weren't "soccer people"; that "Rothenberg and his cronies have more in common with a meeting of the California Bar Association than anything to do with soccer."

Rothenberg bristled. "Our job is to put on a great event. We don't have to be soccer purists to do that. And without denigrating soccer people, the fact is there have been so-called soccer people who've spent almost eighty years promoting soccer here, and they've fallen on their ear. But then, how do you define a soccer person? Gardner says only if your pores bleed soccer balls are you a soccer person—well, I never played the game. But I was the lawyer and general manager of a team, and I ran the Olympic tournament. I think I know a bit of something about soccer."

As to bringing the World Cup to America, he switched into hype overdrive: "This will be the greatest World Cup ever." But that's his job—and after a week in L.A., I was converted from sceptic to enthusiast. That's partly because it's obvious, no matter what corporate machinations go on behind the scenes, that for a fan USA '94 will be fun—and it's partly because, between live-wire Rothenberg and the slumbrous smuggies at the English FA, I'd take Rothenberg any day.

But, I said, if his tournament was to succeed, it would certainly help if the U.S.A. did well. So he smiled and said, "I'm a businessman. I'd like to see the big-drawing teams do well—and it would be improper for me to support the U.S.A."

Italy 1990

For the first time in forty years, the U.S.A. qualified out of CONCACAF for the World Cup finals. They were aided by the suspension of Mexico, the strongest team in the region; the Mexicans fielded over-age players in a youth tournament, and had a two-year ban in all competition slapped down as a result. The punishment seemed sufficiently harsh to raise eyebrows here and there, but the return of the Americans to the top table in 1990 was something of a marketing necessity for FIFA, given the gamble they'd taken over '94. Even so, the U.S.A. struggled to make it, scraping draws against the likes of Guatemala and El Salvador, and it came down to the wire.

On November 19, 1989, they flew to Trinidad and Tobago for the 312th and last qualifying match of Italia '90. The hosts needed only a draw; for the Americans, it was win or bust. Win they did, 1-0, with a bizarre 35-yard looper of a shot from Californian midfielder Paul Caligiuri; a shot the USSF publicity types are pleased to call "the shot heard around the world." But while I'd not wish to seem rude, the truth is that, around the world, we weren't listening.

Still, there you were—drawn to play Italy, Austria, and Czechoslovakia in Florence and Rome. A few of your players had a little experience round the lower divisions in Europe—but with no league to play in at home the rest weren't far out of college, the squad had the lowest average age of any in the tournament, and the coach Bob Gansler had never been to a World Cup. Against a big, physical Czech side in Florence, it showed; they beat you 5-1, and an American journalist said it was like watching a train wreck.

The joking began. Against Italy in Rome, we said they should move the match from the Olimpico to the Colosseum; Italy had looked ravishingly good against Austria, and if they didn't get double figures we'd be amazed. When I watched you walk out under the screaming, flare-lit, smoke-laden stands I feared for you; lined up for the anthems, it looked like you'd all throw up any minute—and after eleven minutes, Italy went a goal ahead.

Seventy-nine minutes later the score was still 1-0. Outplayed and outskilled, the U.S.A. nonetheless ran their hearts out, strove and tussled and defended like Spartans, and along the way even managed to attack a bit; it wasn't always pretty but it was brave, and with a different roll of the ball it might have ended 1-1. The Italians were mightily embarrassed; the Americans were quietly proud. Striker Peter Vermes said, "We've no experience to draw on, it's difficult for us—we're not involved in this, ever. Sometimes we're taken aback in awe of it; but tonight people will respect what we did."

In Italy and elsewhere, we did; in America, few noticed. Back in Florence you lost an ill-tempered fracas 2-1 to Austria, and went home—but for those who paid attention in the Olimpico, you were evidently not as bad as we'd thought. Not good, not yet—but not bad either.

If it was good you wanted, you went to the San Siro in Milan. World Cup openers tend to be drab—teams tense after waiting through bloated ceremonial TV spectacles freeze and scuffle to 0-0 after 0-0—but nobody told Cameroon. They came out cautious enough, playing 5-4-1, then after twenty minutes they looked at this Argentina lot, these world champions, this bitching, gesticulating little Maradona bloke, and said to themselves, Hey. We can beat these. Their attacks became more bold, Argentina looked more fraught—and then, after a little over an hour, Cameroon had a man sent off. It was harsh, but 74,000 were behind them, and three minutes later they scored anyhow; the most amazing first goal of a World Cup ever, watched by two in five of all the people on earth—and I'll bet every one of them outside Argentina was grinning his socks off.

Then they had another man expelled, this time rightly; Cameroon played high-octane football but they didn't mind thumping you either, and when an enormous defender named Massing tried to separate Claudio Caniggia at the waist, it was a red card, no doubt about it. So, down to nine men with a thin one-goal lead, what did they do? They went on attacking . . . it was wonderful, it ended 1-0, and when it was over an African radio commentator in a flowing robe of many colors came dancing to the British press crying, "We have avenged the Hand of God!"

But the Hand of God wasn't done with yet. Against Russia in Naples, an early flurry of Russian attacks produced a shot surely goalbound—and Maradona, standing on the goal line, stuck a hand out to stop it. So he'd scored with his hand, now he'd saved with it, and again the referee was looking the other way. It should have been a penalty, Russia should have gone ahead, and maybe then an unimpressive Argentina might have cracked and gone home. Instead they stayed and won, and it was Russia who were out, coldly furious. "Is Maradona untouchable," asked their manager, "that he can do what he likes?"

It seemed so. But at twenty-nine, kicked to bits, damaged so badly he was virtually playing on one leg, pumped to the gills with cortisone down the years, short, fat, mad, he was also seethingly determined not to lose his World Cup. You didn't want to watch, but it did have a horrid fascination.

Beckenbauer's Germans opened with unmistakable purpose. With Matthaus magisterial in midfield and Jurgen Klinsmann and Rudi Voller sharp as razors up front, they stuck four past Yugoslavia, five past the United Arab Emirates, and looked the best team in it by a mile. Italy were dazzling, but they had trouble finding the net; Brazil were trying to play like Europeans again, and goals eluded them too. Both did enough to win all their group games—but, as ever, much of the entertainment in the first phase came from unexpected quarters.

The first side to make the Round of 16 were Cameroon; with Argentina beaten they took on Romania, a skilled and pacy outfit marshaled in midfield by Gheorgi Hagi, "the Maradona of the Carpathians," and they beat them 2-1. Both their goals were scored by thirty-nine-year-old "supersub" Roger Milla, a national hero who'd played in Spain '82; he'd been pleaded out of retirement by everyone in Cameroon from the president on down. So now he entered the game late, won it, and went after each goal to do a jinking, slinky-waisted little shimmy of a dance with the corner flag, one arm up, one finger pointing in sexy good cheer to the sky. And we'd be seeing more of that.

Colombia were even more flamboyant, with hairstyles from outer space and a keeper from another dimension altogether. René Higuita said he was the world's first "sweeper-keeper," by which he appeared to mean that hanging around in goal was dull, and that he'd rather come out and join in playing with his defenders. It seemed insanely risky; it didn't stop them pinching a draw off the Germans.

But the best game in the openers was a storming 3-1 win by Belgium over Uruguay—while the most surprising entrant in the next round was tiny Costa Rica. First they took on Scotland—and the quadrennial ritual of Scottish hopes ignominiously shattered was duly completed after fifty minutes, when one Juan Cayasso scored. As the headline put it, SCOTLAND PLUNGED INTO CAYASSO. Costa Rica then beat Sweden and on they went, their success ascribed to the crafty management of the same man who took Mexico to the quarter-finals in '86, Bora Milutinovic. He'd had Costa Rica for ninety days, and he'd worked a miracle.

In the Round of 16 Yugoslavia put out Spain, and Italy dealt comfortably with Uruguay; an unknown little Sicilian named Salvatore "Toto" Schillaci, responding to the elegant promptings of midfielder Roberto Baggio, scored his third goal of the tournament.

In Genoa, Ireland's relentless long ball had the Romanians flummoxed (in their opening group when they played Egypt, it was said the Egyptians would have seen nothing like this raining down on their heads since the plague of frogs). So now the Irish lumbered to a 0-0 draw and on to penalties, and won through to the quarter-finals 5-4. As for Costa Rica, the Czechs were too much for them; a big lunk named Skuhravy outjumped them every time, and they lost 4-1. But their achievement was notable all the same—as Costa Rica's president observed, his country had been "driven crazy with satisfaction"—and one who noted it was Alan Rothenberg. Nine months later, the USSF appointed Bora Milutinovic coach of the U.S.A. national team.

In Milan, meanwhile, the Germans and the Dutch played a ferocious, thrilling game that boiled over when Rijkaard was sent off for spitting in Voller's face; Voller went off with him for retaliating. With ten men apiece, the extra space saw both sides attacking from all angles—but the Germans had the better of it, and ran out 2-1 winners.

In a surreal game in Naples, Cameroon also beat Colombia 2-1. It was a game in which no one did anything for 105 minutes, the teams idling around like it was a Sunday kickabout—then, from kickoff in the second period of extra time,

Roger Milla pounced forward, beat one man, hurdled another tackle, thwacked it in, and went dancing to the corner flag. A few moments later the lunatic Higuita came to join his back line; again Milla pounced, dispossessed him, and raced off to pop the ball in the empty net. It was, Higuita bravely admitted, "a mistake as big as a house," and though Colombia got one back in a surging finale it wasn't enough, and an African side were in the last eight for the first time in history.

In Turin, Brazil couldn't do to Argentina what Cameroon had done. For eighty minutes they won corner after corner, fired shot after shot, were immeasurably superior—and Argentina clung on bloody nails. Then Maradona stirred; from somewhere in his bruised bones he found his old glory. He took the ball in the center circle, meandered a yard or two, then jinked, turned, and was gone. He left the first man, rode the second tackle, and now Brazil panicked; three defenders fanned out in a line trying to cover him, and they left Caniggia free. When Maradona slipped a pass to him inch-perfect between the feet of the second and third defenders, the first by then already had a hand on Maradona's shoulder, pressing him to the earth, so the pass was made even as his body was flattened horizontal—but made it was, and Caniggia's finish was exact. For the last few minutes Maradona remembered himself then, and was all too briefly a joy to watch—unless you were Brazilian. Men and women in the gold and green wept all round the stadium, as their dream died for the fifth time since 1970—and Argentina advanced.

England did too. The games in their group, with Holland, Ireland, and Egypt, had been awful; five out of six were drawn, most of them numbingly. Quarantined on the island of Sardinia, their sullen fans were encircled by hordes of armed police who on one occasion went berserk, gassing and beating a largely innocent crowd on their way to the stadium—while their team, crashing about brainlessly with the Irish, struggling glumly past Egypt, seemed the drunk at the party, the boor no one wished to deal with. Except . . . against the Dutch, Bobby Robson played a sweeper.

For the English, going to a sweeper from 4-4-2 was the soccer equivalent of abolishing the monarchy, and the liberation felt by Chris Waddle in particular was exhilarating. Instead of tracking back down the wing all the time to help out his full back, suddenly he was free to roam—and against Belgium in Bologna, he roamed to devastating effect. But so did Enzo Scifo; the Belgians were fast and free too, and a white-knuckle game coursed, poised and even, from end to end for two hours. Shots bounced off the woodwork, chances shaved wide of either goal, both keepers were busy until it seemed, with only one minute of extra time remaining, that it must end 0-0 and go to penalties. Then Gascoigne flighted a perfect free kick into the Belgian area, Platt swiveled as it dropped over his head to volley home with punishing precision, and England were through with bare seconds to spare.

Looking round the field, there seemed to be only two teams in it. The potent, unfaltering Germans, who beat the Czechs in the quarter-finals with a lot more to spare than Matthaus's one goal suggested, were rolling toward the cup with the smooth weight and strength of a top-line Mercedes—while the rapid and clinical Italians, for whom Schillaci ended a brave Irish challenge in Rome, were a Ferrari of a side, the only team with an engine that might match them.

In Naples, meanwhile, Cameroon pissed gleefully in England's gas tank; in a stirring match, after sixty-five minutes they were 2-1 ahead. But inexperience undid them; they were too prone to knock people about in the wrong places, and now twice they bundled Lineker to the turf in their penalty area. Twice he stood up, brushed himself down, and slotted home the spot kicks; 3-2 England.

As for Argentina, what kind of car they were driving nobody knew. They ground past Yugoslavia in a shoot-out after a horrible 0-0 tie, and Maradona by now was plainly bonkers. Facing Italy in the semis in his adopted hometown Naples, he made the wildly foolish error of asking the Neapolitans to support his side instead of Italy. His brother squared up against the police after being stopped in Maradona's sports car; Maradona started raving about conspiracy.

Come the game, Schillaci scored his fifth of the tournament—but Argentina ground their teeth, started battling and playing too, got an equalizer, dragged it out again to penalties, and clung once more to their screaming nerve ends to win the shoot-out 4-3. To universal astonishment, the Italians were out; as the host nation fell stunned and silent, Argentina rumbled on.

England went out against the Germans in the other semi as fired up as it's possible to be; they knew, should they win, that revenge over the Hand of God was theirs for the taking in the final. What followed was the best game I've seen in my life, one of the World Cup's all-time finest, clean, fast, impassioned, unforgiving, an honor to both countries. In the opening period the Germans were rocked on their heels by the ferocity of the English onslaught; gradually they hauled their way back in until, early in the second half, they took the lead.

Now it could have gone either way; the game pulsed from goal to goal, bold and unceasing, and the crowd in the Stadium of the Alps filled that glamorous bowl of light with a tumult of desire, a great roaring of song, England's much-maligned fans who'd been pushed and shoved and truncheoned from one end of Italy to the other for four weeks now seizing their moment of glory as, with ten minutes left, a long cross flew to the edge of the German area, and Lineker latched onto it like a wolf. Harried and bumped he shot past two men, he scored, the game was back from the brink at 1-1, and the noise was unending.

> *Walk on, walk on*
> *With hope in your heart*
> *And you'll never walk alone*
> *You'll never walk alone*

I cry every time I have to write about it. I followed that team for a year; I saw them go further than anyone thought possible, and play better football than anyone dared to dream of. Extra time powered magnificently by, both sides hit the post, it ended a wholly appropriate 1-1, applause rang out in awed admiration of both teams—and for a fan, those two hours were of an intensity for which the only comparable experience is to see the birth of your child. That is how important this game is to us. We watch a great game at the World Cup with our bodies and souls taken over by something so much greater than we can ever be, filled with pride and passion, forgetting to breathe, thunderstruck.

The Germans won the shoot-out, and I sat weeping in my seat—and I pray that in my life, just once, I'll be at a game that good again. It was the real final; the foul charade in Rome afterward, in which Argentina were finally defeated by the Germans, with justice, was neither here nor there.

When it was over, while the great Lothar Matthaus lifted

the World Cup high for Germany, Diego Maradona sobbed uncontrollably, and refused to shake João Havelange's hand. Nine months later he tested positive for cocaine.

The World Cup Record

	winner	runner-up	3rd	4th
1930	Uruguay	Argentina	(U.S.A./Yugoslavia)	
1934	Italy	Czechoslovakia	Germany	Austria
1938	Italy	Hungary	Brazil	Sweden
1950	Uruguay	Brazil	Sweden	Spain
1954	W. Germany	Hungary	Austria	Uruguay
1958	Brazil	Sweden	France	W. Germany
1962	Brazil	Czechoslovakia	Chile	Yugoslavia
1966	England	W. Germany	Portugal	U.S.S.R.
1970	Brazil	Italy	W. Germany	Uruguay
1974	W. Germany	Holland	Poland	Brazil
1978	Argentina	Holland	Brazil	Italy
1982	Italy	W. Germany	Poland	France
1986	Argentina	W. Germany	France	Belgium
1990	W. Germany	Argentina	Italy	England

19

Cold Blow Lane

When I told Alan I was going to watch Millwall play Luton at the Den in Cold Blow Lane, he grinned. He said maybe I should shave my head. Maybe I should get the word DEATH tattooed on my front teeth. Millwall's anthem:

No one likes us
We don't care

Millwall Football Club's ground is in a shattered corner of southeast London by the wreckage of Rotherhithe Docks, a place all dank brick tunnels and old bomb sites. People on Brian Flynn's coaching staff recalled going there in their playing days, and said it was the most intimidating environment in English football.

To this place, a young American goalkeeper had come to make his living. Kasey Keller was twenty-three, six-one, one hundred ninety-five pounds, and he grew up with forty thousand chickens on an egg farm in Olympia, Washington; now he drove a silver Alfa Romeo in which, after a year and a bit, he'd more or less figured out where he was in south London. The first four months he was in a hotel; now he had an apartment with his fiancée, Kristin. Blandly convinced of the superiority of all things American, they were amiably uncertain as to whether to be more stunned by the price of things in London, or the shoddiness of them. But the cultural gulf (lousy opening hours, indifferent supermarkets, impenetrable road systems) was easily traversed thanks to one salient fact: Keller had made the grade in pro soccer.

He started playing when he was six or seven. As he grew up he played on district, state, regional, and finally national teams; at the World Youth Cup in Saudi in '89, where the U.S.A. made the semifinals, he was named Second Most Valuable Player of the tournament. The next year he was in Italy with the senior squad, understudy to number one pick Tony Meola, and in any other country he'd have been signed with a club for years by then; in America, he could only go back to school.

He got a full-ride scholarship to the University of Portland; his coach there was Clive Charles, who'd played at West Ham, and Charles worked his contacts in London. As a student under NCAA regulations, pro clubs theoretically couldn't approach him; Keller says he didn't know where Charles had fixed for him to try out until three days before he got on the plane on December 4, 1991. But he was advised he'd have a better chance of a first-team place with a First Division side like Millwall than he would in the Premier League, and that was important for more than just pride. It was important because no place, most likely, meant no work permit.

The permit came through two months later. He got his debut with the first team in the last game of that season, May 1992—then the new season began the next August, and he was back in the reserves. The first game Millwall lost 3-1, the second they drew 2-2, the third game Keller started, and he's been first pick ever since. So what was it like?

"It's nice," he said, "it's definitely nice. In the States you have these wannabe coaches, wannabe soccer experts, who think England's all kick and rush, and they want to play fifty-five passes and not go anywhere, and they have no clue. Even in the long ball game here, there's five times as much skill as anything's that's played in the States."

So I asked what he was learning and he said, "Everything. I remember my first reserve game against Arsenal, and the *pace* of it—it was a tremendous shock. The way the players' first touch didn't let them down, the way the majority of the shots were at least near the goal—I was afraid if I looked away for one second the ball was going in the net. It was like, if you're used to driving thirty miles an hour and suddenly everyone's going sixty, you look around and think, things are passing me by here."

And now?

"Now, I feel extremely comfortable. But it's still an education every time I step out on the field, a tremendous education. I was successful in my first ten games, but I'd still love to play them again on what I've learned now."

I asked how he thought he'd improved and he said, "Decision-making is the key to goalkeeping. Of course, if you can stop a ball in the top corner, that helps—but decision-making is the big factor. And when things were coming as fast as they do, I seemed not to make proper decisions at first. I was lucky—I've got good reflexes, I'm a shot-stopping keeper—so I was able to say, if there was any question in my mind, no, I'm not coming for that ball, and then stop the shot. But I think what's happening now is, I'm able to intercept things better, and not have to make the save any more; I'm making decisions earlier. Goalkeeping's a game of mistakes, and I'm still making them—but it's improving."

Mark Morris at Wrexham said he'd seen a couple of American keepers passing through—and, he said, they were leaping all the time, they were always *leaping* . . .

Keller smiled and said, "There are a lot of those. The coaching in the U.S. is very agility-oriented. But technique is the answer to everything in goalkeeping, so at home it's been frustrating. I've had coaches who've had me diving through hoops, flipping over hurdles—and I'm standing there saying, Well, at some time we should probably bring a ball into this. It's great that I can jump over that house—too bad the ball went through my hands."

England's an education in more than technique. He said, "I've been beat up more in the forty games I've played this season than in two hundred in the States. No question. It's a whole different ball game." And he said, obviously, for the money, he'd prefer to play in Italy—but for the game, he preferred it in England, because "people aren't just passing it around and going nowhere here. The ball's in and around the box more than in any other country. So this is where I need to be to learn."

The U.S.A. has a squad of players training at Mission Viejo near San Diego under Bora Milutinovic; they play a more-or-less random round of international friendlies against whoever they can lay their hands on, as that's the only way to get experience in the absence of a league. It's possible, however, that only two or three members of that squad will make the starting lineup at USA '94—because most of the best Americans now make their living abroad. So Milutinovic won't see the bulk of his best team until four weeks, or less, before the tournament begins:

	Age	Position	Club	Country
Thomas Dooley	31	Defender	Kaiserslautern	Germany
John Harkes	26	Midfield	Derby County	England
Frank Klopas	26	Forward	AEK Athens	Greece
Hugo Perez	29	Midfield	Ittihad	Saudi
Tab Ramos	26	Midfield	Real Betis	Spain
Ernie Stewart	23	Forward	Willem II	Holland
Roy Wegerle	28	Forward	Coventry City	England
Peter Woodring	24	Midfield	SV Hamburg	Germany
Eric Weynalda	23	Forward	FC Saarbrucken	Germany

I asked Keller whom he'd advise the home crowd to look out for, and the first he mentioned was Dooley. Dooley's the son of a GI-German marriage who grew up in Germany, and in 1993 he didn't speak too much English—but as captain of a Bundesliga championship-winning side, "He's definitely seen it all, more than any of the others." As for Harkes, "He's a very good utility player, he works tremendously hard, he battles like hell—he's a good fighter, definitely. He's something every team needs."

But the players to watch above all were Wegerle and Ramos. "The skill factor with those two is tremendous. They're both able to beat any player they come up against, they both have great shots; they're definitely our most explosive players. Other people like John or myself, Tom Dooley, if we play well, then we do—but those are the two to look for."

What does soccer need in America if it's ever to take off, and let these players come home?

"Higher quality. My father was a baseball player, got drafted by the Yankees, and he knew nothing about soccer, he still hardly knows anything about it. So I sent him a tape of when we played Newcastle at St. James's Park this year, and he was amazed."

I asked what had happened in that game, and Keller

grinned. "I got Man of the Match . . . it was 1-1. But apart from me being there, he just said it was a very enjoyable game to watch, better than any game he's seen me play in the States—and it takes that level to pull people in. We need better players, in better games, on better fields."

But if you can't make a living at it, the best will always go abroad, and you'll never get that.

"No. The opportunities aren't there. Basically, there's the national team, or you're semi-pro. Here, there are so many options. You can have a nightmare with one team, go on loan somewhere else, get your bearings back and start over. But at home, if you have a nightmare with the national team, you're at the top level—and there's no place to drop. That's why at Italia '90 we had the youngest team—because when you're twenty-eight and maybe you've had a rough spell, as every player does, then you're dropped. And then the coach has to bring someone in out of college, because he's the only one who's been playing. And the one who's been dropped, he's twenty-eight—he's thinking about his family, he can't make a living, so what do you do?"

The USSF promised FIFA a pro league before USA '94; now they say they'll definitely be one afterward—but in a saturated sports market they know they have one hell of a task. One World Cup organizer told me that if it didn't come about then no matter how successful the tournament itself, overall they'd have to say that they'd failed—that if they didn't get a league now, he'd not see it in his lifetime.

Keller said, "I wouldn't say that. People have tried to pull that make-or-break crap, but I don't think so." And he certainly thought the tournament would help. He said, "The World Cup will break all attendance records that any World Cup has ever seen. People ask me, Why? Will people go out and watch other teams than the U.S.? And I laugh—they'll probably watch those teams more than the U.S. They're not stupid; they know we're not the great soccer nation. But look, at US Cup '92, Italy–Ireland got 44,000 people. You think they'd get that at Wembley? No way in hell. And that's what's so nice about the U.S.—if they think it'll be enjoyable, the people will come."

So how will the Americans do?

"I think we'll make the second round."

After what happened in Italy?

"Gansler did a very good job with the youth team in Saudi.

But I don't think either he, the coaching staff, the federation—
I don't think anybody knew the magnitude of the jump from
there to the World Cup. And they wanted to keep it American
only, and that was a mistake; they needed to get someone in
who knew what was going on. Instead, the first game, they
just got it wrong. They said we were going to overpower
Czechoslovakia physically—so we came walking down the tunnel to do some warm-ups and we looked at Skuhravy and we
thought, This guy's a *monster*. So, *oops*, that scouting report's
a little wrong . . . and that was the naivete. We came out
thinking we were going to attack, do this, do that—whereas
every other team in the World Cup, even Germany, they'll hold
back a little and assess the opponent first, right?"

But what was it like as an experience?

"Oh, tremendous. Even not playing, I learned what the level
was. When you step into a stadium and you've got 80,000
people and they don't care about anything in life besides what
their country's doing in there, and the whole country's glued
to that game . . . it's so intense. How do I explain it? It's like
a father sees the birth of his first child, it's of that magnitude,
it's unbelievable. You look in the past, when Uruguay beat
Brazil in the Maracana to win in 1950—people were jumping
off the stadium killing themselves." He shook his head. "It's
unbelievable."

The Olimpico in Rome was a howling cauldron, dense with
the smoke of the flares drifting through an ear-splitting ca-
cophony of whistles and hooters and chanting. I said, they
can never have seen anything like it in their lives.

"Oh no. Being in stadiums with big numbers is something
you're used to in the States. But that . . . it was totally different. And they were a friendly crowd—nicer than a lot of countries I've been to. Maybe"—he smiled—"because we were
supposed to get killed in there."

Yet they only lost 1-0—and with four more years' experience
since then, you might find that your team could surprise us
all. Two summers after Italia '90, Portugal, Ireland, and Italy
came to play in US Cup '92, a round-robin tournament set up
to promote the game in America, and to serve as a dry run for
the big one. Keller suggested that the other sides might not
have taken it too seriously; he said the Irish had won their
first USA '94 qualifier a few days beforehand, so they'd been
in the bar and on the golf course ever since. And there may be
something to that—but nobody likes to lose, do they?

The tournament's six games in Boston, Washington, and Chicago drew average crowds over 30,000. The U.S.A. beat Ireland 3-1, Portugal 1-0, and drew 1-1 with Italy to win the thing. An omen?

Experience: "At home you might play one hard game and when it's over it's like, OK, now I get to hang out for a couple of weeks. But here, you have a great game, that's cool, you go home, have some dinner—then it's like, oh shit, three days later I got another. And that last game's over. Maybe on the way to the stadium somebody'll say, Hey, you had a good game the other day. Then it's like, But don't you let one in today. Or we're going to blow up your house."

Millwall aren't a big club; they average maybe 9,000 at the gate. But they're intense . . . the game against Luton, said Keller, would be difficult. Luton had the most draws in the division at this point—and at their place, "They took it to us. I got the shit beat out of me." He was, he said, off anti-inflammatories for the first time in months.

I watched with Kristin, and the other players' wives. The Den's a cramped, crumbly little place; they're moving next season from Cold Blow Lane to a 25,000 all-seater in Senegal Fields down the road, and it was easy to see why—the Racecourse is better than this place. And maybe it was sitting with the wives—but with due respect to Millwall's fierce reputation, compared to standing in the Kop, this was a more genteel experience altogether.

But Millwall's reputation is worse these days than the reality. Kristin was mystified to watch the fans jumping the barriers at Southend to go after the police one time—she inquired mildly, "Isn't that an offence?"—but generally they don't riot with the zest they were once famed for. And on the park, meanwhile, they play football—well enough, indeed, that they were in contention for a spot in the Premier.

They won 1-0. They're an attractive side, and they have a good keeper—quick off his line, strong in the air, with a hefty long kick on him—but in this game he didn't have a great deal to do. Luton had four corners, and he came for them decisively; he made four saves, one of them a fine flying lunge to tip a screamer round the post. So it wasn't a big contest—but still Kristin said, "I just cannot imagine how any American can find American football more entertaining than this." She said, "Just look at the *pace* of it."

She passed round a pack of Starbursts, treats from home, on a Wednesday evening in a derelict corner of South London, while her man made his living jogging on his line under the glare of the lights, and the crowd in Cold Blow Lane sang

> *There's only one Kasey Keller*
> *Only one Kasey Keeeeehhh—ehl—ler*

20

Away Day

April 27, 1993
Northampton Town v. Wrexham

Two games to go, two points required. So two draws would do it—but a win would be sweeter. . . . Northampton's one hundred thirty miles southeast toward London, a two-hour trudge down the Midlands motorways through the dingy sprawl of Birmingham. I drove down there in a dull blare of burnt fog and heat haze, head empty, heart tight.

The town's got a one-way road system designed by Jackson Pollock, and a soccer team called the Cobblers who aren't any prettier; they're nineteenth in the table, scrapping for their lives. The woman at the counter in the tourist office said, "Please don't beat us. If we go down, they'll never let us back in again. Not with a ground like ours." It's only got three sides, see—the fourth side's the boundary of the county cricket pitch.

I got a room at the Fish Inn at 4:30. There were Wrexham fans at the bar already. One said, with ominous contentment, "Town's full of Wrexham." Three hours later the attendance at the game was 7,504—bigger by three thousand than Northampton's previous best this season, and two thirds of them down from North Wales. They could barely fit us in; at the tatty little burger cabin, if you wanted sugar in your coffee, they had two teaspoons for all those people. If you wanted Coke, it was warm.

We were packed onto half a terrace of crumbling concrete.

At the far end there was the only thing you could call a proper stand, where the Town fans were; it was a shabby antique. Above the dressing rooms on one side there was "the Meccano Stand," a ratty box held together with scaffolding; it seated three hundred. Then the fourth side was a line of two-foot-high hoardings with the cricket pitch beyond. And Northamptonshire, as it happens, has a good cricket side; their pavilion beyond the pitch was all gleaming and swanky, a silent taunt to the sorry plight of the town's lesser sport.

The Wrexham fans looked around with sympathetic astonishment. They know what it's like to be down at the bottom, but to be down at the bottom in *this* . . .

In the bright warm evening, shadows stretched long across the grass as the terrace filled. Morris, Connolly, Owen and Jones came out to warm up, smiling at the fans, and the fans cheered back for them. Then Watkin and Paskin came out and jogged up and down, breaking into short sprints. And it seems we always do this before a game—come out and kick about how we want. At the other end, Northampton were in a pack doing regimented exercises; most teams seem to be that way, and I think that's instructive. The way we warmed up, like the way we played, was free and relaxed, and that's why we were winners—with just two points required. . . .

The terrace was bubbling, boisterously good-humored. All the flags were out, waving over peoples' heads, tied round their necks, pinned to the railings around and behind us— the Welsh dragon, mostly, red on a white-and-green ground, with local identifiers sewn on—Chirk Reds, Red Army, Wrexham Robins.

Waaaaaaay—ay—uhls
Waaaaaaay—ay—uhls

Someone was throwing a huge inflatable blue whale about; an enormously obese youth in a joke plastic horror mask with mad scientist hair danced by the hoardings. The crowd sang out to him

You fat bastard
You fat bastard
You ate all the pies

Benno took the mask off him and jogged away to warm up in it. Then he came back and Pieman went in goal to save a shot—the goal was just a few feet in front of us—before the stewards hustled him back onto the terrace. Benno embraced other fans for their snapshots. Over by the Meccano Stand, Flynn made a presentation to retiring linesman Larry Watson; after ten years running the line this guy was offered Liverpool, Manchester United, or Arsenal for his last game and he said, No thanks—he came here instead, because the County Ground was the first place he did the job. That's football. And a local side of schoolboys walked round the pitch showing off the trophy they'd won and we gave them a warm hand, because that's football too. The atmosphere was happy and eager; when we sang

> *Shitty ground*
> *Shitty ground*
> *Shitty ground*

it wasn't malicious. But that'd change when the whistle blew. It'd get serious then—because we all know, chasms apart in quality or not, anyone can beat you on the day. When Northampton came to the Racecourse in October, they were the worst side we'd seen in the division—and they won 1-0.

When Wrexham run out in their away strip of white they get the best roar we can muster, and a great quick shower of homemade confetti from all over the terrace. The linesman checks the net in front of us, the players form up—and away at the far end they go thundering into us from the off; with three minutes gone they get three corners in a row. Morris comes for them, sure hands, high and brave among the bodies. You think, That's the way, calm it down . . . but they come again. It is, frankly, terrifying—and sure, I want peace on earth, contentment among nations, food, health, and liberty for all—but right now all I want is two points.

They take a free kick; Morris comes to claim it. So long as *he's* strong . . . the ball comes out, Cross collects, beats two men like they're simply not there, whips the cross over for Watkin

> *please please score*

but he falls in a heap with the defender. My gut's heavy, weighted with an indigestible bolus of desire and despair.

Cross comes again, flying, dancing, electric down the wing; then Owen comes, surging, steaming through the middle. You think, Yes, this is it, they've had their little flurry, now *do* the bastards . . .

A throw-in comes to Watkin, near post. He brings it down and lays it off for Lake, arriving late; Lake fires, and it flies a foot wide. You can hear every chest fill, pregnant with the scream, and every lungful sighing out in disappointment. My own chest feels constricted; there's so much emotion in there, there's no room left for oxygen.

Cross has his full back in ribbons; he streaks past him again, the guy left spinning and helpless. The ball comes in hard and low to the box, and Watkin's there. He fires instantly, close range; the keeper dives, he stops it, he drops it, and Benno's on him like a wolf. He crashes into the net with the ball—and then he's hanging there in the back of it with his fingers clenched through the string, his mouth as wide as it'll go in a great spasm of joy, a goal, a score, the round-ball orgasm. People are in the air all around me howling at the sky, and there are others spilling over the hoardings to seize Benno in ecstatic embrace through the netting, and others dancing in a frenzied trance on the pitch.

Among the older men around me the joy converts to rage. "Get off the pitch you BASTARD IDIOTS, we wanna go up not BALLS it up, we wanna win the bastard MATCH, you fucking lot STAY HERE, you fucking morons get back HERE."

When it's tidied up, a long cross sails way too close for comfort past Morris's top corner. Up this end, we've got a line of thirty police between us and the game now, and more of them just off to the sides. One lad gets taken away, arms behind his back, not doing what he's told and staying on the terrace. People mutter, "He wants to get himself thrown out, let him go. Idiot." They've brought a couple of police dogs too. One guy next to me mutters, "I really don't know what it's about. Let's win promotion first and *then* go on the pitch."

Morris collects high in the air again. When it comes out, Northampton's player-manager Phil Chard cracks a drive from twenty yards and it's only inches wide. Then another of them plunges in with a diving header; one-handed at full stretch, Morris tips it away. There are moans of panic all about me— and lots of people think Morris is the weakest link in the team. But he's playing tonight like if we're going up, then he's damned if he's having Flynn buy another keeper when we get there.

And 1-0 is the thinnest margin. The goal came in the thirteenth minute, but if anything the agony after it is worse. You're that much nearer the peak—but that only means when you look back below you, the fall if it should come will be all the more horrendous. The guy next to me's talking to himself, chewing his lip, a man in his forties: "Come on, keep it going. Ten years of watching *bloody crap.*"

Jones floats in a teasing cross to the top corner; their keeper takes it as Benno slides in beneath him.

"Keep it going. Take your time."

Benno wins a corner. Every time we come forward, they're flailing.

> *We're going up tonight*
> *We're going up tonight*

Morris makes another cracking save; then he's out for a clearance, hoofing the ball miles away onto the cricket pitch. They're still having a go, this lot—and I'm burning and frozen all at once here, numb, shaking, heart like a drum. There's an hour left to go on the end of this extraordinary nine months—and you really doubt whether you can take it.

Then it's their corner, our clearance, a long ball up and Watkin's chasing it, and their boss Phil Chard's on his shoulder in the area seeing red, seeing all his horrible season of nine months of defeat upon defeat in this shabby place staring him in the face—so he decks him. Penalty, no question, and Chard's blown his fuses. He kicks the ball in a blind fury at the referee and it smacks him in the leg. On the terrace we're leaping, taunting, it's impossible to be still. The ref books Chard; Benno puts the ball on the spot. The police appear, *whoosh*, in a long line down before us again. There's a guy among them I recognize, a Wrexham cop, hands up, palms out, pleading, *stay there, stay there*, as Benno pelts the ball past the diving keeper. 2-0. Then Benno's running to the fans, fists clenched, and the ref's frantically after him telling him not to do that, for Christ's sake don't do that—but he does, he can't not do it, it's in his blood, and he's booked for it. And mercifully, we do stay on the terrace this time—ringing bells, beeping horns, waving flags, standing on the crush barriers, swaying against the fading blue sky, singing our dumb delirious songs as Lake frees Watkin and Chard's in his face again like a mugger, cracked, twisted, desperate. He's close to throwing punches before his keeper pulls him away. The ref talks to him; more of that and he'll be off. When it restarts, Connolly wins the ball, frees Hardy, he's down the flank like a rocket, one look up, *ping*, and Watkin's right *there*. As he leaps he heads the ball, immaculate, sharp as a boxer's jab—and it rifles away just inches the wrong side of the post. And then it's halftime.

The interval was a party, hands in the air, kids on their fathers' shoulders clapping and grinning. The guy next to me says, "We've just got to hold on to it. When you think of the decline we've been in all these years, it'd be a marvelous occasion to go up here. But it's a cruel game. So we've just got to hold on to it."

And you should understand that away from the dementedly exuberant boys chanting over the hoardings at the smiling policemen, there are also so many older men here, some silver-haired, some balding, all silent—and their faces are filled with the strain of knowing they're forty-five minutes from a prize they probably thought they'd never see again in their lives. They have years and years of Saturdays behind them and now, at the end of all those years, there are forty-five minutes left before an away day to Northampton turns into a trip to heaven, an excursion to rainbow's end where the pot's filled full with a satisfaction so vast, so all-embracing as to be undefinable. And I'm standing there among them trying to throw my mind forward over those forty-five minutes, trying to see what's there—and the honest truth is I don't know. Promotion . . . *this has never happened to me before.*

So we wait in all the turbulent noise, the blue evening deepening round the cream shadow of sunset at the far end of the ground. The floodlights are burning splashes in the dusty sky; a brilliant crescent moon hangs high above them. We wait, and every one of us in our private heart is praying, while the jubilant boys prance.

Second half—and I don't like to run the other lot down but the truth is, it was embarrassing. Every move they made, our defenders were there before they'd made it—so they had next to no chances, while we had plenty. There were periods when they simply never had the ball; we'd be passing it around, short stuff, long stuff, back, forward, and then wide when the time was ripe—when all that futile running they'd been doing had pulled them way out of shape, and then Cross or Connolly (or whoever) would be free in so many acres of space, he could have written a thank-you note to the guy who gave him the ball before he did anything with it. So we stood behind Morris and we sang, and we sang.

> *The Lord's my shepherd, I'll not want*
> *He makes me down to lie*
> *In pastures green, He leadeth me*
> *The quiet waters by*

Now break that up so, the next time you sing it, each phrase has a great snaredrum roll of rhythmic clapping before the next phrase comes, every pair of hands coming together as one. And then there's the greatest hymn of them all:

> *Walk on, walk on*
> *With hope in your heart*
> *And you'll never walk alone*
> *You'll never walk alone*

In the crowd your soul soars; you float away into the night over the beautiful game on the brilliant green grass, high on a great cloud of football and song. Eleven men before you weave their never-ending patterns, the ball a white jewel flashing from foot to foot. There's simply no game like it.

Mark Taylor said afterward, "Make sure you put in there that Mark Morris played a blinder. He came for *everything*." And Pejic was a rock, Humes cool as ice; Jones and Hardy were quick as terriers, sharp as knives. Owen tackled like a lion, Lake seemed to be everywhere; Cross and Connolly were up and down, up and down, beating men when they had the ball, working back to get it when they didn't, while up the front Watkin and Benno ran all night, pulling the defence ragged. We were so much better than them—more skillful, more inventive, quicker of foot, quicker of mind. It was a display, a master class.

> *We're proud of you*
> *We're proud of you*
> *We're proud of you Wrexham*

Different sections of the crowd fell cheerfully out of sync with each other as they edged down the terrace toward the pitch beneath their flags—and the second the whistle came they were gone, spilling in an urgent mass across the field, dancing, cheering, shrieking, jumping, springing like lambs in inarticulate delight. The players vanished among them.

And me? I just stood there; I don't know what I felt. Numb, I think. Drained, certainly. I stood there, and I stared; I watched them wheel like birds around the pitch, and a great big smile spread across my face on its own while my empty head echoed and rang. I was a well; you could have dropped a stone down there and never heard it find water; I had a period of the sweetest stillness, a purely wordless contentment. I hope death will be like this—standing there smiling, all your business done, all your fears dispelled, and, as they say in Australia, no worries. No worries at all.

I walked down the terrace through a litter of confetti and coffee cups, burger boxes and burst balloons; I stepped over the flattened billboards and onto the pitch in a daze. There were people embracing; there was a guy on his knees, head bowed to the ground, kissing the grass. The mass of them packed together before the Meccano Stand where Jacko the cheerleader in his Wrexham shirt and his red fez climbed into the scaffolding, and conducted the singing from there.

> *Are you watching?*
> *Are you watching?*
> *Are you watching Eddie May?*
>
> *We—want—Brian—Flynn*
> *We want Brian Flynn*

A Northampton steward sat on the pitch apart from them with his head in his hands, weeping. Because while we go up this other lot have only one game left, and the trapdoor is yawning wide. . . .

And the fans climbed all over that scary old structure of wire and tin, yelling and chanting. Flynn came out briefly and was buried in a flood of embraces; as soon as he graciously could, he dived away again down the tunnel. And the singing went on, and the lunatic clambering, and I turned and walked away. I didn't want to see someone falling, or something collapsing, and they get so crazy . . .

I went in the players' entrance from the street, around the other side of this sorry little stand. The celebrating crowd, seen from the tiny foyer, was a booming mass in the block of bright night at the end of the tunnel. Then the cop from Wrexham told them there'd be a party at the Racecourse when Colchester came, and they'd be better off saving their energy for that—so eventually they eased up, and roamed away into the town.

Back at the Fish, the landlord said he'd had no trouble; the papers reported none the next day. And there's been thousands of them going here, going there, for all these months—and they may be crazy, and some among them may be thick as short planks—but for the most part they're good as gold. After they'd been to Chesterfield, the landlord of The Prince of Wales in that town wrote this letter to the club:

"On Easter Monday my pub was invaded by an enormous number of Wrexham supporters on their way to the match. They were loud, they were boisterous, they were bloody marvelous. If possible I would like to thank them, and extend a warm welcome back to the Prince, if they happen to pass this way again." And I just throw that in, by way of a little balance against all the stuff you'll be hearing about hooligans.

In the foyer there was a crush of people, Wrexham directors hugging and shaking hands among them, bleary with champagne already. "About time," they said to each other, grinning enormously, "about time." Joey Jones went through looking like someone had plugged him into the outlet, shaking every hand that reached him. Kevin Reeves was calmer, smiling from ear to ear. The club secretary said to me, "Twelve years of work finally came to something."

Tubby Welsh journalists scribbled happily in their notepads. In the *Daily Post* the next day we were front-page news, the second lead after Lady Di talking about eating disorders:

WREXHAM SEAL PROMOTION
COCK ROBINS ARE BOBBING AT LAST

Humes said when the whistle went he looked up and there was a group of thirty or forty people on him before he could move. "They just carried me yards and yards back, there was nothing I could do. This one fellow had my shirt up round my shoulders, he was yelling in my ear, Giss yer shirt, giss yer shirt. And I didn't have a lot of choice." Then he grinned and said, "They were all right."

In the dressing room they drank champagne, and looked at each other. Humes said, "We didn't know what to do. None of us have ever had this before."

Hardy said, "The boss is just sat in the corner grinning. He's just sat there with a cigar. He's made up. He's just *made up*."

And he said, "I'm lost for words. I played when we beat Arsenal, that was unbelievable. And I've been picked again for Ireland, and that's unbelievable. But this is better. This is the best thing yet."

· So we drank in the clubhouse until Northampton Town's drink was all gone, and then they got on the team bus to go home. As I walked past it to go back into town there were thumbs up and broad smiles in every window. Then the ground fell away behind me in the night, and ten minutes later I was walking through some deserted shopping area and I just broke out dancing right there, and I danced grinning all the way back to the Fish Inn.

Round-Up

One hundred thirty miles northwest, where he's glued to the radio, Alan's wife looks at him and says, "You're crying."

A small tragedy: At the Fish Inn, I meet a Wrexham fan and his girlfriend who got lost. He's one of the stalwarts, this guy, he's been up and down the country to watch his team play— and on the night we got promoted, he got lost. He said, "I could hear the singing, and I couldn't find the ground. I could see the lights, and I couldn't find the ground. It sounds soft, I know—but I couldn't find the ground."

A large tragedy: The plane carrying Zambia's squad to a World Cup qualifier in Senegal goes down in the Atlantic after a refueling stop in Gabon. Eighteen players are lost. They'd been strongly favored to go through, and that only makes this dreadful thing worse.

And the World Cup goes on. Scotland get mauled 5-0 in Lisbon, so that's the end of them. Ireland stay in it after a 1-1 draw with the Danes; Wales ditto, after a sterile encounter with the "Representation of Czechs and Slovaks" ends 1-1 in a sauna of a stadium in Ostrava. And they're pleased with the point, after a crowd in the street outside their hotel keeps them awake all night before the game.

Phil Hardy's got a trip with Ireland to Albania coming up. According to the rules, you're supposed to get into these places with forty-eight hours to spare before the game. Albania's so grim, however, that Ireland have asked permission to fly in, play, and fly out again.

At Wembley, the English throw all the gloomy jeering back in the faces of their detractors; they play a cracker with the Dutch, and are desperately unlucky when it ends 2-2. So that group's a real dogfight now—England, Holland, Norway, Poland, perm any two.

But at the bar in the Glyn Valley, what do we care? We have May 8 to look forward to, Colchester United, and a promotion party. And who are Colchester? Alan sniffs. "Just some Third Division side."

21

Ugly in Steel City

When I met with him, John Harkes was playing midfield with Sheffield Wednesday, widely considered in the spring of 1993 to be the most attractive side in England. A month after I saw Keller in the Den, I watched them play bitter rivals Sheffield United in the Premier League—the Owls against the Blades— and when you go from First to Premier, from Cold Blow Lane to Wednesday's Hillsborough, you vault into something more rarefied altogether.

Hillsborough takes 40,000 spectators. On the west side of the city, where the Peak District rises against the South Yorkshire sky, it's a glorious stadium—four steep, deep banks of blue and silver stand packed tight right on top of the pitch. As at most of our grounds, there's no running track; there's nothing between you and the game.

Two hours before kickoff we walked round the pitch toward the tunnel to the dressing rooms. Sprinklers played over the shining grass; pairs of kids sat in big string bags inflating balloons from gas tanks, filling up the bags for pregame release. Harkes pointed high into the empty sweep of the stand above the tunnel and said, "When I was on trial, I used to sit up there. I used to watch them running out in all the noise, hear everybody screaming for them." He said, "I wanted nothing more on this earth than to have them screaming for me."

Three days earlier, before 74,007 people in the Coca-Cola Cup Final against Arsenal, John Harkes became the first American to score a goal in a big game at Wembley. The match was nine minutes old; Wednesday had a free kick on the corner of the box. Sheridan slid the ball down the flank for King to cross it in behind the wall; Arsenal's O'Leary stabbed it clear from the goalmouth and twenty yards out, Harkes met that ball like a freight train. The shot was going in from the second it left his boot. Arsenal went on to win 2-1—but still that goal must have felt truly sweet.

He said, "You hit the ball, you hear the ball go, and then it's like slow motion till it hits the back of the net. Then there's the rush of adrenaline, *whooomph*, and all the people screaming . . . it was ecstasy, it was all the dreams come true. It was like I wanted to keep on running forever."

Harkes had played at Wembley three times now, with the FA Cup Final to come—so I asked what it was like, running out under the twin towers before all those people, and he said, "It's unbelievable. Everything's tingling, everything's moving—and it's a great stadium, it's massive, it's so vast. The pitch itself probably isn't all that much bigger than Hillsborough, but it *feels* so big. And when you're a kid you hear about Wembley, you watch tapes, you dream about it, so to be there . . . it's an inspiration. It's sacred."

Harkes is twenty-six, five eleven, one hundred sixty-five pounds; he's compact and good-looking under jet-black hair. His parents are Scottish; both had emigrated to the States, and they met at the Scots American Club in Kearny, New Jersey. Before he crossed the water, his father, a joiner, was on the fringes of the team at Dundee; in the States he carried on with the game, coaching youth teams.

Harkes was four when his father first threw him a shirt. It was a joke, it came down to his knees—but he went out and started kicking the ball anyhow. Kids, when they begin, all follow the ball; what you get is a disorderly pack of bodies meandering round the park, the ball tangled up in among them. But Harkes was one of those who saw early that if you stood off the pack you had space; if you got the ball then, you could work with it. His father saw he had that awareness; he coached him right through to his late teens.

He was voted best player in the country coming out of high school; he got a full-ride scholarship to the University of Virginia where, he admits, he wasn't the most diligent student. But all he wanted to do was play soccer; he was on the national youth side, then got his senior debut in 1987 in South Korea. Three years later, he went to Italy for the World Cup.

He said, "It's the best thing, the biggest thing for any player. I'm finding out now there's other things—but for us as a national side then, it was brilliant to be there. And it was a learning experience; we didn't think, Let's go show these people we can play. We just wanted to earn a little respect."

So he walked into the Olimpico . . .

"Your heart's pumping so hard you can hardly hear yourself speak. There was so much noise, you could hardly hear the national anthem. There were Italian flags everywhere— 80,000 people at that game and it seemed like 79,000 flags, green, red, and white every place you looked . . . I can go back to everything that night. You're in the dressing room and you're telling yourself relax, relax, just try to relax—that's all you can tell yourself. And everyone expected us to get beat 13-0, so there wasn't a lot of pressure—but at the same time, you're playing the best in the world. You think, Jeez—we really gotta try and hold our own out here."

Which they did. Harkes says now, "I've watched the tape over and over and I see certain plays and think, *Whoooh*—I was so immature. But the more experience you get, the more confident you're gonna be."

I asked if Gansler knew what he was doing in that tournament and Harkes said, "A lot of people criticized him, said he shouldn't be there—but who should have been? He progressed the team through the qualifying rounds, he was the one who got us there. We had to win in Trinidad in the last game, it was like a red sea down there, 40,000 people in red shirts, we were on our own—he helped us get through that."

So if they failed when they got to Italy, he said, that was inexperience all round. He said they'd approached the game against the Czechs like it was just another friendly—a notion of which they were rapidly disabused. But, he said, you'd not see them getting caught like that again.

He first came for trials with Wednesday in January 1990. Ron Atkinson was the manager then; he told Harkes he'd like to keep him, just on a month-to-month contract, but Harkes felt he ought to stay with the national squad, and not let the others down as Italy approached. Then, after Italy, Atkinson asked him to try out again. He returned to Sheffield in September, and started playing in the reserves.

"The hardest thing was being accepted as an American. Everybody's going, Why should we let him play here, he's taking a job off someone else—so I had to play twice as well as anybody, every single day."

His debut was October 31, 1990, against Oldham Athletic. He said, "It was the biggest *relief*. Those six weeks . . . I didn't know what my future was gonna be, I didn't know where I was gonna go, there were phone calls coming from the U.S. Federation saying, How's it going, we want you to go to Denmark, or wherever, and I didn't know *what* I was doing. I was sitting in a hotel on my own, eating on my own, I didn't know anybody and I was thinking, shit, let's pack it in. It was really, really difficult. I can remember times phoning home and saying, I don't know what the hell's going on. I can remember phoning Cindi [his wife] and she was going, *stick it out, I know you can do it*, and I was getting upset, I was throwing the phone down—so that debut was just the biggest relief. But I think the key thing was, we had an international against Poland. And I thought I was on the verge of showing Atkinson I could do it, 'cause he had to take a gamble on me—would I make it here, living-wise, or would I get homesick six months down the road? I had to prove I really wanted to stay—so I pulled out of the international. The next night we played Leeds in the reserves, and I scored two. And that was it."

Determination: after the game with Sheffield United a group of us went out for a drink. Among the group were Greg Milone, whose Lanzera boots Harkes is signed to wear for promotion in the States, and Sam Zighelboim, a soccer kit retailer. So of course these guys have an interest—but when Milone said, "John's unique. He's got a special drive," I thought of him sitting in that hotel room, hanging in there not knowing if he'd get the only future he ever wanted.

Zighelboim said, "He's got three lungs." And, as in any sport at the top level, you need that off the pitch as much as you do on it.

I asked what the football was like when he got off the plane and he said, "It was a big adjustment for me; it was a lot faster, a lot more physical. In the States all we're up against is CONCACAF, El Salvador, Guatemala, and they're skillful, they're Latin, they stroke it about—but here there's a lot more running around, getting on the end of things, playing the ball forward as quick as you can, two-touch football. So I've become a lot quicker in my pace, and my decisions about things, because you have to be. You shift gears right away."

And you get knocked about.

"Yeah. But you pick yourself up, dust yourself off. I remember I got concussed against Notts County, I went for a ball, *boom*, elbow in the temple, out cold. I woke up and the doc was there saying, Are you all right, John? And I was saying, Who the hell are you? Totally out of it. But you get used to it."

So I asked how he felt he'd become a better player, and the answer was immediate: "Professionalism. Dedication to the sport. Discipline—when you become a pro, it's such a difference. On the national side you'd enjoy yourself, go to Florida, play a game here, a game there, go back to your family for a week—and there was not a great deal of responsibility put on you. But here, every single game, every single training session, you gotta perform, you gotta be there—mentally, and physically. So it's not just lifted my game, it's made me grow up, it really has. I came over here twenty-three, and I've grown up so fast."

In the three years since he came, the odd injury's had him in and out of the side; he's filled in at different positions, right midfield, or right back. He'd never played the latter position in his life but it was play there, or don't play; it was tight, squeezing into a class side. On the other hand, in his first year he scored the Goal of the Season—that helped—and he's been a regular pick for a while now, becoming in the process a more creative, attacking player than the defensive midfielder we saw in Italy.

This season, Wednesday didn't get going until January; the team was mixing and changing, shuffling around. In December, Harkes's ankle went—but since New Year the left side of midfield's been his. Things gelled; the club reached the two cup finals, and went surging up the table. Running out against United tonight they stood seventh, with games in hand.

And everyone in the country—everyone except, it would seem, the England manager Graham Taylor—knows that an inescapable part of that success is the presence of Chris Waddle on the other side of midfield from John Harkes. Fresh back from Marseille, he is, without question, the most purely skilled player in England; on his day, he's one of the best in the world.

Mark Bright, one of Wednesday's strikers, said Waddle could

do things other players couldn't do, couldn't even think of doing. He described passes that found him so he could go on to score when, even as he was making the run with defenders on either side of him, he was wondering how on earth the ball could reach him—and yet it did. He said Waddle's passes beat the defenders, not him, and a striker loves that; he's free then to do what he's there for, and put the thing away.

Harkes said, "He's a mentor. I've learned so much from him. The skill he possesses is unreal, he can take on two or three players and pass them—and he never panics. When there's pressure on him, he never panics with the ball. If we're in trouble, if there are a lot of attacks coming in, you give it to Chris and it seems like he holds it for five minutes. It may only be ten or fifteen seconds—but it seems like so long, and that gives us a breather. He's got to be the best player in the country."

So why doesn't Taylor pick him?

"Jeez, I don't know. It's a mystery."

When I asked Harkes which Americans the home crowd should look out for in USA '94 he smiled and said, "All of us."

He said, "I'm really looking forward to it. I don't want to reach too high, I don't want to say how well we're going to do, but I think we're going to gain more respect. We have already, at US Cup '92—and that could have been a fluke, OK, but we did it anyway. There's not many beat Ireland 3-1."

I asked if Milutinovic had made a difference and he said, "Yeah, a great deal. A lot of players are more relaxed on the ball now. He's got a great deal of knowledge, he's really been around—and he's a character, he's a funny man, he's not a strict disciplinarian; he lets us enjoy it. But the thing I still think we need to do is play more direct, put the pressure on—because Bora's great on us keeping possession, but we're not Mexico. We can't knock the ball side to side, side to side all day and then *vwhoom*, straight through—but then, he's still experimenting. He's got to find out what he's got."

But the best of what he's got is abroad . . .

"Yeah. He must be frustrated. And he'll get bad results—like they went to Italy, played Fiorentina and Juventus, got beat 3-0 and 4-0—and he comes back and people say, shit, there goes the World Cup. But that's not the full team. People have got to know that."

It's frustrating for Harkes too, not being able to turn out for his country in their preparatory games. But as with Keller at Millwall, his club pays his bills—and, he says, "The more experience we get here, the better it's going to be for the U.S. in 1994. People complain about it, they say we've got players in all these different countries, so when we come back we'll all play different styles—but reporters who print that have no clue, no clue at all. The Dutch have players in Italy, in Spain, so do the Germans, everybody's everywhere—and any player at the international level will show professionalism. He'll get back with the others and he'll play, just like we did in 1992. I got back for that tournament three days before the first game. No problem."

Professionalism: When I asked him which was the biggest game he'd played, he mentioned Italy in Rome—but then he shrugged and said, "They're all big games. Sheffield United tonight—it's another big game."

After Wednesday knocked United out of the FA Cup in the semifinal two weeks ago, United want revenge. More important, they're down at the bottom in relegation country—they want points as well.

Wednesday, meanwhile, need to pick themselves up after losing the Coca-Cola Cup to Arsenal three days ago—and then, local grudge matches, it's blood and thunder anyhow. You never like to lose, but especially not to the guys from down the road. And this goes on every year, round and round—Liverpool and Everton on Merseyside, Rangers and Celtic in Glasgow, United and City in Manchester . . . they're called derbies, these games, after the traditional riot with a bladder played down the centuries between the parishes of St. Peter and All Saints in the town of Derby—and there's no quarter given.

As for style, Wednesday are sweet—they pass it around, they play football. Harkes is in good company; aside from Chris Waddle, his side tonight has England's number one keeper, Chris Woods, and five or six others who are or have been internationals. United, on the other hand, are long ball and muscle. They're not as bad as Wimbledon—but, said Harkes, "It'll be ugly."

Hillsborough was a furnace; the crowd was 38,688. The packed stands rose around the pitch, shrieking cliffs of humanity; the United fans yelled out, *Arsenal, Arsenal*, taunting the Owls with Sunday's defeat. The noise echoed and boomed through the spider's web of blue girders in the silver tin roofs. Then the PA hollered, "Ladies and gentlemen! Here are the players!" and as they came from the tunnel the roaring became enormous, swelling and swirling over the crashing chords of a Simple Minds tune. Balloons spilled off the terraces at either end; in the United stand they lit brilliant red flares, burning splashes of crimson fire held high over the sea of faces, pouring smoke down the rippling masses and out across the pitch—the noise thuds in your bones, your body's hollow, you boom and reverberate like a big bass drum. And you think, C'mon, lads. What you going to show us tonight?

When Harkes got his first touch the crowd's encouragement was potent; he's evidently liked. Gwwaaahhhn JOHN, they growled, Gwwaaahhhn HARKESY . . . the guy sitting next to me said he'd had a good season, he was popular. In his first year they'd got on his back—Yank go HOME, you're fuckin' USELESS, go play your OWN SHITTY GAMES—but, said Harkes, he was a Wednesday player now. Gwwaaahhhn HARKESY . . .

The game wasn't ten minutes old when Wednesday's nineteen-year-old midfielder Ryan Jones dived in low and brave among the boots for a flying header. As soon as United's keeper had seen the ball past his post, he was screaming for the referee. Harkes ran over; he said afterward it was like something out of a horror movie. He could see the livid bruise on the kid's temple swelling, blood running from his nostrils, his legs twitching and shaking on the ground. He was stretchered off, and taken to hospital for a brain scan.

But it'd take plenty worse than that to give the Blades any pause. In flew the tackles, bone-crunching, remorseless—but it's hard to kick Chris Waddle. You fly at him full pelt, studs first—and he lightly touches the ball, skips away, leaves you flying through empty air in his wake. The man's a ghost; it's a treat to watch a player this good. He gets the ball and he leans, pauses, feints, ducks, bursts away, and you're wood left to petrify behind him. And the precision of his passing, the timing, the curling of the ball past defenders so it swings in just where the front man wants it . . . I sat wondering if I should sell my house and move to Sheffield.

Harkes isn't in the same league (no one else is either) but he can play. He says he's not the best in the air—but after three years in England he looked OK there to me. Otherwise he's got good control, he's strong when he's running with the ball, he puts himself about, he gets in good positions, he tackles hard, and he's dogged, he doesn't give up. When one guy decked him he was up straight off with a finger in the guy's face, Don't you try that again . . . and then he does the business, he knows the tricks. He gets crosses in, wins corners, hassles his full back—and if the chance opens up, he can hit the ball like he wants it busting through the net and ending up in the next county.

Wednesday weren't at their best, but they were still plenty better than the other lot. United got naggy; they're not just thugs, they're crotchety too. They throw the ball away when you've won a free kick or a throw-in; they barge and shove and grumble—but they go crashing forward on the break, and just before halftime they scored.

Harkes's wife, Cindi, said during the interval, "You can't play football against these people." She knows what she's talking about; she plays for Wednesday's ladies' side and if she hadn't torn her knee ligaments, she might have done well in the American women's game.

The American women became world champions at Beijing '91, but the only thing United'll ever be champion at is making business for doctors. With fifteen minutes left, they finally nobbled Waddle—studs to the inside of the thigh. He limped off, applauding the Wednesday fans, then drew gales of delight from them as he turned to indicate with his fingers to the United end what the final score would be: 2-1. And sure enough, in the next minute Wednesday equalized.

With Waddle gone, they also switched things around; Harkes went from left midfield to right back, and started digging in the tackles. With ten minutes left, he neatly dispossessed United's Glyn Hodges as he charged into the area; the ball was cleared and the play streamed upfield, and the referee with it—so he had his back turned to what happened next. Harkes and Hodges picked themselves up, and as Hodges ran back past Harkes he smashed an elbow into the American's face. Harkes went down clutching his nose, and stayed down. While the stadium erupted in outrage and Harkes lay motionless, a brawl broke out in the middle of the park, just about all the twenty-two players who could get there pushing and jostling, squaring up and throwing punches—and that's a Steel City derby.

A linesman had seen how it started; Hodges was sent off. Gingerly fingering his nose later that night, Harkes said it wasn't broken or anything—then he grinned. He said he'd stayed down until he knew for sure Hodges had got the red card—and that's a pro.

In the dying minutes Wednesday stormed over United's ten men; Harkes cracked one screamer that their keeper did well to parry, and Bright was unlucky not to put the rebound in the net. There was such chaos in the United defence, they were fighting each other—but it ended 1-1, Waddle's prophecy not falling as true as his passes. So I didn't like the result, and as Harkes had promised, it was ugly—but it was English football, and it was a good night out.

We went for a beer at Milone and Zighelboim's hotel. Pubs and nightclubs, for Harkes they're out—what if he met some United fans? There'd be trouble flaring before you knew it. He said he'd got used, for the most part, to being public property, loved by half a city, hated by the other half. The tabloids were a pain in the neck and Cindi found it a bit weird at first, him getting letters from women who wanted to marry him, go to bed with him—but he shrugged it off; he was enjoying himself. He had, he said, not one thing in his life to complain of.

And Greg Milone said, "For us, he's a focus. An identifiable American." He smiled and said, "We don't need to look for an Italian any more."

He said sales of soccer kit in the States were showing consistent growth, 10 to 15 percent year on year. And the USSF saying there were sixteen million playing, that was pushing it—even if that number was real, most of them were kids, and in the words of one USA '94 organizer, the sport without a league was "the biggest free baby-sitting service in the world." So to get to sixteen million you're counting kids, and you're counting people who only play once or twice a year. But, said Milone, if you're talking thirty games a year, the numbers were up to maybe five or six million—and there was a hard core of two million playing twice that much.

He said, "It'll take time, but the kids get more and more aware. And this World Cup will be a success—but the one thing we can't provide is the passion. We'll go to the games all right, but the passion—you've got to bring that."

Then he described how, when he was twenty-four, he went to Barcelona to watch Italy play Brazil for a place in the semifinals at Spain '82, one of the great games of all time. He described being on Las Ramblas in the heart of the Catalan capital, seeing the Brazilians march from one end to meet the Italians coming from the other. The Brazilians had their bands, the street was filled with the samba; the Italians had their earsplitting hooters and their enormous banners, their pennants and their mediaeval heraldry waving and fluttering, splashes of color on the electric night air. In the middle of Las Ramblas they met, and they danced together.

Harkes said, "I've had family and friends over here and every one of them, no matter what type of game they've seen, it's the best sporting event they've ever been at in their lives. Because there's so much passion and excitement, it's peoples' lives, it takes you by storm, it's such a beautiful game—and I think people will see the beauty of it in '94. On the best stage they could ever possibly see it."

Postscript

In September 1993, unable to come to terms in a new contract with Sheffield Wednesday, Harkes was sold to Derby County for $1.2 million. Coincidentally, Derby plays at a stadium called "The Baseball Ground."

The Pryce Griffiths Stand

Observing a group of idlers close at hand with their backs
against the wall I went up to them and addressing myself to
one enquired whether I could see the church. He and his
mates were probably a set of boon companions enjoying the
air after a night's bout of drinking. I was subsequently told
that all the people of Wrexham are fond of good ale.
—George Borrow, *Wild Wales*, 1862

When the Romans built their legionary fort at Chester, Wrexham was forest and swamp; it doesn't turn up in the records
until the twelfth century, the site of a manor in the Welsh
lordship of Maelor. In 1277, the area came under the English
fiefdom of Bromfield-and-Yale; whether there's a connection
I don't know, but Elihu Yale, benefactor of Yale University
275 years ago, is buried in St. Giles's churchyard. Our main
stand at the Racecourse is the Yale Stand, with Yale College
behind it.

The name Wrexham may mean the "ham" (settlement) of
men from the Wrekin, a range of hills over the border in Shrop-
shire; it may not. Most early spellings are English—Wristles-
ham, Wrettesham—though as late as the seventeenth
century, 80 percent of the population bore Welsh names. But
whatever you call it, it was a little town with a market, a
church, and a place of execution on the banks of the Gwenfro.

Today, it's the largest town in North Wales (since North Wales is mostly mountains, sheep, and tourists, that's not saying much) and the population's 40,000. But within the boundaries of Wrexham Maelor Borough Council—142 square miles of urban villages and farmland—the head count rises to 117,000. Further afield in West Cheshire and North Wales, if you wanted to run a business—or have people come to watch a football side—you'd figure a catchment of about a quarter million people.

The town used to have coal mines and steelworks; they're all gone, and thousands of jobs with them. The brewery's still there—can't be doing without that—but the work now is in electronics, packaging, food manufacture; it's moved from sweat under the ground to tin sheds on the ring road. There's Kellogg's, JCB, BICC making cables, Monsanto doing chemicals, a Japanese outfit named Hoya making eyeglasses; of fifty Japanese firms in Wales, seven are in Wrexham. Sharp Corporation employs 900 making typewriters, microwaves, CD players, and VCRs at the silicon coal face.

Unemployment in the borough in May 1993 was 6,000 people, 11.4 percent of the insured workforce—a percentage point over the national average. And the cattle market's closed, so we can't say "market town" any more; we have to say "provincial center" instead. There's a bit of office development, there's a graduate medical school, there's the North East Wales Institute aspiring to university status. . . .

According to the council's chief executive officer, Bob Dutton, Wrexham was identified by the Henley Centre for Forecasting as "a hotspot for the nineties." He talked about regeneration, reclamation, tourism; so I said, if you were thinking of taking a break in Wales, Wrexham might not come top of your list.

He said, "It's not top of the list *yet*."

At the Racecourse, chairman Pryce Griffiths and a consultant sidekick eyed the developer's drawing in the glossy brochure, and glowed. The handout opened onto a picture of the Racecourse of the future, bright colored and airbrushed, a sci-fi vision of a little Welsh San Siro with retail space, multiscreen cinema, swimming pools, parking lots, orderly decorative vegetation. There'd be a virtual reality arcade . . . seemed a good description of the whole deal to me.

They were talking about a $65 million development, twelve hundred jobs, three years of work; they were talking banqueting facilities and fast-food outlets, a bingo hall and a bowling alley, a health club and a ninety-bed hotel where the Turf pub is now. They want an Omni-max cinema behind the Kop. I wondered how much the consultant was being paid, and whether his fees might have paid to build us a decent urinal.

Where the old Mold Road Stand now lies in a crumbly heap behind the builders' billboards, Pryce Griffiths ran his fingers over what looked, in the picture, like a cross between Harrods and an airport terminal. He breathed, with reverence, that this would be the Pryce Griffiths Stand.

Some months ago he'd thought they might be getting there—they had American investment dollars lined up on the table—but the council didn't get planning permission through fast enough. Griffiths grumbled that they'd refused to call a special meeting on the grounds that it would have set a precedent—and he wanted to know, if this development didn't set a precedent, what did?

But they had planning permission now. The consultant said they'd have the money again too, they'd have it in a week. The chairman ran his fingers over the drawing . . . you get promoted, you can dream whole new worlds up then.

Griffiths said the last fifteen minutes at Northampton were hard to bear. "And when the whistle went it was elation, it was wonderful. When you're down and out and an hour before the match you're praying it doesn't rain, because that'd knock five hundred off the gate—there's no pleasure in it then. So I've been waiting a long time for this, it means everything to me. This last two months I've hardly slept. But Brian's always saying, Don't worry, Chairman, we'll be there, don't worry. And he was right, and it's wonderful."

Griffiths was born sixty-seven years ago, a mile from the ground. His father was a miner; he was the fourth of eleven children. He left school at fourteen and began work as a shop assistant, and with a wage—five shillings a week—he could afford the two pennies to get in the Kop. "In those days there were droves of people, you used to get fifteen, twenty thousand just for a pre-season match. And where I lived up the road here, the people used to pass the house coming to and from the game, and I used to run down the road to meet the first one back and ask what the result was. Because until I started work, I couldn't afford to go."

After the shop he was in the steelworks, and he did some laboring; the Kop then was cinders and ashes, and Griffiths was one of those wheeling barrows of cement when they covered it. During the war he was in the army, mostly in Italy; in the fifties he went to work for his brother-in-law, the town's newspaper distributor. When his brother-in-law fell ill, the business went to Pryce; it grew, and he made his stash. In the seventies he started buying shares in the football club; today, he has 80 percent of it. So how was it, I asked, that two years ago we nearly went bust?

"It wasn't just two years ago—seven or eight years ago, I was putting money in for the paychecks. And we've been well off since then, and we've been down again, and I'd be surprised if we don't go down again in the future—I don't mean in the league, but financially. Because if you have a bad run, the crowd's fickle; they want to see a winning side all the time and, flipping heck, you'll never have that. This season, if we'd have lost a couple of games six weeks ago, our gates would have gone down by a couple of thousand—when we needed them more than ever."

So why does anyone put money into it in the first place? These are businessmen, and they must know what happens to money in football. . . .

"Oh, good gracious, I make decisions here that I wouldn't dream of in my own business. But I've always been proud to say I'm chairman of Wrexham Football Club—because when I was wheeling cement round the pitch out there, I never dreamed I'd be able to afford to sit in the stands, let alone own the club. So I think, to answer your question, it's pride."

The club's buying the players a week's holiday in Majorca; the chairman's going, so he can drink beer with his boys and be proud of them. The prospect struck me as comical; I imagined the players trying politely to pop off and get good and lewdly drunk without this fond old gent aglow with his pride in their ears—but I was wrong. One of them grinned, and said of course they'd be in the same bar as the chairman—he'd buy the drinks.

Griffiths said, "I'd like to think I've always been a popular guy round the town. The type of job I had, I met the man in the street all the time, and to this day I will boast that I haven't forgotten myself. But these young boys here, they show respect, as perhaps you've noticed. They won't let me pass without saying, Hello, Mr. Chairman. And I can't remember all their names, so I call them all 'son.' "

And he said, "When I was laboring, I was a hod carrier on the council houses in Overton. And now I live in the biggest house there. The nicest house in Overton, without question. And that's not a brag."

If ever there was an archetypal chairman, you're meeting him now—a small-town personage, a self-made, local businessman who's bought what he views as privileged membership in an exclusive club. A man who says he always buys British—and in the parking lot he's got a BMW.

We were in the directors' lounge; when we finished talking Griffiths unplugged the phone and put it away behind the bar. He said he might be daft with his money in some ways, but in other ways he was tight—and when they'd been counting every penny two years ago trying to stave off bankruptcy, he'd not wanted the directors of other clubs making long-distance calls back home after the game, not on his phone bill. He smiled, and said the habit had stuck.

Back then they'd had bailiffs knocking at the door, and fans raising money to help pay the players' salaries. Now, the next thing he was going to do was hang a bigger picture of himself on the wall of the directors' lounge. He wanted to see how it looked, now he was pleased as punch with his life and his club. And why not?

And we have these grand schemes; a 16,500 all-seater at the heart of a multipurpose leisure complex, a dream decked out in fulsome copywriter's blurb—a dream about a place where right now you've got to be Carl Lewis if you want to take a piss without getting your feet wet, a place where if you want a cup of nasty bitter coffee you've got to wait in line fifteen minutes. . . .

You'll have detected that I'm uncertain. I do want it to happen; I want jobs in Wrexham, and I want a decent, modern little ground where Wales can play internationals and not be embarrassed. And I'll miss the Kop, but that's sentiment; I know this is 1993, and it's well overdue that we get ourselves in shape—but what will a ticket cost? The bedrock of football, the lads, the laborers like Pryce Griffiths once was, the unemployed—will they be priced away from the game, as they've been priced away from so much else? And what will the atmosphere be like then?

Attendance has risen around the country season on season for some years now, even as new seating and safety standards have seen capacities shrink. But ticket prices have risen too, and somewhere there's a limit. Somewhere, at the bottom line, the game becomes middle class; somewhere, it falls forever out of our hands into the hands of King Sponsor and his legions in their suits and their sky boxes. Somewhere, in short, the whole game goes Coca-Cola. Already, Rupert Murdoch's satellite channel Sky TV has exclusive rights to live Premier League football—so in Oldham and Liverpool and Wimbledon and Sheffield we're seeing troupes of soccer cheerleaders prancing around plastered with Murdoch's logo, and we've got sumo wrestlers in the center circle at halftime, and men pulling nails out of planks with their teeth, and the whole baloney of ersatz razzmatazz and packaged spectacle. And we're standing in the Kop—for perhaps the last season before the future arrives with a wrecking ball—and we're wondering what the hell ever happened to our game.

We're standing in the Kop realizing that USA '94 is, in fact, the most obvious and natural development for soccer you could think of. And I really hope you enjoy it—but it won't ever be the same.

May 8, 1993
Wrexham v. Colchester United

It's the last day of the season, and issues remain to be settled the length and breadth of the land. Come 4:30 this afternoon, as the last ten minutes unfold, millions will be listening to radios, punching remotes to get the latest news on the TV, playing panicky fingers over calculators, lunging for tranquilizers, diving to the fridge for beer.

At the top of the Third, Cardiff, Barnet, and Wrexham are promoted already—but what we don't know is who'll end up as champions. Here's the math: if Cardiff lose at Scunthorpe and don't score, and Barnet lose or draw at Crewe, then if Wrexham beat Colchester and score four in the process, they finish top. In the papers Flynn's talking about "a platform of a couple of goals, so we can go for an onslaught in the second half." But it's unlikely we'll be obliged a second time with good results elsewhere, and what the hell—we're going up, and today we have a party.

The Turf was heaving, raucous with the red army in full song in their red shirts, men and women with red eyes and shattered teeth and shaven heads. Around the corner in the ground, people had their faces painted red and white; they had Viking hats and inflatable bananas, inflatable hammers, inflatable champagne bottles. The PA played Free's "Alright Now"; we stood in good cheer and guitar noise and sunshine, come through another winter to claim our reward. We had the warmth in our hearts, the beer in our bellies, and the delicious anticipation before a game, for once, of knowing for ninety minutes we wouldn't have to worry one bit.

Mind you, says Alan, "I want them to win. Put a bit of a dampener on the celebrations, losing, wouldn't it?"

Never satisfied, that's us.

Then the Colchester players formed an avenue to greet Wrexham onto the pitch, and to the march "Men of Harlech" out they came, and the Kop disappeared in a blizzard of confetti and balloons and streamers, and the horns and hooters beeped and tooted, and the people jumped and clapped and cheered, and here and there some stood with tears running down their cheeks after all those Saturdays, all those wet Tuesday winter evenings, all those hopes . . .

And in a torrent of song we attacked them. Connolly played the deftest chip over the head of his full back, running onto the ball as it passed him, then over sailed the cross and Cross was waiting on the end of it, and he tried a first-time volley—and if he'd made contact that strike would have been sweet sweet sweet. Then Watkin and Bennett combined, lacing their way through, one-two, touch, touch, and Bennett looked up and Connolly was arriving too, all alone at the far post, so Bennett slung it over on the floor and Connolly said thanks, I'll slip that away, keeper nowhere, Wrexham 1-0.

Showtime. Cross slipped by two men like they were holograms, looked up—and then he gave it away and *whoomph*, one quick ball and their striker was free, charging down on Morris. The keeper stood up, spread himself, the guy looked and shot, we could see it rolling in . . . it hit the inside of the post and bounced out. This bloody game. It strokes you, then it bites.

Colchester had more chances; at the other end, Benno

spooned a shot into the stand. If he got one, it'd be his best season ever—twenty-four goals—but he wouldn't get one like that. Then Owen released him with a perfect pass over forty yards, he beat the center half and fired—and the keeper dived to touch it away. Then we had a free kick; Cross thumped it in, the ball bounced off the keeper, and a defender trying to clear it headed into his own net from six inches out. It was 2-0, halftime, Flynn had his platform—and Cardiff were beating Scunthorpe so it didn't matter anyhow—but we were going up, we were winning, we were happy, and when Colchester came out for the second half we even applauded them.

That dried up pretty quick. A long ball sent over for Watkin to chase set him free and clear on goal—so the Colchester full back raised a hand and punched the pass off course before it went through. That's a red card offence for a "professional foul," where you've brought down or otherwise hindered the man clear on goal—and the ref didn't even book him. We bawled in fulminating outrage . . . but Pejic said afterward the ref had been good. He might have given a few soft decisions, and not done us any favors—but, he said, any time things looked hot he'd always say, Don't spoil the day. He said, "I could have been booked a couple of times. But he called us over and said, 'Let's make the most of it. Let's enjoy it.' And you appreciate that."

But he still should have sent that guy off. This ain't basketball . . . and then Colchester scored. The guy shot, it hit Phil Hardy's legs, spun in deflected, and there was nothing Morris could do about it. 2-1. That wasn't supposed to happen. And Benno was going frantic, screaming at Morris when he had the ball to get on and turf it upfield—and Morris was getting the ball a lot more often than we'd have liked.

Pejic said, "It was too easy. And when it's like that we're our own worst enemies sometimes."

Cross and Benno went through, Benno fired high over the bar, and Cross was fuming. He was right there, free—and Benno learnt his lesson. He may desperately have wanted one himself, but when Connolly put the next cross over, Benno at the far post turned it across goal for an open Watkin this time, and a simple tap home made the score 3-1. That was more like it—and Cardiff were winning 3-0, we couldn't catch them—but we'd said we needed four, so we'd surely get them anyhow.

That was in the sixty-fifth minute—and fifteen minutes later the score was 3-3. This bloody game . . . their second goal, our defence was asleep; their third, God himself couldn't have stopped it. The guy shot from outside the D, *thwang*, top corner like a rocket. Morris dived for it, but he said afterward he knew it was going in from the minute the guy struck it; he only dived for the cameras. "It was in all the way, that one. I was just watching it go past."

So on the Kop there were some peeved people now. We were 9,705, and there were voices screaming everywhere SHOOT! SHOOT! Someone bloody SHOOT! And someone did, and he was a Colchester player . . . Morris saved with his fingertips. From the corner they tried again, and hit the side netting. What was this? We didn't come to this party to watch the other lot get goals. . . .

In the eighty-ninth minute, Connolly crossed one last time; Benno headed against a defender, and the ball squirted out to Cross. He looked up, played it back in, Watkin stopped on the penalty spot—and there it was, 4-3. What a way to end a season. And we were shrieking for the whistle as Watkin damn near scored a fifth, and Benno was chasing everything, and Cross nutmegged some hapless defender—that's when you beat a guy by slipping the ball through his legs so he looks *really stupid*—and everyone that wasn't yelling was purring with joy. Then we had a corner and Watkin headed it down to the keeper and the ref blew, and the Racecourse burst out roaring and clapping, and Benno had the little kid mascot riding on his shoulders, and they were embracing and punching fists at the blue sky, and they went to clap the hundred or so Colchester fans who'd made the long journey from the far side of England, and the Colchester fans clapped them back, and then they ran round the ground in all the outpouring noise, down the length of the Yale Stand as the chanting pumped and surged, and back at last to the Kop, the players dancing and clapping, and then sprinting for their lives as the crowd spilled out and not making it, no chance, and they had Benno stripped to his jockstrap in a nanosecond, hunting sacred garments to be taken home and treasured, and Barnet lost at Crewe, and after nine months and forty-two games we were second and we were up, and I haven't had this much fun since Italia '90 and roll on USA '94, because this is *the best game in the universe.*

* * *

We went to the Cotton Club, a kind of nightclubby bar on the first floor in the Yale Stand. Some kids got in, wanting autographs on their inflatable hammer, and they didn't recognize Phil Hardy, and asked artlessly if he was a player. Pejic chuckled. "He tries to be. Scored a goal today though, didn't he?"

Tony Humes's wife said of her husband, "He's a different man. They've done him such a favor. He was thinking of giving up, at Ipswich they had him training with the kids—he was so down. And when he said they'd come for him here, I didn't even know where it was, I had to look it up on a map. But I'm a convert now."

Humes pointed at the carpet and said, "My chin was down there. I could see myself fizzling out of the game, ending up as a bloody dustman or something—then I talked to Brian Flynn, and he was so *relaxed*." So he said, if he spent the rest of his career here now, that'd do him just fine.

Postscript

Benno was found not guilty of handling stolen goods on the day before this game.

Round-Up

The long quest for the grail finally ends. With the relegation monkey hooting on their shoulder, Oldham go to Villa Park and beat Aston Villa 1-0; Villa can't catch Manchester United, Alan loses five quid, and after twenty-six years the biggest club in the country are champions again. They beat Blackburn and Wimbledon in style to confirm it.

United first won the championship in 1908, and again in 1911; on both occasions, Villa were runners-up then, too. After Munich, Villa were also one of the clubs that transferred players to Old Trafford to help them rebuild their shattered squad—and the question inevitably asked is whether the new champions can match those great teams of the past. In short, can they win the European Cup? When the draw is made, the first club they're set to play is Honved of Hungary, the old home of the Galloping Major.

By a grim turn of irony, the day United become champions is also the day when, after another plane crash in another continent, the bodies of Zambia's footballers are flown back to Lusaka to be buried next to the Independence Stadium.

The regular season's over. Now there's the FA Cup Final, and the meeting of AC Milan and Olympique Marseille for the European Cup. Then there's the summer. Mark Morris says he'll get his fishing gear out. While the others celebrate, he's angry that he's let three goals in. Flynn says he'll offer him a new contract; he also says he'll be looking to buy another keeper. When they come back for pre-season training on July 15, he says, it all starts again from scratch. When I ask him what sort of challenge the Second Division will present, he only smiles and says, "The next one." And Pryce Griffiths says Flynn will be managing Wales before he's done.

Kasey Keller's Millwall miss the play-offs for the Premier League by one spot. After the last game in the Den, fans invade the pitch, tear up the turf, tear down the goalposts, and hurl missiles at the directors' box for daring to take them from their beloved shithole to some fancy new stadium. Other fans weep.

The lad in my village shop reveals that he came home from the Racecourse with Jonathan Cross's left boot, and that it stank.

A season ends, but the game goes on. In CONCACAF's final qualifier Mexico beat Canada 2-1 in Toronto, and become the first nation to book their place at USA '94. Earlier scenes in this region have included fans in the cheap seats at El Salvador's Cuscatlan Stadium hurling dead cats and iguanas, bags of piss and shit, rocks and stones and two-by-fours onto the pitch; the cheap seats are known as "Vietnam."

In Sweden, where local government bodies are still owed several million dollars for police overtime during the '92 European Championships, the police suggest that the country should host no more such events until it's clear who's going to foot the bill. You have been warned.

At Wembley on Saturday, May 15, Arsenal and Sheffield Wednesday play the 112th FA Cup Final. The game's oldest fixture is seen by 79,347 in the stadium, and by a TV audience around the world, live and recorded, of 750 million. This is embarrassing, because the showcase of the English game turns out to be dreadful. Drawn 1-1 after extra time, it goes to a replay five days later.

Why so bad? It was Arsenal's 58th game of the season, and Wednesday's 62nd; the absurd demands of the league program had seen them play their last five games in eleven days, before they finally stumble out under the twin towers.

Harkes plays well; he has as much energy as any player on the pitch, battling on as others fade. His opponent, Arsenal's right back, is England international Lee Dixon, and Harkes is his equal—and when Wednesday score, it's Harkes who, deftly and unselfishly, nods the ball into the striker's path to make the goal, when he might have tried for glory himself.

In London before the game, in a sports bookshop, by chance I meet an official of USA '94. With thirteen months to go before kickoff, he says 650,000 tickets are sold already. And he says if England don't qualify, it'll be a disaster—but given their present form, I don't know about that.

The replay of the FA Cup Final is an English paradigm. Seen live in forty countries, it kicks off half an hour late after Sheffield fans are delayed by pile-ups on the motorway coming south from Yorkshire. Wednesday's chairman hires a special Pullman from British Rail to collect himself and a group of colleagues from Chesterfield—so they stand on the platform, and the train roars straight through without stopping. As for the game, it's more of the same—a caveman's catalog of clattering tackles, long balls, and offside traps. After ninety minutes, it's 1-1 again; in the last minute of extra time, neither side finding a way through in open play, an Arsenal center half with a broken nose and a broken finger scores the winner with a header from a corner. Harkes plays well again, and goes red-eyed with tears up the steps to the royal box to collect his loser's medal.

The following week France and Italy show the world how to do it. 109 countries watch Marseille beat Milan 1-0 to win the European Cup; both sides play stylish and incisive football. The contrast between the two fixtures is ominous.

The day after the FA Cup replay, England's squad join up to play two qualifiers for USA '94. The squad includes six Arsenal men, and two from Sheffield Wednesday. They go to Katowice in Poland; while the riot police fight on the terraces with warring groups of Polish fans, the team fight snapping and snarling with the Polish players on the pitch. The Poles deserve to win, and are desperately unlucky when Arsenal's Ian Wright— with a broken toe and a sprained ankle—scores a good goal against the run of play for a 1-1 draw. But it still means that if England don't win in Norway five days later, you can pretty much write them out of USA '94.

England haven't lost a World Cup qualifier since 1981—but that last loss was against Norway in Oslo . . . on the night before the game, Norwegian riot police clash with English fans; seventy are detained and deported, and the bar on which the trouble centers is smashed to bits.

Norway win 2-0, and they could have had four. It's the worst England performance I can remember; jaded, uninspired, gutless. The tabloids scream for the manager's head; in the broadsheets, calls for his resignation move from the back pages to the editorial columns. The front page of the *Daily Sport*, a tits'n'sleaze rag, says: VIKING AWFUL.

Two events parallel this catastrophe in the bawling, loutish turbulence that passes these days for English public life. The day of the game is the fortieth anniversary of the queen's coronation; back then it was a new dawn, but now it's merely occasion for more wondering at how the head of state's family has become an anachronistic bunch of adulterous mediocrities. And secondly, Conservative Prime Minister John Major is found in an opinion poll to be the most unpopular leader of the country since World War II. Our royal family, our govern-

ment, our soccer—all the same, dreary and incompetent. So
the ticket salesmen may say otherwise, but while it pains me
to say it, the way things are, USA '94 can do perfectly well
without England.

The Republic of Ireland will most likely be there, and that's
fine. But since 1950 there hasn't been a World Cup in which
at least one of the home unions—England, Wales, Scotland,
Northern Ireland—didn't make it. So British hopes now rest
with Wales.

23

Richmond Kickers

The Friday night before Cardiff mugged us in the league, I went for a drink in the Turf. It's the only pub in Britain on a football ground—select insiders watch Wrexham play from the balcony—and on a Friday night, it's packed out and grungy. A three-piece band fronted by a stocky, throaty young woman belted out loud dirty rock. I heard one ragged character in a leather jacket asked by another, how did he get his black eyes? The ragged one looked at the other like he was thick as a brick and said, "I got beaten up." Obvious . . .

In these dense, smoky surroundings, a squad of teenagers from Virginia celebrated the end of a successful eleven days' soccer tour. Being able to get a legal drink was a hoot—but the drinks that were bought for them were mystifying. One stirred his finger round in the white, creamy head on his pint of black Guinness. It was OK, he said, not looking too certain about it, but what was this scum you had to drink it through?

I went to see them the next morning. There'd been a party laid on, then they'd slept in a heap of bodies on someone's living-room floor. While they woke complaining about the stink of one anothers' feet, I talked to their coach—because while the likes of John Harkes fly the flag at the summit of the game, it's these boys who are the bedrock. If you want more like Harkes, it's here you've got to find them.

The coach was Bobby Lennon, thirty years old, from Washington, D.C. He started playing when he was nine; in 1979, he captained Annandale Boys' Club in the Under-16 national finals. The NASL was in business then; he supported the Washington Diplomats, he worked the locker rooms and the press box, he loved it, and he missed it. But it was too big, too costly, and America wasn't ready—and Lennon didn't think it was ready now either.

In his twenties he played indoor soccer with the Jacksonville Generals, but in the late eighties they folded. Before then he'd brought a youth team to Britain on tour, and they'd passed through Wrexham; when the franchise folded he came back. He was here for a year, mostly working in a nightclub, training by day; he played with the reserves a few times, but he never got on the staff. He readily admits he wasn't fit enough, and he wasn't good enough.

So he went back to Florida, and tried to get an outdoor team together; he nearly managed it, he thought he was getting there—but the recession set in and the prospect died. Upset, he packed his bags and went off to Taiwan. He was traveling, making money teaching English; but in Taipei he started playing for a team called, absurdly, the Salem Cigarettes, and he started a soccer school there. He got sponsorship, he had a thousand kids come through, he made money at it—then he was offered a coaching job back in Virginia.

So he shut up shop, flew home—and found the college had put their money into baseball instead. At a loose end, he stopped in Richmond for the U.S. National Youth Championships, and liked what he saw. It was well organized, there was local corporate support, they sold 24,000 tickets over the five days of the tournament—and he saw his opportunity.

An outfit named the United States Interregional Soccer League was starting up. First formed in 1986 as the Southwest Indoor Soccer League, it had evolved through various mutations, started playing outdoors, and was on the way to becoming the biggest league in the States. Lennon knew there was a good player pool in Virginia; he'd seen in Richmond that there was audience potential, and they were investigating having a club there anyhow. So he went to the parties concerned, the Metropolitan Richmond Sports Backers, he talked to the USISL, and the Richmond Kickers were born. Those boys sleeping in a heap on a Welsh living-room floor are their youth team.

The approach of the USISL is sensibly modest. You lodge a bond of $10,000 to join; you get exclusive rights for that money to a territory of fifty miles' radius. The league's thirty-nine teams are separated into five regional divisions, so travel costs are low; the Kickers play in the Atlantic Division, and the range of their competition looks like this:

Baltimore Bays
Charleston Battery
Charlotte Eagles
Columbia Spirit
Connecticut Wolves
Delaware Wizards
Greensboro Dynamo
Raleigh Flyers

The other divisions are South East, South Central, South West, and Pacific—so you've got soccer organized here from San Francisco to San Antonio, from Tulsa to Tennessee, with the top teams in play-offs for a national title. But, like I say, it's modest. Lennon's goal is $125,000 in sponsorship (he says he's 80 percent there, two weeks before the opening game on April 30, 1993) and his *modus operandi* is to live on a shoestring. There are, he says, three expenses—players, travel, and marketing.

Players: for the first few years he won't pay them. He can't, and that's that. They're mostly coming out of college into jobs, so it's just a place for them to keep on playing; he knows for some it means the team is the second priority, but there's no way round that. He's found jobs for a few of them, coaching on the Inner City Youth Soccer Program—and that might lay building blocks for new players in the future—but otherwise, for now, if you're a Kicker you do it for love.

Travel: he's got accommodation sponsored, and he's got the van sponsored. So that's down to food and gas.

Marketing: a lot of it's traded out to local TV and radio. In a small city, he says, you can do that.

Working on this basis, he's allowed a roster of twenty-six. They'll play in a 4,000-seater at the University of Richmond, and he hopes to sell out at least the first few games. After that, he'll see—but in this form or some other form like it, he said this was the future of American soccer.

He said, "The World Cup is free soccer promotion, it's wonderful—but I don't think there'll be any miracles once it's gone. The game will get stronger and stronger, but it'll take generations; over here, you've got a century's head start on us. So we're not going to fill our stands just because of the

World Cup. Hopefully, the crowds will go up—but it's a long-term thing, and if you aren't willing to go in there and really sweat, work long hours, it's not going to happen. But I think the people involved are committed, they're in it for love of the game—so it isn't a great business adventure, but it is the way the game can succeed."

Alan Rothenberg talks about maybe ten or twelve big city franchises up and running for '95—but he concedes that he can't say it'll happen for sure. It would take so much money—and money in this world is tight right now.

And if you were going to start a soccer league in England tomorrow, OK, you wouldn't start it from where we are now. You wouldn't have Wimbledon in the Premier League, with their tiny gates; you wouldn't have ninety-two clubs, with all these half-bankrupt little outfits down the bottom playing in mud baths before fifteen hundred souls in a garden shed.

But if you want the passion, if you want the beauty, if you want the spirit of the game to move in your hearts—then you have to understand that it's built up over so many years, and that these funny little clubs with their crumbling terraces and their dismal urinals are the heart of the game every bit as much as Manchester United or Milan. Scarborough, Northampton, Halifax Town—there's barely a chairman in the land with the decency to admit it, but these clubs *belong* to their fifteen hundred diehard souls, and it's from these clubs that the big game grows and flows. Owen, Watkin, Hardy, Connolly, Cross—if they go to the Premier, we know where they came from.

And Wimbledon—you might not like them, but they're where they are because they got the results. All the money in the world can't buy you goals—so while we fret and grieve at what seems the ever more pernicious effect of bigger and bigger money, it remains the case that everything depends in the end on how you do on the park. Milan, in short, can be beaten. Or there's the guy who put $15 million out of his pocket into Derby County this season to buy promotion from the First to the Premier—and they finished up ninth.

So promotion and relegation are the essence of our game, and money can influence that—but it can never determine it. What a squad does over nine months, rocking up and down the table, causing all that fear and joy, all that hope and dread in our hearts—can you tell me that's down to their wages?

But, said Kasey Keller, if a big league's to get going in the States, it can't have that crucial element. He asked, what American squillionaire will invest his treasure in a team, if there's the possibility of that team *going down*? Yet if you take out that threat you will, I'm afraid, turn drama into soap. Glossy soap, no doubt—but soap all the same.

Lennon said he'd never thought about that. Promotion, relegation, a big league? "It's a long way away. And in the meantime what I'm doing is small potatoes. I don't exaggerate when I say I work fifteen-, eighteen-hour days—and the major stuff's not where my interests lie. My interest is quality semi-pro. So, sure, I hope a major league comes along, I really do—we'd all go and watch it. Maybe if they regionalized it, had a player cap at $30,000 a player, $50,000 . . . they can't make salaries like the NBA, no way. And they can't be stepping on airplanes, there's just no way. And if anybody thinks they can, if anybody thinks it's going to happen just because the World Cup came, they're fooling themselves."

Lennon's teenagers played a youth tournament at the University of Keele in Staffordshire. They beat a French side 2-1, beat a local English side 3-1, then lost the final 4-3 in the last minute of extra time to another English side by the name of Ball-Hay-Green. Lennon was so proud of them, he'd have glowed in the dark.

Then they drew 1-1 with Wrexham's apprentices, and lost to non-league Southport's junior side 1-0. To cap it, they watched Aston Villa play Coventry at Villa Park, and Arsenal down in London. And they saw Cardiff mugging Wrexham— but we'll not dwell on that . . .

And at first his kids, said Lennon, came off the field saying, *Whoooh*, this is *different*. He said, "They close you down so much quicker here than in the U.S., you have much less time to react—and they're so much better in the air. Wrexham just thrashed us in the air, the difference was night and day. But despite the results, they were the only team who were actually better than us—they did clearly dominate that game. If it wasn't for our keeper, we'd have lost by three or four; we didn't start figuring it out until the last ten minutes. But if we played them again we'd do better; it was definitely a learning experience."

A midfielder named Preston Flowers was invited back to train with Wrexham for three weeks in the summer. Lennon said, "He'll get an edge, a competitive attitude that you just can't get in the States. I'm not cutting down American players, but the attitude here—players come out of the woodwork here, quality players. For us, it's a part of life; here, it's a *way* of life."

Flowers said, "In America, if I get the ball, I can usually turn, run with it a bit. Here, you better play it on quick—or you'll be down on the ground."

I asked what he thought he'd get from training here, and he smiled. "I'll be in better shape, that's for sure."

Tim Garnett was a striker; he started playing when he was nine. He loved the game, he said, "because it dictates itself. Every moment there's something original or new. And except for free kicks it isn't plays, it *flows*—so once you're on the field it's your game, and nobody on the sideline can do a single thing about it."

He said, "We came over, we were pretty scared. We'd been thrashed at a tournament in Florida by American teams, so we thought, what's going to happen to us now? And as we expected it was a lot faster, a lot more physical—it was just exhausting. Not necessarily during the match, but after—you could feel every tackle in your joints. So you can really tell, if you're going to have success over here, you're going to have to play one hundred percent at all times."

I asked what he'd learned and he said, "The trip definitely solidified the concept of knowing what you're going to do *before* you get the ball—of reading the game ahead of time. And the importance of constant thinking, constant awareness; it became more than obvious that to be successful, you have to know what's going on all over the field—not just in your zone."

But his favorite part of the trip was seeing two games in the Premier League. He said, "To see that many people share the love and the passion, and to be so close to the pitch like that—you could reach out and touch them. And they play so fast, it's incredible. You'd think it'd be out of control, but almost everyone's in *perfect* control. I've seen the U.S. play, it was good quality, but it wasn't the same. There wasn't the *intensity*."

He said, "It's all of our fantasies to get out on a pitch in front of a crowd like that, and have them cheering with all their hearts the way they do here."

He said, "I wish it'd be like that at home. And hopefully one day it will be."

24

US Cup '93

The bus from JFK juddered into Manhattan. On rough grass behind chain-link fencing by Shea Stadium, kids played soccer—but when I told friends this they shrugged. They said, "There's a lot of Latinos out there, Colombians, whatever." They said if they hadn't known me, they wouldn't have known the World Cup was coming at all.

It was June 6, 1993; Brazil beat the U.S.A. 2-0 in New Haven, Connecticut, and in my room I scanned the stations for news of the game. There was Clinton, Somalia, tornadoes; a boatload of Chinese illegals washed up on Rockaway Beach, and RKF was remembered twenty-five years on. Then there was a spectacular twenty-five-minute baseball brawl between Baltimore and Seattle, along with ice hockey, golf, George Foreman, and Bruguera beating Courier at Roland Garros. Of events in New Haven, beyond a few seconds on ABC, there wasn't a peep.

The New York Times the next morning gave it one column on the inside pages. Headlined APOCALYPSO NOW FOR THE AMERICAN TEAM, the piece said the home side "really had no clue." So you can't play, you don't care, and you shouldn't have the World Cup.

Wrong. When I got off Amtrak's Mayflower at Boston's Back Bay Station the next evening, every other pillar in the concourse had a poster promoting USA–England. It was the second game of US Cup '93, the biggest soccer event ever held in America—and while coming top over Ireland, Italy, and

Portugal last time was not to be sniffed at, this time you were really putting your hands in the fire. To take on Brazil, England, and Germany in one go—this was a micro–World Cup.

The Boston papers, and many more besides, went to watch England manager Graham Taylor run a training session, and were mystified. If, after the loss in Norway, the guy was in the doo-doo so deep, how come he was so cheerful? As for the training, why wasn't he filming it? What was this? Where was the jargon, the science, the sporting technocracy? The business pages didn't care; Boston hosts six games at USA '94, the last of them a quarter-final, and a $250 million input into the local economy was being projected as a result.

I went to a press conference; Taylor was diplomatic, Milutinovic was witty, and his syntax was anarchic. He tried to explain to the American press—I would see him doing this again and again—that, "It is important to know who you play, and to know who you are." Victories in 1994 were what mattered; every game now was just education, for the team, for the media, for the public. He said, "It's very important for the public to understand how is the soccer exciting game."

Afterward I spoke with Taylor, who was affable and charming. He wondered mildly, as every English manager since Winterbottom must have done, if the tabloids sell more papers when England lose. Asked about the mess in Norway he asked the Americans in return, "Did you never have a bad day at work?"

The Americans were staying in the Sheraton Needham in the leafy west 'burbs; the hotel was as big as a palace, the kind of place where you need a road map to find your way to the john. Finding Bora was easier—the U.S.A. was in open-house mode, wanting all the world to know about them. So I sat with him to watch Marseille–Paris St. Germain on Prime Sports Channel America.

He's a puckish man with French pop-star hair, glossy and all over the place. Born in 1944, he played for Partizan Belgrade in the sixties, then moved via France and Switzerland to Mexico. On his travels he's picked up Spanish, Italian, French, a spattering of Russian, and some jovially fractured English. But whatever language he works in, it does the trick; his successes with Mexico and Costa Rica in 1986 and 1990 we know about already. But the Americans, people thought, that was different altogether; this was a team, I said, about whom the English in particular tended to be snottily derisive.

He shrugged. "It's normal. I understand why. But it's not my problem, and I think it's more important for the English to watch how is English soccer."

His problem, instead, is that he never has his best players—and then, "We don't have league, we don't have nothing to make training every day. And when you have a hundred players to choose best eleven, OK. When you have only thirty, this is also a problem."

Of starting a league he said, "You need to live in America to understand how difficult to building something is." Then Marseille scored. "Ah so nice, 'scuse me, 'scuse me, you see how is so nice goal? Voller, incredible, look, so nice. Jump, turn, lovely."

He said he'd like his own team to play like Marseille, like Milan, like Brazil—to play "nice." But in America as much as anywhere else, "They watch more the result." With his entire first-choice strike force and midfield playing pro overseas, results in 1993 so far read: W1 D9 L5. But, he said, "I need to think about what is more important, to find our best players, and not to think about the press." And with his best team all in off the plane now—against Brazil he'd been missing Ramos, Dooley, and Wynalda—he said of a league, "If we can have chance to help with our results now, then I be most happy in the world."

The NASL may have folded but among the American squad, you'll find every native-born player grew up with a team and a star in his eyes. For Harkes it was the Cosmos, for the striker Eric Wynalda it was Johan Cruyff of the Los Angeles Aztecs—and the idea that these guys don't know soccer is baloney. Wynalda said, "The American team can play with anybody. They can call us the green-card team, they can call us underdogs, they can call us whatever they want, that's fine. We've got a great coach, we've got some great players, so let's just see what happens."

Bora got Harkes and Wegerle to tell the team everything they knew about the English. Harkes said they should expect them to come at their throats—"they won't be thinking about Norway, they'll be thinking about thrashing us 5-0"—and knowing our press, he had a lot of sympathy for Taylor. He said, "It'll be embarrassing if they lose," and he had no doubt that they might.

Game day dawned gray and murky, with a severe thunderstorm watch posted over parts of New England until six o'clock—kickoff time. In the heartland there'd been forty-eight tornadoes sighted in as many hours; now, the heavy weather was rolling in out of Pennsylvania, the vanguard of a humungous storm system running back down the Ohio River through Kentucky and Missouri to Oklahoma and West Texas—two thousand miles of lightning.

I spent the morning talking with USA '94 people, and there wasn't one of them didn't feel cockahoop. The attention they were getting was unimaginable even two or three years ago; of 1,200 accredited press at US Cup '93, 500 were American, and every major paper in every city, they said, now had at least one writer who wasn't just soccer-literate, but who actually liked it as well.

But the media was still the hardest sell. The public was out there—the Brazil game in New Haven drew 45,000, and advance sales for Boston were 28,000—but the older sports editors tended not to know about soccer, and it was easier for them to knock it or ignore it than to learn about it. The younger journalists who'd grown up with it said they were hammering on their editors' doors, and wedging them open was hard—but, they said, here we are.

As for television, USA–Germany in Chicago would be broadcast live and commercial-free on ABC—an unprecedented slice of network exposure. The other games were carried on Telemundo, reaching 90 percent of Hispanic-American homes, and on Prime Sports Channel America, another cable outlet with a potential reach of 41 million households. The World Cup itself will have eleven games on ABC, and all the rest on ESPN—but right now, when I called Prime, they said they figured their soccer audience split 80/20, maybe even 90/10 in favor of non-native-born people—Russians, Germans, Brits, Irish, Italians, whatever.

Since, according to the 1990 census, there are 22 million people in America who weren't born there, that's still a sizable chunk of audience. So when people say the World Cup shouldn't go to America, think: Do all those people not deserve their turn? And, more important, do the millions of American kids who play the game not deserve their turn too?

Gus Martins, one of the Boston journalists, was the son of immigrants from Cape Verde, and he'd grown up loving soccer; he said if he could cover nothing else that'd suit him just fine. And if you think Americans don't care about the game, you should have heard the passion in his voice when he said, "We're starving for this, man. We're starving."

Foxboro's a concrete box in a wood, and God knows for why, but it's thirty miles out of town. I drove there with an American writer; it was his first game, and he was intrigued and bemused in equal measure. When he saw the extent of the security round the stadium—highway patrol all over the shop, state and county police with batons and handguns—his eyes widened. But on the security front as on all others, this was dry-run time—and, happily, I'd hear later that among maybe a thousand English fans, there'd not been one hint of a hoolie. So they ended up with no one to practice on—and by the looks of them, I'd not be wanting to give them any practice either.

Closer to the ground, the Adidas logo was everywhere—on volunteers' T-shirts, and exclusively at the Foot Locker Team Shop. Marquees and stands did steady business; the crowd was thin, but growing. I went inside and sat down to write my notes; a security guard asked, "Hey. How long's a soccer game last anyhow?"

With an hour to go, the sky grew heavier. They'd expected a brisk walk-up sale, but I could see people looking out their windows and thinking, No thanks. We agreed this would have to be a brutal place to watch gridiron in January—but the Americans grinned, and said the Patriots were always out of it by January anyhow.

Clumps of people slowly occupied the stands. The English put out their flags, West Ham, Woking, Leyton Orient, Bath City Blues World Tour; the Americans eyed them with interest. Their own crowd seemed mostly to be kids bringing their parents; the USA '94 mascot, a mutt called Striker, wandered around getting his picture taken with children. The floodlights came on; the sky was dense, the air tangy with the smell of thunder, the wind whipping about. With thirty minutes to go it was raining, and the horizon was a wall of dull, metal-gray threat. Someone in the press box wandered by, headset crackling: "We may have to delay. We got a severe thunderstorm crawling in, we may have to delay." There was a pale far flicker of lightning; people milled about uncertain.

The English press fretted. A six o'clock kickoff meant they'd not be filing before one in the morning at the earliest, London time, with quotes from press conferences way later than that; any delay, and they'd miss the next day's papers altogether. Worse, however, was the fact that while the crowd were out there in the rain, this American press box was a cosy wee room behind glass. A roar out there would be a whisper in here—and it's hard to write a game when you can't hear the crowd.

So the storm slithered past and the game began, and it was like watching it on TV with the sound turned down. There was England attacking for a while, and the American defence looking wobbly—and then, *ping*, a sliderule pass from Harkes to left back Jeff Agoos, he broke down the flank, crossed, and Wegerle was firing straight at Chris Woods. And the Americans had skill, no doubt about it. They didn't shut people down like the English did, and they'd get caught being slow at the back—but after fifteen minutes, there wasn't much in it. Then John Barnes shaved a curler just wide by thin inches.

Under clearing skies of pale scud, the Americans held out. Then suddenly, *zoom*, Tab Ramos was skinning Leeds United's Tony Dorigo; ahead of him Wegerle was the best forward on the pitch, tricksy and mobile, while Wynalda was bullish, cocky, in your face. English clearances were getting a tad hectic here—and Dooley pushing up through midfield was strong in the tackle, while his teammates around him were getting nifty now, selling dummies, playing backheels, chipping their markers. They weren't Brazil—but like Bora wants, they were "nice."

Ramos unzipped Dorigo again; at the other end, Lee Dixon hit the post. So it was still evens when Harkes released Agoos with another pinpoint pass, Agoos crossed for Ramos on the byeline but the cross was too long, yet somehow Ramos still managed to keep it in and turn, a brilliant little piece of control—and he looked up sharp and there was Dooley arriving late and free near post and he fed him and *thump*, header like a bullet, 1-0 USA on the edge of halftime.

And if that scoreline was a staggering fluke in Brazil in 1950, tonight, forty-three years later, there was nothing fluky about it at all. England looked exhausted, maybe, at the end of a season ten months long, but they weren't playing remotely as badly as they had in Norway—and weren't Harkes, Wegerle, Dooley, Wynalda, Ramos all coming off a European season too? So if the Olimpico at Italia '90 was the coming of age, let me tell you, you guys were getting the keys to the car tonight.

I went outside for the second half. Here you've got a result on the cards that could ring round the world, and the crowd were little noisier in the flesh than they'd been from behind glass. One USA '94 guy said later that while he was pumped up in every other regard, he was a little upset that these people—near 38,000 on a Wednesday night, grim weather notwithstanding—were so quiet in the face of a piece of soccer history.

In the second half, Taylor sent on Arsenal's Ian Wright; he fired a string of ferocious drives at the American goal, and Tony Meola kept everything out. Word is a lot of people figure Meola's not as good as Keller these days, and there's another keeper challenging for the number one spot named Brad Friedel too—but on this form, you'd pick Meola every time. We're talking world-class saves here, saves of phenomenally rapid and athletic reaction, we're talking the man who kept you dramatically in the game—and still the crowd stayed too polite for words, a creature of sporadic hoots and claps without cohesion or real noise of any kind. The sorrowful chant of the despairing English boys—"What a load of rubbish"—was the only thing that sounded like football.

Then the U.S.A. had a corner, and a great lunk of a guy named Alexei Lalas soared at the near post, and his glancing header was immaculately placed, and the Americans were 2-0 up—and Lalas was spilling like a streak of wild light across the turf to the crowd, yelling, sliding on his knees through the spray, arms high to the sky, and at last they were shouting too, U.S.A.! U.S.A.! U.S.A.! So the place did hum a bit then, and it deserved to.

Before the game, USA '94's senior press officer Jim Trecker said if the U.S.A. won, it would be "a great, a potentially defining moment for the national team." Sure enough, they were front page now: COLONIALS 2, RED COATS 0.

In the press box, English voices, voices bitter, angry, dismayed, spoke harshly down the phones of disaster and humiliation. Outside, a TV newsman spoke solemnly into the camera of "One of the darkest nights in the history of English football."

Bora said carefully, "Only we win one game, nothing more." But in the following days, he tried another tack in the education of the American media, a tack dubbed immediately "Milutinovic math." Forget the record overall, he told them, and look at the record of this team, my real team, that have played together four times only—against England, and in US Cup '92: W3 D1 L0.

As for Taylor, defeated on a shabby plank dais behind railings in a dismal marquee, he was a model of dignity. Told that after Norway, there'd be "a temptation to interpret this as something of a national disgrace," he smiled wearily and said, "I'd have thought there'd be more than a temptation."

Certain members of the English press were not so dignified. When I got to the Back Bay Hilton after midnight the girl in the lobby bar was trying to shut up shop, and half a dozen of them wouldn't leave. When she said she wanted to go home, one of them said to her, "Well fucking go home then." Distraught over the result they stood shouting and swearing at each other, until one said something unforgivably insulting to another and then slouched off snarling, and the other said, "I'm not fucking having that, I'll fucking have him," and he went after him primed to throw punches. If the security guys needed practice, they could have found a lout or two to go to work on right there.

The Americans were jubilant. So long as they didn't go to Chicago and get beat 7-0 by the Germans, for their own purposes they'd now won this tournament already. At Logan Airport in the morning, I met Willie Banks, the world triple jump record holder, now on the staff with the L.A. organizing committee. Asked how he felt he grinned, and opened his jacket. His shirt was stars and stripes from collar to waist.

Another day, another stadium—it felt like the World Cup already—and at RFK in Washington for Germany–Brazil, Rothenberg was brimming over too. But then he always is. Show him a rock, this guy, give him five minutes, and he'll have you thinking you're holding gold. So I asked, would they have a league in 1995?

He said, "To me, professional soccer in the U.S. is absolutely inevitable. Its imminency is the only issue—and doing it right is the most important thing, so if it takes a little more time, a little more effort, a little more money, then we'll take that extra time, we'll make that extra effort, we'll spend that extra money to accomplish it."

They won't be short of money; USA '94 is projected to run a surplus of $20 million or more. And their plans for a league go before FIFA on December 1—but if it starts in 1996 instead of 1995, I said, then so be it?

"Absolutely."

They say they'll not make the mistakes the NASL did, going too big, too fast; they'll look for crowds of ten to fifteen thousand. And they say there are all those people playing now, they won't need to fill the teams with foreigners this time—and then, of course, if the U.S.A. does well . . . the England win, said Rothenberg, was "a real shot in the arm. You do all these various things to try and get it ready, but you need that magic moment to captivate the public. So it gives us enthusiasm, and it gets our fans believing we're on to something real."

Now it had been reported that he'd joked that if England didn't qualify, his security bill would be lower . . .

"I don't joke about that. I've said that if England don't qualify, it's a mixed blessing. On the one hand, obviously, a country with that tradition in the sport, a country where 99.99 percent of the fans are phenomenal, fans that we'd love to have here—it's unthinkable in some ways that they wouldn't be part of our World Cup. But on the other hand, if they don't come, and their crazy hooligans don't come either, I can catch a few hours' more sleep. It would be one potential problem removed. But it wouldn't mean all our problems are over; we've got the last phase of the Asian qualifiers coming up, with Iran, Iraq, North Korea, South Korea all in there—and you can only imagine the kind of security detail we'll have to engage in if one of them ends up here."

I asked what his biggest headache was and he said, "We have no headaches."

No headaches, Germany–Brazil, and wonderful RFK for them to play in. On a Thursday afternoon 35,000 came, and the two best teams in the world treated them. First half, Brazil played the loveliest soccer I've ever seen—endless one-touch stuff, chest, head, knee, foot, the ball stroked like a baby passed among adoring relatives, and the Germans never saw it; after forty-five minutes, Brazil were three up and strolling. So then the Germans came out aggrieved in the second half and got three goals back, and the Brazilians, coshed, got a bit nasty—an elbow here, a little hack there—and the crowd loved every minute, cheering everything nice with festive impartiality, jeering anything naughty with good-humored vigor. Like Gus Martins said, they'd been starving—and now here was someone bringing them a five-star banquet.

And the English press were in town—England would play Brazil here in three days' time—and apart from a few worthies from the qualities, they didn't even bother showing up. One of those who did said wearily, "I suppose they think they're not going to learn anything."

In the dim and cavernous bowels of the stadium after the game, German manager Berti Vogts was asked about America's win over England. He offered congratulations, and said his scout's report suggested "a strong team both in fighting, and in technical performance. I've said before that it'll be hard to beat the U.S.A. here, and we look forward to playing them." And the way that came over sounded ominous to me.

I took the Amtrak to Chicago, and talked over dinner in West Virginia with a construction worker called Scott from Seattle. An avid reader, he'd had the misfortune to read Bill Buford's *Among the Thugs*—a meretricious, misleading, morally repellent piece of work—so when we found in the lounge car that a tattooed grotesque with a waxed handlebar mustache and a drink problem was falling over on his fellow passengers, Scott grinned. He said, "An American hooligan."

Kayvon Bahramian heard us talking, and joined in. He was seventeen; his parents were Iranian immigrants who'd arrived in the sixties. He'd played the game since he was seven, and he was going soon to Miami University in Ohio where, he said, he'd like to go on playing, but only for fun; he wasn't good enough to make it competitively. He said, "It's not an open tryout. The soccer guys are all recruited; the college coaches and scouts go around all the high schools. There are always players with names."

He wasn't one of them, but he loved the game big time, and he knew a lot about it. In his locker at high school, he'd had tapes of all the games at Italia '90 from the quarter-finals on, and one day they'd been stolen—all except the horrible final between Germany and Argentina. "This most discriminating thief"—Kayvon smiled ruefully—"had to leave me that one."

So I was astounded when he said the World Cup shouldn't be coming to America. "It's not practical," he said. "It's not going to have the feel a World Cup should have, all the distances. Any other country, everybody'd focus on it—like, that's what's going on. But here people'll still be going to the baseball, whatever."

I asked how it was to grow here if it didn't come and he said, "How did it grow anywhere else? Isn't just loving it enough?

And as far as youth is concerned, it can't grow much more anyhow. So if it's going to grow as a spectator sport, something else has to go. And how are you going to bring people away from Michael Jordan?"

He said if it did succeed, "Once soccer gets a hold it's like a disease. There's no way the others would survive." But I went to bed knowing he had a point. In the vastness of America, for example, the national team isn't really a national team yet, but only a team of merely regional interest to whatever region it happens to be in. A Boston paper might send a man to cover them as far as D.C.—but when they move on to Chicago, in Boston they stop being a story.

So in contrast to Italy, where 58 million downed tools for a month and thought of nothing else—the game is like food in that country, it's the air you breathe, the wine you drink—fans in the U.S.A. could find themselves passing instead through nine cities where the World Cup's happening, and great voids where it isn't. And if it isn't that way—if the World Cup does capture the imagination of your whole vast nation, with so much else of its own going on—then that would be a remarkable triumph.

The omens in Chicago were good. USA–Germany at Soldier Field on June 13, 1993, was up against the biggest of all possible competition. That evening, Jordan and the Bulls were playing the third game of the NBA Finals against Charles Barkley's Phoenix Suns, 2-0 up in the series and aiming for a clean sweep and a three-peat. So the fact that 53,000 turned out to watch soccer there (with 56,000 watching England–Brazil in RFK at the same time) says firmly that if this game's a disease, then a lot of people are coming down with the symptoms.

Before the game, Lothar Matthaus was honored; he was playing for his country for the hundredth time. The world champions then proceeded to stomp all over you. The American defence, by some margin the weakest part of your makeup, looked bewildered and just fearfully slow. You'd have some guy with the ball at his feet just putzing about looking lost with Jurgen Klinsmann in his face and you'd be screaming, Get it out of there! Don't you know who that guy *is*? Sure enough, on thirteen minutes, Klinsmann tore through once more, and it was Germany 1-0.

And the Germans kept coming—until, on twenty-five minutes, the U.S.A. scored the best goal of the game. Ramos played the sweetest long pass wide and diagonal to Wegerle, Wegerle went pelting down the left, looked up, there was Dooley getting free far post, *ping*, he whipped it in on the button, Dooley stooped, *bam*, clean off the head, 1-1.

The Germans were not best pleased, and from here to deep in the second half they put on a show. It was 3-1 at halftime, 4-1 soon after. In the midfield Ramos turned to Harkes and said, "John, I feel helpless out here."

An American in the press box said, "If this is a war, we better learn some negotiating skills fast."

Harkes said afterward the Germans were, by a mile, the best side he'd ever played—so fast, so strong, so organized. You'd get the ball, and there'd be no one anywhere you could give it to. So you'd grit your teeth and beat a man, and before you'd looked up to try and find someone again, there was another German in your face. So if you didn't beat him too you'd lost it, and seconds after that they were down Meola's throat again.

An American journalist said to Ramos afterward that it looked like the Germans had nine midfielders out there, and Ramos grinned. "It felt like they had nine midfielders, nine forwards, nine defenders. So I think around the world it's going to raise eyebrows, what we did."

What they did was they didn't lie down. What they did, with eighteen minutes left, was pump a long ball wide right for Ernie Stewart. He tore after it, with a German defender stretching long legs at full speed round his knees, and somehow he stayed upright and he made that ball, the German left sliding on his back in his wake. So now the keeper came haring out and, still sprinting, Stewart nutmegged him from the tightest angle; the ball went through him, and trickled long yard upon slow yard toward the line. And the crowd fell silent, and right there you had one of those great soccer moments where the world goes slo-mo, and Michael Schulz was racing back toward the goal trying to make it before the ball did and clear it away, and the ball beat him by a yard, and the score was 4-2.

Five minutes later, Harkes flighted a free kick into the area. Dooley rose—and then the astonished crowd were screaming and hooting and bawling as ball and keeper together got punched in a heap over the line by the force of the header. So the final score was 4-3, and who scores three goals against the Germans? Brazil, OK. But the U.S.A.?

Dooley subsequently announced that with his contract up at Kaiserslautern, he'd be moving to Mission Viejo to join the American national squad. That'll put some meat in your training sessions.

Berti Vogts said, "The German team played extremely well for seventy minutes. Then we seemed to remember that we will be a guest here in twelve months, and we gave away a few gifts. But," he said, "you can see if you give them the opportunity to come forward, they're perfectly capable of taking their chances." The shot count was 28-7 in Germany's favor—but three goals in seven strikes, that's shooting. Vogts said, "They are indeed a team to be reckoned with."

And seven goals live on ABC? Bora smiled. He said, "I'm very happy for the people, because it's so important for our future."

And now, that future is the World Cup. I wish you well in it.

25

USA '94

In the end, after the little guys dropped out—bye-bye to the likes of Liberia and Liechtenstein—490 qualifying matches decided twenty-two nations to join Germany and yourselves at USA '94. A total of 1,429 goals were scored, and none was more astoundingly weird than that scored by San Marino against England 8.3 seconds after their game had begun. Kickoff, ball to English full back, he fluffs his pass back to the keeper, the Sammarinese striker nips in, 1-0, cue hysterical laughter globewide. It was the fastest goal scored against England in 700 internationals; their ignominy was complete.

It was November 17, 1993. In Buenos Aires, Argentina scraped past Australia 1-0 in the second leg of the South America/Oceania play-off; all around Europe, eleven other games took the final issues to the wire. For England, after losing 2-0 in Rotterdam, their last faint hopes rested on Holland losing in Poland, while they themselves had to score seven against San Marino. They did, too—they won 7-1—but a manifestly superior Dutch side, their forward line led by the lethal Dennis Bergkamp, beat Poland 3-1 anyhow. And few would deny, given England's calamitous decline since the 1990 semi-final, that the outcome gives the tournament the better side.

There was more sympathy for the Welsh. Needing to beat Romania in Cardiff, the game was tied 1-1 when they missed a penalty; they went on to lose it 2-1. So you'll not be seeing Ryan Giggs—but again, any impartial observer will tell you the better side is through.

Harder to explain is the absence of Eric Cantona and his stylish fellow Frenchmen. But, needing only to tie one of their last two home games against Israel and Bulgaria, they somehow contrived to lose them both, the latter when the Bulgarians scored the winner in the final minute.

Japan's exit was less surprising, but equally dramatic. They were home and dry, leading Iraq 2-1 in their last game with just seventeen seconds remaining, then the Iraqis equalized, the Japanese dropped a point, South Korea slipped past them on goal difference, and a stunned nation wept. It's a cruel game . . . for whose highest prize the following entrants did make it, listed by their world rankings at the time of the draw:

Italy	1	Nigeria	16
Holland	2	Mexico	17
Germany	3	Colombia	21
Brazil	4	Belgium	22
Norway	5	Bulgaria	23
Spain	7	Cameroon	24
Argentina	9 =	United States	27
Switzerland	9 =	Morocco	30
Sweden	11	Greece	32
Romania	12	Saudi Arabia	38
Ireland	13	South Korea	39
Russia	14	Bolivia	59

The big players missing are European champions Denmark (ranked 6), who were squeezed out on goal difference by the Irish, along with England (8), France (15), Uruguay (18), the Czechs and Slovaks (19), and Portugal (20). The surprise packages are Norway and Bolivia—the latter, in December 1992, ranked eighty-seventh—but you should take these rankings with a weighty dose of salt. Recently introduced by FIFA because, one suspects, they figure Americans like this kind of thing, they're updated monthly, they take into account everyone's record over the previous six years, and they can't suggest for one minute what'll happen on the day. Sides from different continents only meet in meaningful competition at the World Cup every four years, so the criteria by which Nigeria or Mexico rank higher than Uruguay or Portugal are, frankly, ethereal—and it will all mean nothing when the real thing begins.

* * *

The draw for the first round was held in Las Vegas on December 19, 1993. It was farcically gerrymandered, and stained by a nasty outbreak of politics when Joao Havelange refused to allow Pele to take part. Pele had accused Havelange's son-in-law, Ricardo Texeira, the president of Brazil's football federation, of corruption over broadcasting contracts for the Brazilian championship, and lawsuits were in progress. But when it was suggested to Havelange that Rothenberg and the Americans might be disappointed that the world's greatest player was barred from their inaugural gala, his sinister reply just sums the guy up: "Mr. Rothenberg would be disappointed if we withdrew the World Cup from the United States. But he has the World Cup, and one person is not going to change that." Not even Pele . . . Havelange is seventy-seven and, God help us, apparently means to stand for reelection in 1994.

While the boss was snubbing his game's greatest star, his adjutant Sepp Bladder (as Americans are pleased to pronounce him) tried to explain the carefully manipulated intricacies of the draw to the world's soccer press. Eventually, he despaired. "I have had great difficulty explaining the draw to you, and you are specialists. Imagine what it must be like for the public." I will not, therefore, even attempt to explain it here, but merely tell you how it turned out.

Group A

Sat. June 18	Detroit	Switzerland v. U.S.A.
Sat. June 18	Los Angeles	Colombia v. Romania
Wed. June 22	Los Angeles	Colombia v. U.S.A.
Wed. June 22	Detroit	Romania v. Switzerland
Sun. June 26	San Francisco	Colombia v. Switzerland
Sun. June 26	Los Angeles	Romania v. U.S.A.

So did you get an easy group? Me, I wouldn't call this lot easy at all. If you don't take three points off the Swiss in your opener, basically you're really up against it.

The Swiss are well organized, a resolute outfit ably marshaled by English manager Roy Hodgson, and in Knup and Chapuisat they have two dangerous front men. But they're not experienced at the top level (they've not been to a World Cup since 1966) and a reliance on workrate may hurt them in the heat of an American summer. So Dooley, Harkes, Ramos, Wegerle, and Wynalda should have enough to get you past them—and they better have, because containing a Romanian side orchestrated by Gheorghe Hagi will be a much stiffer challenge.

As for Colombia, they're a strong outside tip to go all the way. Freddy Rincon and Carlos Valderrama are two of the best midfielders around, while Parma's Faustino Asprilla is an electric striker, instrumental in his club's recent success in *Serie A*. In the qualifiers, they beat Argentina 2-1 in Bogota, then thumped them 5-0 in Buenos Aires—this second result producing dozens of deaths as drunk and/or coked-out Colombian celebrants jubilantly crashed cars and shot each other. God knows what'll happen if they win the World Cup . . . I predict Colombia to top the group, Romania and the U.S.A. to go through with them, and Switzerland to go home. But it'll be very, very tight.

Group B

Sun. June 19	Los Angeles	Cameroon v. Sweden
Mon. June 20	San Francisco	Brazil v. Russia
Fri. June 24	San Francisco	Brazil v. Cameroon
Fri. June 24	Detroit	Russia v. Sweden
Tue. June 28	San Francisco	Cameroon v. Russia
Tue. June 28	Detroit	Brazil v. Sweden

This is the pick of the groups, a mouthwatering prospect; Brazil-Cameroon should be a cracker. Brazil will go through; with Romario and/or Rai up front, plus Muller, Elivelton, Careca, Bebeto, Mozer, and plenty more, Brazil should win the whole thing.

As for the others, perm any two from three. Cameroon want supersub Roger Milla, now forty-two, to appear yet again, but it's hard to believe the old talisman can work his magic twice. Look out for Makanaky in midfield and a striker named Omam-Biyik, but don't count on them making the last eight a second time; Sweden and Russia will likely press them too hard.

Tragically, the Russians lost a fine player just days before the draw. Sergei Cherbakov played for Sporting Lisbon who, unforgivably, sacked their manager Bobby Robson in early December, after a defeat in the UEFA Cup. I say unforgivably because, apart from that defeat, Sporting were joint top of their league at the time, and had lost only two of their previous sixteen. The players plainly disapproved, and went to a valedictory dinner with Robson—but while the others went home, Cherbakov went on to a bar. As he was driving home at five in the morning without a seat belt, he ran one red light too many and crashed; he may never walk again, let alone play football.

Which is sad—but it won't make Russia any easier to deal with. In Kiryakov, Yuran, and Kolyvanov they have three threatening front runners, and they're technically gifted all through; on the other hand, they have a tradition of not realizing their promise, and went home last time after the first round.

So did Sweden, one of only four sides in Italy to lose all their three games. This indignity, however, belies their ability; they were semifinalists in the European Championship in 1992, and in Thomas Brolin of Parma, and Martin Dahlin of Borussia Moenchengladbach, they have two formidably able attacking players. So in short, anything could happen in this group—and whatever does, it's likely to be good.

Group C

Fri. June 17	Chicago	Bolivia v. Germany
Fri. June 17	Dallas	South Korea v. Spain
Tue. June 21	Chicago	Gemany v. Spain
Thu. June 23	Boston	Bolivia v. South Korea
Mon. June 27	Chicago	Bolivia v. Spain
Mon. June 27	Dallas	Germany v. South Korea

I don't know about the U.S.A.'s group, but this group's so easy it's ridiculous. Germany and Spain will beat the other two, the other two will go home, and that's that.

If Matthaus, Klinsmann, Hassler, Moller, and the rest don't go on to make the final, it'll be a big surprise; outside of Brazil and Italy, it's hard to see who can stop them. As for the Spanish, Barcelona's keeper Andoni Zubizarreta can stop just about anything; a 3-1 trouncing of the Irish in Dublin (where virtually no one ever wins) showed how good they can be going forward, too. Quarter-finalists, but probably not more.

South Korea, by contrast, are sure to go home early; Bolivia ditto. They got some cracking results in the qualifiers (they twice put seven past Venezuela) but the other sides all grumbled that Bolivia were just running up points at altitude. Certainly, playing at home in La Paz—the world's highest capital city, 11,000 feet above sea level—does give you an advantage. They beat Brazil there 2-0, both goals scored in the dying minutes as the Brazilians panted like beached fish for the final whistle. But when Bolivia came back to earth for the return in Rio, Brazil stuffed them 6-0.

Still, they may have more about them than just leather lungs this time—thin air in La Paz, after all, hasn't helped them qualify since 1950—but while much is expected of their only European-based player, midfielder Erwin Sanchez, it's probably too much. Germany and Spain, in short, to walk this one.

Group D

Tue. June 21	Boston	Argentina v. Greece
Tue. June 21	Dallas	Bulgaria v. Nigeria
Sat. June 25	Boston	Argentina v. Nigeria
Sun. June 26	Chicago	Bulgaria v. Greece
Thu. June 30	Boston	Greece v. Nigeria
Thu. June 30	Dallas	Argentina v. Bulgaria

Argentina-Nigeria's the pick of this bunch; I expect those two to go through, with maybe one of the others snatching a third-place slot, but overall it's a hard group to read.

Argentina made a fearful meal out of qualifying, but they should still go far. They'll be hellishly hard to score against, and look out for Fernando Redondo in midfield. And the only question is whether they bring Maradona. Now thirty-three, back playing in Argentina and supposedly rehabilitated, if he comes he's as likely to be a disruptive influence as an inspirational one; I'd leave him out myself, because the shadows some heroes cast can get too long. But they're candidates for the last four either way (unless someone can turn them over like Colombia did) because they're hard as they come, and they don't give up.

Nigeria, meanwhile, are Africa's best hope. They've never been to a World Cup before, but I doubt that'll bother them; all their players play in Europe, among them a zippy striker named Efan Ekoku in England, and the burlier front man Rashid Yekini in Portugal. There's also John Fashanu ("Fash the Bash") who plays for my favorite club, Wimbledon, and who's said to be working on getting himself a Nigerian passport . . . but whoever plays, expect them to be lively.

Between Greece and Bulgaria, the latter are more likely to get through, with Barcelona's Hristo Stoichkov and Sporting Lisbon's Krasimir Balakov making the difference. In sixteen games at previous World Cups, they've not won one—but, after ousting the French, 1994, I think, will be the year they lay that bogey to rest.

Group E

Sat. June 18	New York	Ireland v. Italy
Sun. June 19	Washington	Mexico v. Norway
Thu. June 23	New York	Italy v. Norway
Fri. June 24	Orlando	Ireland v. Mexico
Tue. June 28	New York	Ireland v. Norway
Tue. June 28	Washington	Italy v. Mexico

On paper, Jack Charlton's Irish could hardly have had a worse draw; they didn't even get to play in Boston, which they'd been hoping to turn into home terrain. And, on paper, you'd have to say that the all-or-nothing Irish game will wilt in the swampy heat of these venues; you'd have to say they'll be going home after three games. Except, except . . . Charlton, a single-minded mix of the wry, the blunt, and the boorish, has molded a team with as much unforgiving self-belief as any around. With the exception of Glasgow Celtic's Packy Bonner, they all play in England, and they've been together so long they're virtually a club side. They're getting on a bit, maybe— but they're boundlessly bighearted, and the likes of Aldridge, Staunton, and McGrath (if he's fit) are canny with it too. Watch also for Manchester United's midfielder Roy Keane, a twenty-two-year-old with one hell of an engine on him.

If they can bustle their way through, it'll probably be at Norway's expense. Like Ireland, ironically, Norway could also field a side employed entirely in the English game, and they too have progressed on the strengths of workrate and organization. But with all due respect to their performance in the qualifiers—they finished ahead of Holland, England, and Poland, beating all three along the way—a world ranking of 5 is just silly. Still, from Tottenham's Eric Thorstvedt in goal to Sheffield United's Justein Flo up front, they've got muscle and courage, and more than a shade of skill too; their game with the Irish will be a dogfight.

Mexico look more certain to advance, with skillful players running up a good record in 1993, but they may prove brittle. They'll not often have played sides who get in your face the way Ireland and Norway do—but on the other hand, they're likely to last better in the heat. Watch for their keeper Jorge Campos; like René Higuita for Colombia in 1990 he is, shall we say, just a little bit eccentric.

So I figure two of these three to go through, but I wouldn't want to call it; Italy, meanwhile, should beat all three of them, and go on to be semifinalists at least. They looked shaky in the qualifiers, and they've a history of being slow starters, so an upset along the way is always possible, stirring epics of trauma in their media—but they have far too much quality to blow it. In midfield, Roberto Baggio of Juventus is the best player in the world; Signori and Melli are clinical finishers, and there's no better left back around than Maldini. Moreover, to all intents and purposes, in New York they'll be playing at home. In short, Italy to walk it.

Group F

Sun. June 19	Orlando	Belgium v. Morocco
Mon. June 20	Washington	Holland v. Saudi Arabia
Sat. June 25	New York	Morocco v. Saudi Arabia
Sat. June 25	Orlando	Belgium v. Holland
Wed. June 29	Orlando	Holland v. Morocco
Wed. June 29	Washington	Belgium v. Saudi Arabia

Boring. The Dutch-Belgian meeting will decide it while, like Bolivia and Korea, the Arab sides go home. Expect Morocco to be a tougher proposition than the Saudis, and maybe to nick a point or two—but they won't have the flair of Cameroon or Nigeria. In Nourredine Naybet they have a handy young sweeper, but I doubt he'll hold up Bergkamp for long. As for the Saudis, they've got pots of money and they've bought a Dutch coach with it—Leo Beenhakker, who managed the Dutch in Italy last time—but you don't score goals with your wallet.

Of the four, the Belgians are the seeded team, on the strength of recent World Cup outings, and in Michel Preud'homme they've an excellent keeper marshaling a miserly defence. Enzo Scifo's worth watching in midfield, too—but the Dutch will most likely have the better of them. Aside from Bergkamp, they have two scarily fast guys attacking from midfield, Bryan Roy and Marc Overmars. Further back, Jan Wouters or Ronald Koeman would knock a bus over if they had to. Quarter-finalists, certainly, with the proviso that, as ever, they're arguing with each other.

They were managed to qualification by Dick Advocaat, who knew that if he succeeded he'd lose his job; his ingrate bosses wanted Johan Cruyff for the actual tournament instead. It now seems, however, that Cruyff's asked for too much money, and the bosses have turned back to Advocaat. The trouble with this is that Ruud Gullit—his career rejuvenated since he moved from Milan to the Genoese club Sampdoria—isn't talking to Advocaat, and took no part in the qualifying . . . but if they didn't need him to get there, why take him now they've arrived?

In conclusion, I'll say that the predictions above will be in tatters before the first round's half done. Bolivia and Morocco will take mighty strides forward under the banner of the underdog, Germany and Brazil will go down in flames, Greece will win the final 5-4 after an epic struggle with South Korea. . . well, it won't be that weird. But in truth, anyone could make the last sixteen, and once you're into the knockout, the only certain thing then are the dates and the venues.

There'll be a Round of 16 game in each city bar Detroit, two games a day from July 2 through July 5. On July 9 there'll be quarter-finals in Dallas and Boston, on July 10 in New York and San Francisco. The semifinals will be in New York and Los Angeles on July 13, the play-off for third place in Los Angeles three days later, and the final in the same place on July 17. And while you're watching all this with, I hope, mounting interest and enjoyment, there's one thought I'd like to leave you with.

On the day before the draw, the players of Tottenham Hotspur and Liverpool stood in silence around the center circle at White Hart Lane in North London, paying tribute to the memory of Danny Blanchflower, and a crowd of 31,394 kept silence with them. Blanchflower, captain of Tottenham and Northern Ireland in the late fifties and early sixties, was a great player, a much-loved advocate of the beautiful game, and he once said this: "The great fallacy is that this game is first and last about winning. It is nothing of the kind. The game is about glory; it is about doing things with style."

In keeping with that thought and that man's memory, Tottenham and Liverpool then played a wonderful 3-3 tie, a swirling, fluid match blessed with pace, invention, skill, and, yes, with glory. And it's too much to hope João Havelange might ever remember that that's what it's about—but if Alan Rothenberg gets his twelve-city, million-dollar "Major Soccer League" off the ground when the World Cup's been and gone, just write him a letter and remind him for me, won't you?

Glossary

4-4-2   A team formation with four defenders, four midfielders (qv), and two forwards (qv).

4-3-3   A formation with three midfielders and three forwards, at least one of whom is a designated "winger" (qv).

4-2-4   A formation with two midfielders and four forwards: two wingers and two central "strikers" (qv).

5-3-2   This formation has five defenders, one of whom, the "sweeper" (qv), roams the defense, tidying up and acting as the link man to the attacking players.

The area   The penalty area: the rectangle in front of the goal (qv) where the keeper (qv) may handle the ball and within which a foul results in a penalty kick (qv).

Backheel   A pass made to a fellow player with the back of the heel: usually unexpected, occasionally a little technical gem from the game's more skilled exponents.

The bar   The crossbar which, supported by the two "posts," makes up the goal (qv). Alternatively, the place where most journalists may be found during a game.

Booking   For a transgression of the rules like a bad foul, abusive language, or deliberate hand ball, the referee (qv) can "book" the offender. (So called because the player's name is noted in the referee's little book.) To show the player and crowd that this has come to pass, the referee waves a yellow card at the player. A second booking in a game results in a sending off (qv). Also known as "being shown the yellow card."

Center half   The two central defenders are center halves. Usually tall, to deal with crosses (qv), they should have pace to keep up with quick forwards (qv), but often aren't. *See also* **Donkey**.

Center forward   An attacker, traditionally tall and adept at heading the ball, often slow and unadept at skilled play with the ball on the ground. A target of crosses, his job is to find his colleague or go for goal. A position favored by British teams but, in the faster modern game, often an anachronism. Hence nearly always described as "an old-fashioned center-forward."

Clean sheet   When a goalkeeper does not concede a goal in a game, he has kept a "clean sheet," i.e., a shut-out. Note: Soccer is not as obsessed with statistics as other sports. Beyond individual goalscoring and appearance records, not many stats, including clean sheets, are maintained and discussed by the average fan.

CONCACAF   The Confederation of North and Central American and Caribbean Federations. They've said lately that they'll come up with a less boggling acronym, but they've said that before so don't hold your breath.

Corner   When a defender plays the ball over his own goal line, the attacking team is awarded a corner. The ball is placed on the apex of goal line and touchline (qv), and is kicked back into play. As a set piece, there are a number of plays that can be attempted: the "short corner," when the ball is passed to a nearby teammate who can gain a better angle for a cross (qv); the "near-post corner," when the ball is fired toward a player on the near post for a header toward the goal; or a "far-post corner," where the ball is lofted in the path of onrushing attackers beyond the far post.

Cross   A ball played from the flank toward an attacking player or players. Most effective when curled away from the goalkeeper.

Cup-Winner's Cup   A European club competition for the winners of the national, domestic cup competitions. 1993 winners, Parma of Italy.

Dead-ball situation   Nothing to do with the old baseball. Corners, free kicks (qv), and penalties (qv) are "dead-ball situations," when the ball is kicked from a fixed mark, and attackers and defenders dispose themselves to deal with it accordingly. This is the nearest soccer gets to a "play" in the American sense of that word.

Donkey   A British supporter's term of abuse for a slow, ungainly player, usually a center half or center forward. (C.f. many other terms of abuse, e.g., galumph, toe rag.)

European Cup   A European club competition for the winners of national league championships. Olympique Marseille of France won it in 1993. They were barred from defending their title after an alleged match-rigging scandal.

Extra time   Overtime. In the World Cup, a tied score at the end of ninety minutes results in two fifteen-minute periods of "extra time": if no winner has emerged, a "penalty shoot-out" (qv) takes place.

FIFA   The Federation of International Football Associations. World soccer's ruling body, whose president since 1974 has been Dr. João Havel-ange of Brazil.

Foul   A challenge deemed illegal by the referee who awards the other team a free kick (qv) or a penalty (qv).

Forward   A player whose role is in attack: a winger (qv), a striker (qv), or center forward (qv).

Free kick   When the referee deems that one side has committed an offence, a "free kick" is awarded to the other side. The ball is played from the site of the misdemeanor. Serious transgressions merit a "direct free kick" from which a shot may be taken directly at goal. (qv) Most teams have a specialist for such eventualities. Lesser crimes only result in an "indirect free kick," which must be touched by someone else before a goal can be scored.

Full back   The two defenders who play on the flanks, the right back (qv) and left back (qv) are the full backs. An ancillary function is to support the offence by providing crosses from the flank. Known in this role as an "overlapping full back."

Goal   Both (a) the structure defended by the goalkeeper and (b) the physical crossing of the goal line between the posts by the ball—the object of the game being to score more goals than the opposition.

Hand ball   An offence: any intentional handling of the ball by any player other than the goalkeeper in his area.

Hat trick   The individual feat of scoring three goals in one game. Originally, the three goals had to be consecutive, but this is no longer the usage.

Jules Rimet trophy   The trophy awarded to winners of the World Cup until Brazil were given it for winning their third cup in 1970. Named for the longtime president of FIFA.

Keeper The guardian of the goal, the goalkeeper or "keeper."

Kop The largest standing section of a British stadium is often called the Kop, named after a hill in South Africa made famous during the Boer War.

Lay-off A ball pushed aside to a fellow player with more room than you have yourself.

Left back The full back patrolling the left side of the pitch. Usually left-footed.

Linesman The officiating team consists of the referee (qv) and two linesmen, who run the touchlines (qv), assisting the referee and looking for offsides (qv).

Manager A team official. In British football coterminous with coach, but international teams often call the people who select and train the side the coach.

Marking A defender stays close to an attacker and tries to prevent him getting the ball or finding "space." (qv) Most noticeable at free kicks and corners, when defenders try to "mark" each attacker and prevent a goal. Often a player will be assigned the job of marking a particularly dangerous opponent the whole game.

Midfielder The players linking defense and attack, who operate, as the name suggests, in the middle of the field. Although they should be able to do a bit of everything, individuals specialize and teams often have a "ball-winner" (a tackler [qv]); and a "play-maker" (a passer, analogous to a quarterback) in midfield.

NASL North American Soccer League

Net The mesh in the goal originally introduced to capture a ball fired hard between the posts (qv) to make it obvious that a goal has been scored.

Offside An offence committed when a player, in the

other team's half, has fewer than two opponents between him and the goal he is attacking when the ball is played to him. See Chapter 14 for fuller explanation.

One-two   A passing maneuver in which player A passes to player B who immediately passes back to player A who, in theory, has run into "space" (qv) to receive the ball. Looks nice when it works.

Penalty kick   A foul in the area committed by a defender results in a penalty for the attacking team. The ball is placed on the "spot" twelve yards from goal and the penalty taker only has to beat the keeper to score; everyone else must retreat at least ten yards behind the ball. A discretionary award from the referee and thus often the subject of rancorous debate on the field.

Pitch   The field. Also, colloquially, the "park."

Post   The poles supporting the crossbar and holding up the net (qv).

Possession football   In which a team attempts to advance the ball by careful passing. The opposite of the "long-ball game" which is often little more than a succession of Hail Mary passes lofted in the general direction of the forwards.

Premier League   The top division in England below which are the First, Second, and Third divisions and the GM Vauxhall Conference, between which teams are promoted and relegated, although you cannot be promoted from the Premier League—there is nowhere higher to go. Beneath the Conference are a whole series of minor leagues.

Professional foul   A foul committed deliberately to stop a forward from getting a clear run on goal. Cynical and unsporting, it should result in the offender being sent off (qv) forthwith.

Red card   Shown by the referee to a player to indicate that he has been sent off.

Referee   The single arbiter of the rules on the pitch.

Right back   The full back patrolling the right side of the pitch. Usually right-footed.

Sending off A player who has committed two bookable offences or a single particularly heinous foul is "sent off" and can take no further part in the game. Indicated by a red card from the referee.

Serie A   The top league in Italy, universally acknowledged to be the best in the world.

Sitter   A chance to score so gapingly easy that it should be taken sitting down. Generally referred to when the chance isn't taken, thus "He's missed a sitter."

Space   A vital part of the attack is to find unguarded territory from which to essay an unhindered cross or shot.

Striker   A forward player whose job is to score goals.

Studs   Protrusions from the bottom of the soccer boot (shoe) that provide grip. Much like cleats.

Suspension In the World Cup, one red card or two yellow cards mean a one-game suspension. Unlike in baseball, the length of the ban is not determined by the severity of the offence on the pitch.

Sweeper   The fifth man in the 5-3-2 system whose job it is to "sweep" up around his area and bring the ball forward. A free role (thus sometimes called the "libero" in deference to the Italians who invented it): the sweeper does not mark any particular player, rather he deals with attackers who have evaded the other defenders. A demanding role that only a few can perform well.

Tackle   The attempt by a player to take the ball away from an opponent in possession. Subject to endless qualifications such as "late" (a foul); "sliding" (the spectacular, feet-first launch of a player for the ball from distance); and so on.

Throw-in   When the ball crosses the touchline (qv), a

throw-in is awarded against the team that touched the ball last. The ball must be thrown in with both hands, over the player's head. A "long throw-in" right into the goalmouth can be attempted by the adept who can reach that far and this is as good as a corner.

Total football

A style of play where all the players are able to play all the roles, thereby befuddling any rigid opposing system. Used to describe the play of the great Dutch teams of the seventies, whose defenders had as much skill on the ball as the attackers.

Touchline

The lines between the goal line patrolled by the linesman.

UEFA

The European Union of Football Associations (designated by its French acronym). The governing body of European soccer.

UEFA Cup

The competition, organized by UEFA, for teams finishing second or third or fourth in their league. Each nation receives a number of places based upon the performance of their clubs in all the European competitions. 1993 winners, Juventus of Italy.

USSIL

United States Interregional Soccer League

USSF

United States Soccer Federation

Wall

The collective noun for players lined between a free kick, from which an opponent is likely to try to score, and the goal. Designed to block shots and obstruct the view of the kicker. According to the rules, it must be at least ten yards from the ball but it never is. A wall can be circumvented by skillful shooting, an art much beloved by South American teams.

Winger

A forward who plays wide, near the touchline, whose main role is to provide crosses for his strikers.

Yellow card

Shown by the referee to a player to indicate that he has been booked.

Further Reading

Although these books may not be readily available in this country, they should be kept in mind for a rainy day in a bookstore in the U.K.

Bryon Butler, **The Official History of the Football Association**, MacDonald: Queen Anne Press, London
Butler has been BBC Radio's soccer man for twenty-five years, and strikes the desired tone of sonorous worthiness accordingly; but this is very much better than might have been expected of something "official" all the same.

Pete Davies, **All Played Out**, Mandarin, London
"This could well be the best book ever written about football."—**Time Out**

Eamon Dunphy, **A Strange Kind of Glory: Sir Matt Busby and Manchester United**, William Heinemann, London
A masterful biography, fueled with love of the game, and righteous anger at the idiots who run it.

Brian Glanville, **The History of the World Cup**, Faber & Faber, London and Boston
Compendiously knowledgeable, acerbic, witty, not infrequently surreal—a soccer junkie's bible. Revised and rereleased in this country in 1993.

Nick Hornby, **Fever Pitch**, Gollancz, London
A wonderful book, bittersweet and very funny, in which Hornby performs an invaluable service by explaining one of life's great mysteries—how anyone ever becomes an Arsenal fan.

Arthur Hopcraft, **The Football Man**, Sportspages, London
A collection of attractive and thoughtful essays from the sixties, when journalists could still employ words of more than one syllable, and romance about the game was still easy to believe in.

John Moynihan, **The Soccer Syndrome**, Sportspages, London
Like **The Football Man**, an intelligent collection of journalism from the sixties.

John Robinson, **The World Cup 1930–1990**, Soccer Book Publishing Ltd., Cleethorpes
More prosaic than Glanville, but more stats.

Bobby Robson with Bob Harris, **So Near and Yet so Far: Bobby Robson's Mexico Diary**, Collins Willow, London
There are a lot of ghostwritten football books and a lot of them are terrible, but this one's not bad at all.

Vyv Simson & Andrew Jennings, **The Lords of the Rings**, Simon & Schuster, London
Invaluable, cold-eyed exposure of the moral rot now rife in world sport; principally about the Olympics, but very good on João Havelange.

James Walwin, **The People's Game: The Social History of British Football**, Allen Lane, London
Published in 1974, and now probably impossible to find, but really worth looking for—an excellent account of the game's development.

About the Author

PETE DAVIES was born in 1959. He is the author of two novels, *The Last Election* and *Dollarville*; the travel book *Storm Country*, about the American heartland, and the soccer classic *All Played Out* about Italia '90. He writes on sport and travel for magazines on both sides of the Atlantic, and is a contributing editor to the British edition of *GQ*. He lives with his wife and two young children in North Wales, sixteen miles from the Racecourse Ground in Wrexham.